D1391750

LEARN
S

164 017

WORKS TO HISTORIC BUILDINGS: A CONTRACTOR'S MANUAL

GEOFFREY R. SHARPE MSc, MCIOB, FBEng.

LONGMAN

Pearson Education Limited
Edinburgh Gate
Harlow
Essex CM20 2JE, England

Published in the United States of America
by Pearson Education Inc. New York

Co-published with The Chartered Institute of Building through
Englemere Limited
The White House
Engelmere, Kings Ride, Ascot
Berkshire SL5 8BJ, England

First published 1999

ISBN 0 582 36910-X

British Library Cataloguing-in-Publication Data

A catalogue record for this book is
available from the British Library.

Set by 35 in 10/12pt Ehrhardt
Produced by Longman Singapore (Pte)
Printed in Singapore

CONTENTS

FOREWORD

The Chartered Institute of Building has been working to promote standards of excellence from its very beginning. The Institute's origins lie in an organisation called the Builders' Society which was founded in London in 1834. During the Institute's long and distinguished history, membership has widened to include all those concerned with the management of the construction process.

Even before being granted its Royal Charter in 1980, the Chartered Institute of Building had a long tradition in the publication of books and manuals. Over many years these publications have had a major influence on technical aspects of the construction industry. I am pleased to commend the Institute's latest publication, which has been produced in association with Pearson Education. The Institute supports Government initiatives to raise industry standards and this manual is a practical step to achieve greater competence by contractors, thereby improving the service they provide to the public. The manual is endorsed by the Institute's Building Conservation and Heritage Working Group.

The Chartered Institute of Building has a commitment to conservation issues and this manual provides contractors with appropriate guidance when undertaking works to historic buildings. It will also be useful as an information resource for those engaged in the specification, project management and practical application of heritage conservation works.

One of the key requirements of heritage conservation work is to understand the current significance of the place or building. The first part of the manual guides the reader through the issues of conservation philosophy and conservation matters. It also deals with essential requirements in managing projects important to national culture.

The manual then looks into the approaches, special requirements and skills that are needed for all elements of historic building. These include fabric surveying and recording, as well as analysis as part of the need to identify past repair methods and materials. The approach to the conservation of brick and stone walls is detailed and includes jointing, repointing and the options available for cleaning. Principles of repair in roofing and timber work are described along with treatments. Types of historic floors are then considered together with the methods of repair. A range of materials used in ancient construction is shown, with the appropriate repair options. Finishing, both internal and external, is discussed with plasters, renders, wall coverings and historic paints. The manual also considers the types of doors and windows and the approach required when there is a need to conserve historic glass.

Additional guidance is in the four Appendices, the reading list and details of useful technical contacts.

The manual has been written by Geoffrey R. Sharpe MSc MCIOB FBEng. Mr Sharpe is a Chartered Builder who has had a distinguished career of over forty years in both the public and private sectors. He is a respected author on conservation topics. The Chartered Institute of Building is also indebted to members of its Building Conservation and Heritage Working Group who have generously given of their time and provided a substantial level of expertise and informed comment at the various draft stages.

Joseph A. Dwyer
President
The Chartered Institute of Building

PREFACE

Work to historic buildings involves the need to use traditional materials in the original manner and results in a different building operation compared to the techniques used now. This also necessitates a fundamental alteration in the way work is planned, programmed and managed. Most conservation projects present a challenge and when a job has been well done, the true reward is the satisfaction in ensuring the survival of a relic of history for generations to come. The principal aim in writing this book is to guide and inform those contemplating such involvement through the complexities and additional problems which are likely to occur.

I have many to thank in the compilation of the text and the illustrations, but a special acknowledgement must go to Gerald Burbidge, Chairman of the CIOB Building Conservation and Heritage Group. His encouragement, input and support has made a substantial contribution in so many ways. I am particularly grateful for the help provided by Freddie Charles, Tim Donlon, Sara Carruthers, John Hurd, Jane Logan and David Brennan. Others who deserve a special mention are Garry Reeder, Trevor Francis, John Edwards, Mel Smith, Steve Fallon, Ian Wainwright, Joe Bispham, John Gleeson, Paul Mabbot and David Lodge who acted for the Society for the Protection of Ancient Buildings.

Geoffrey R. Sharpe
Surby, Isle of Man
February 1999

CHAPTER 1

UNDERSTANDING CONSERVATION PHILOSOPHY AND PRACTICE

1.1 INTRODUCTION

The aim of this manual is to state good practice and to provide guidance for those involved in works to older buildings, and although primarily intended for contractors who wish to expand into the conservation market, much in the book will be of assistance to others who are concerned with the care and conservation of the historic built environment. There are critical differences between present day building methods and those of the past, which need to be fully understood and correctly interpreted, especially at the contract planning and preparation stages. Moreover, the climate of operation can often be alien to the working criteria and procedures to which managers, craftsmen and operatives are generally accustomed. While modern building operations are orientated around speed and costs, conservation works are more concerned with historical accuracy and a strict adherence to the use of traditional materials and methods. It is a culture change that often calls for patience and a psychological adjustment towards time application and site management, particularly in cases where the activities of conservators are labour-intensive and painstaking. A realistic provision for the likely duration of such work needs to be carefully considered before it can be effectively coordinated into the programme of a main contract.

It is vital for a contractor to be familiar with the additional statutory requirements and obligations relating to protected buildings, structures, designated areas and trees. The contractor should also understand the varying approaches which influence local opinion and official decision-making. In addition, the builders of the past employed different construction techniques from those used today; this influences the approach to alteration and repair work. It is essential to ensure any form of intervention harmonises with the old and is in keeping with the basic tenets of conservation.

In the past, transportation difficulties often meant isolated communities had no alternative but to build in materials which could be obtained locally. This has produced a legacy of buildings constructed from a variety of materials, ranging from unbaked earth to stone, and is a factor which calls for special conservation skills. It is normally unwise to assume that a craftsman who is proficient in modern methods will be able to cope with the applicational variations between the past and the present. Conservation work in unaccustomed hands is liable to create formidable problems, mistakes and delays, which can be costly. The need to engage suitably experienced labour for the key elements of the process cannot be overstressed.

1.2 CONSERVATION PHILOSOPHY AND THE WORKING ENVIRONMENT

The value of an old building is not necessarily confined to aesthetics or historical interest, as the surviving elements can provide vital, and sometimes subtle, evidence of the customs and practices of our ancestors. An ancient structure marks a particular period in time, which may reveal essential clues relating to past living fashions and styles and the different techniques used in construction. Unless evidence of this type is respected and correctly interpreted, any modern intervention is unlikely to combine satisfactorily with the original. Moreover, the surviving fabric is an authentic relic from the past. If it is lost, a tangible link between the past, present and future will have been severed. Replication dilutes the historic worth of a structure.

This is the principal reason why intervention is such a sensitive matter and is further complicated by the many varying attitudes that surround the conservation debate. The factors which govern conservation issues are mainly orientated around emotion, culture, the visual or symbolic effect, and historical attachment. Old buildings cannot escape the inevitability of gradual deterioration and decay and therefore the manner in which they are maintained becomes critical. There are those who are likely to condemn any work which affects the issue of authenticity, no matter how minimal. On the other hand, there are also more liberal attitudes prevailing which are sympathetic to a measure of variation. Going to the other extreme, there is an opposing school of thought which questions the basic hypothesis and the need to conserve.

Change is sometimes unavoidable and this is acknowledged in Government policy documents, which offer useful guidelines when applying for planning permission or listed building consent. The selection and suitability of alternative options go to the heart of the central issue of authenticity and the measures required to maintain the status quo as far as is practicable. In reality, many conservation schemes are the outcome of an objective approach where the need for a degree of alteration or change has been accepted in the interests of continuity and effective use.

It is against this background of controversy and unresolved argument that judgements have to be made which have a profound influence on the approach to and application of building operations. Nothing should be assumed or left to chance and the need to become thoroughly acquainted with the climate of local opinion and the policies being applied by the local authority, English Heritage (or Historic Scotland and Cadw) and any other official organisation is paramount. Local planning authorities are required to consult the recognised amenity and preservation societies before applications for permission are determined. Under such circumstances, adequate preliminary consultations to help overcome any likely objections may be appropriate. Apart from policy statements issued by some local planning authorities, the Department of the Environment, Transport and the Regions has published jointly with the Department of Culture, Media and Sport a policy planning guide (PPG 15) (an HMSO publication) on the operation of the planning system. In a wider context, referral to international declarations such as the Venice Charter and the Burra Charter can be useful additional material at the negotiation stage (see Appendices C and D). Under normal circumstances, new work to an old building should, as far as possible, be kept to the minimum and it is deplorable practice to introduce elements which imitate the original in a manner that deceives.

In most everyday situations, a satisfactory solution can be achieved that permits new elements to harmonise with the old, provided they can be identified as later introductions. Not all historic structures are protected by listing under the Planning Acts nor are they necessarily scheduled as Ancient Monuments. This may mean that statutory permission is not required for some minor works, but such freedom does not negate a general duty of care on the part of the contractor.

It is essential to ensure that all forms of adaptation, treatment or change are capable of reversal to the original state. Where alterations and structural adaptation cannot be avoided, they need to be kept to the minimum. In addition, interference to existing elements and all new work must be distinguishable from the original in a manner that enables the historic development of a building to be positively identified by visual examination, without reasonable doubt or ambiguity.

FURTHER READING
See section on Philosophy in References.

1.3 THE ESSENTIAL NEED TO RECORD

Full and accurate recording of historic structures is an essential feature in the protection and conservation of our cultural heritage. No work of any significance should be undertaken unless the fabric of a building has been fully inspected and documented by an expert before the commencement of works. Moreover, the benefits are not confined to posterity, as the discoveries and perceptions made often enable building works to be carried out more efficiently. Minor works not requiring expert help should also be evidenced in the same way. Any need for recording should be arranged and formalised before site entry. Due account should be taken of any likely delays, interventions or impediments that could occur as a result of this exercise. To be fully effective and reliable, recording should be worked to a systematic procedure covering:

- The type and form of construction and the period or different periods of building (taking particular note of any subsequent alterations or changes).
- The materials used, including how they have been worked and finished (such as the tooling and dressing of stone).
- The architectural characteristics and any issues of architectural and archaeological significance relating to the property.
- Note all past repairs and the techniques used.
- Provide large-scale detail and measured drawings of essential features.

- State the general condition of the elements and the structure.
- Prepare plans giving the layout of the buildings, together with drawings and photographs which adequately project the imaging and state of the structures. The photography is best carried out with a plate camera as this gives larger and more distinct images. This documentation also needs to be accompanied by a written statement giving the history, function and detailed condition of the buildings and any remedial measures that may be necessary.
- A geographical location plan.
- A site plan with boundaries.
- Make a search through archives and old records for any relevant information.

This exercise is best carried out with a standard pro-forma which allows for all likely conditions and circumstances. Where hand-measured surveys are difficult, due to either the height or volume of a building or to restricted access, external elevations and other features including interiors can be expeditiously recorded using photogrammetry. With the aid of highly sensitive equipment, the system can compile with extreme accuracy, and in remarkable detail, two- or three-dimensional images. Advanced analytical photogrammetry is operated through a system of three-dimensional coordinates that feed data into a CAD system from which scale plans and other drawings can be reproduced as prints. It is an option which offers clear savings in time and labour and provides an accurate base on which all subsequent work can be recorded.

A much cheaper but more limited alternative, in response to the need for accuracy and scale, is the use of rectified photography, which enables reliable photographs to be taken for architectural recording without the need for specialist services. A rectified camera lens accommodates the distortions caused by the effects of perspective and camera tilt by means of a rectifying enlarger. The resultant prints can be equated to a scale by taking hand measurements of all key dimensions and inserting a scale rule into the finished image. The technique does, however, have the disadvantage of being unsuitable where the subject matter has excessive depth or penetrating recesses. All completed new work needs to be suitably recorded and dated in the same manner.

1.4 CONSERVATION PLANS

At the discussion stage of a scheme establish whether or not a conservation plan has been prepared and approved. It is a document which is having increasing significance in the approach to the conservation of historic places and areas, and is becoming a critical requirement for applications for grant aid and for official dealings and submissions with bodies such as the Heritage Lottery Fund. In substance, the document has a visionary purpose and sets parameters for policy objectives within an overall historic setting. Nevertheless, the wider perspectives of a conservation statement are likely to have profound implications for any building located within the confines of a plan. As such it can be a useful tool for formulating and planning building conservation and maintenance policy, particularly in the longer term.

A conservation plan encompasses many different needs, including items that may relate to any archaeological, ecological or environmental concerns. The concept aims to encapsulate into one document the critical items that need to be coordinated into the overall process of conservation in the widest sense. A conservation plan can sometimes be supplemented with an additional statement termed a management plan, which describes in detail how relevant items, including engineering and building works, should be put into effect within the provisions of the conservation plan.

1.5   CONSERVATION AND PLANNING LAW

In addition to the normal development controls, the Planning (Listed Buildings and Conservation Areas) Act 1990 makes specific provision for the protection of buildings and areas of special architectural or historic interest. Listed buildings are graded according to value and importance in terms of historic or visual interest. Those of exceptional significance are classed Grade I, while those of special interest are rated Grade II*. The Grade II category relates to those buildings which are worthy of preservation. Different legislation applies to Scotland, where an A, B and C classification works in a similar fashion.

It is a criminal offence to demolish or alter a listed building without the official consent of the local planning authority. This restriction applies to work to the external and internal parts of a structure. When an offence has been committed, the local planning authority may prosecute or issue a Building Enforcement Notice requiring restoration, including additional works to alleviate the effect or impact of the offending works. The Secretary of State has similar powers of enforcement. In terms of general policy, there is always a strong presumption in favour of preserving an ancient building, but this does not necessarily prevent permission being granted to alter, adapt or demolish a structure if a case is considered to be justified. Much depends on the circumstances of each individual situation.

FURTHER READING
See section on Legislation in References.

1.5.1   Ecclesiastical exemption

All listed buildings which are for the time being used for ecclesiastical purposes are exempt from the need to obtain listed building consent for repairs and alterations. This does not include houses provided for ministers of religion, but may include halls, vestries and other buildings which are physically attached to the ecclesiastical building. The denominations which benefit from this exemption are:

Church of England
Church of Wales
Roman Catholic Church
Methodist Church
Baptist Union of Great Britain and the Baptist Union of Wales
United Reformed Church

All these denominations have their own system of granting permission for works to be carried out. The system in the Church of England is known as the faculty jurisdiction, which extends to all buildings (whether or not listed) and includes all works except most minor items. Before works can be commenced it is necessary for a faculty (licence) to be sought by the parish, which must submit details of the proposed works to the diocesan advisory committee. Work can only commence after a faculty has been issued by the chancellor of the diocese, or in some cases the archdeacon. Always seek written confirmation that a faculty has been issued before entering on site and notify the diocesan surveyor of the intended starting date. The other denominations have similar procedures which are given in the Department of Culture code of practice 'The Ecclesiastical Exemption: What it is and how it works'.

1.5.2 Crown buildings

The Crown is exempt from listed building and conservation area controls, but the Government normally adheres to a declaration whereby work to Government buildings conforms to statutory controls which have been enacted. In addition, English Heritage needs to be notified in writing before commencing site work.

1.5.3 Designated conservation areas and their impact on building works

Conservation areas are created under section 69 of the Planning (Listed Buildings and Conservation Areas) Act 1990, where there is deemed to be a need to protect the special architectural or historic quality of an area. While listed building procedures deal with individual buildings, conservation area designations are used to give effect to the protection of a particular area or neighbourhood. Designation introduces more stringent control on the demolition or alteration of unlisted buildings which in isolation may not have particular aesthetic or historic merit, but in group form are considered worthy of additional measures of development control. Individual buildings within these areas may continue to be listed. The collective quality of buildings within a designated conservation area enables a local planning authority to exercise greater control over alterations, additions, user changes and new developments within a defined zone. The critical aim is to maintain or restore the original features of an area and to guard against any future works that would be out of character or inappropriate for the neighbourhood. In the case of new buildings, the issue of scale is frequently important and will need to be compatible with the original in terms of architectural tone, quality and size.

All trees within a designated area are protected and anyone wishing to fell or prune trees must give the local planning authority six weeks advance notice in writing. This provision does not, however, negate in any way the Tree Preservation Order provisions under the ordinary planning legislation. If a Tree Preservation Order is in operation, no work of any kind can be undertaken without formal approval. Most local authorities seek from the Secretary of State additional powers to administer conservation areas by applying for an Article 4 Direction. If granted, this confers greater powers over matters such as the control of advertisements and bestows improved provisions to prevent dilapidated or neglected land and buildings from causing harm to the visual amenities of an area. The scope of this measure is usually extended to control additions, alterations and repairs, including the permissible style and type of doors, windows and roof coverings that can be used. Porches, gates and boundary walls may be affected in a similar manner. In general terms there is a need to be vigilant when operating in a conservation area, as the following or similar restrictions could be in operation:

- The preservation of the skyscape by keeping all new work below the roof line.
- External alterations are likely to be kept to the minimum and be in keeping with the original.
- Materials may need to blend with and match the existing ones.
- Features such as doors and windows will probably be required to be in the same style as the original.
- Porches and canopies may need to harmonise with the period.
- Boundary walls, fencing, gates and gate posts may be required to be rebuilt to the original design.

The criteria which govern the establishment of a conservation area are not always restricted to medieval or very old structures and more recent periods of architecture can be included. The policy in some districts extends to the preservation of areas developed as late as the 1930s, subject to them being approved as worthy of protection.

FURTHER READING
See section on Legislation in the References.

1.6 HISTORIC INTERIORS

Considerable importance is now attached to the conservation of historic interiors, including the original layout, but this does not necessarily imply that a degree of adaptation or alteration will be refused. The criteria used to determine applications are similar to those applied to the external features of a listed building, although expert assistance is likely to be required much earlier in a project. It is vital that those involved are adequately briefed to ensure that they fully understand that all fixtures, finishings and fittings are the subject of statutory protection. This includes features such as wall panelling, decorative plasterwork, fireplaces, internal joinery, wall and ceiling paintings, old bathroom and sanitary appliances, historic tiling, old door and window handles and locks and wall coverings.

Full liaison with the local authority (building control and planning) is also necessary when contemplating work to items such as flooring, the removal of non-load bearing partitions and the installation of service equipment such as fire and security alarms. Considerable care needs to be exercised when preparing walls for redecoration, as many paintings of significance have been discovered buried under layers of wallpaper or have been hidden by coatings of whitewash. Many of these coverings act as a protective layer, leaving the original in a condition suitable for cleaning and restoration. A failure to recognise the significance of a valuable wall covering could lead to legal redress by the local planning authority and the building's owner.

1.7 HISTORIC PARKS AND GARDENS AND THE BUILDER

Many historic parks and gardens form an important part of our cultural heritage and have an intrinsic value worthy of protection. English Heritage maintains a register of parks and gardens of special historic interest and particular care is necessary to ensure site activities do not harm or infringe the objectives of this measure. The listing of a building may also extend to the entire curtilage of a site, including boundary walls, ponds and other similar features, which then require listed building consent before any changes can be made. At times such features can also be scheduled as Ancient Monuments, in which case this legislation takes precedence.

1.7.1 Outdoor sculpture

Outdoor sculpture includes any artwork, decoration, feature or memorial that is either free-standing or attached to a structure. Carved, cast or otherwise modelled from a variety of materials this can include architectural detail, relief panels, friezes, statues, commemorative plaques and garden ornaments. They can be in stone, metal, ceramics, timber and various man-made materials. Often items are constructed from a combination of materials. Sculpture and architectural detail are associated with buildings of all ages and range from fine carving on historic structures such as cathedrals to twentieth-century office buildings.

1.7.2 Inspection and assessment

- To assist future care, the condition should be recorded before any form of work is undertaken. Photographs in both colour and monochrome provide excellent records, particularly if they are supported by measured drawings.
- The varying angles, forms and surface shapes undergo differences in exposure, wear and weathering and deteriorate differently to the flat facades of buildings. Information of this type needs to be recorded precisely and in detail.
- The three-dimensional nature of sculpture results in certain parts retaining absorbed water for longer periods, making them more vulnerable to the action of frost, corrosion, decay, biological growths and other destructive media. It is essential that particular attention is given to these factors.
- Investigations to determine stability and condition need to be non-destructive. In the initial stages, archival evidence can be helpful concerning history, past treatments and problems with blurred design features. X-ray and metal-detection equipment is

ideal for locating armatures and dowels. Ultrasound is suitable for discovering and tracing fractures.

1.7.3 Maintenance and repair

- Sculpture and similar details need to be treated and maintained in an independent and separate activity. Much harm and damage can occur if cleaning and maintenance work forms part of larger works. It is essential to ensure treatment meets the particular needs of the sculpture.
- Before appointing a specialist conservator, seek evidence of previous work, visit examples and obtain references from main contractors and clients.
- Ensure any repair work is distinguishable from the original at close range, in accordance with the philosophy adopted by ICOMOS (International Council on Monuments and Sites).
- For the first twelve months, all treatments and repairs should be inspected and checked every month, with each visit being evidenced and documented with notes and photographs.

1.8 ARCHAEOLOGY AND THE LAW

Archaeological remains are irreplaceable evidence of the development of civilisation, and extra care is vital to ensure they are not damaged or destroyed by default. Protective legislation exists through the Ancient Monuments and Archaeological Areas Act 1979, which provides for the requirement to obtain Scheduled Monument Consent before works can be undertaken to any feature which has been included in a schedule under this Act. If granted, Scheduled Monument Consent can be issued with or without conditions, but there is no right of appeal against a refusal or the imposition of conditions. The procedure does, however, provide for observations to be made by an applicant before determination and consent is usually limited to a period of five years.

In practice, the discovery of archaeological remains often occurs during building operations and for this reason it is advisable for a contractor to take out adequate insurance cover against loss and hindrance. The conflict between historic and commercial interests may not always be easily resolved, especially if the Secretary of State decides to schedule archaeological discoveries during the course of site operations. In situations such as this, English Heritage can frequently provide helpful advice and guidance, but the incidence of this type of contingency occurring can be minimised through pre-operational consultations, with the archaeology unit of the local authority or a museum. In some situations physical indicators may be able to provide an early warning of a possible problem such as slight, unnatural differences in contouring, or a marked variation in the vegetation. Aerial photographs can be highly revealing in this respect. If initial excavations display signs of stratification or the layering of the soil, work should only proceed with extreme caution and immediate advice from an archaeologist may be essential.

1.9   PROCUREMENT: MATCHING OPTIONS TO RESOURCES

With conservation works, the clear and established divide between architect and builder can pose problems for either side unless both are proficient in the application of their respective skills and have formed proper lines of communication. In practice, most builders who have established a good reputation in this sphere owe their success to the dialogue they have been able to form with conservation architects and their clients. In this respect the traditional method of tendering is not always helpful and can engender an atmosphere of distrust and a lack of cooperation. For this reason, negotiated contracts are more likely to provide a better basis upon which conservation works can be undertaken. This creates a climate of discussion and communication and enables those involved to look at alternative options and to consider different viewpoints. It also affords specialist sub-contractors the opportunity to make a contribution to the planning process at a much earlier stage.

Most works are carried out through the traditional procurement route, whereby the design and associated documents are prepared by an architect or superintending officer, with the construction works being undertaken by the builder. In general terms the system works satisfactorily, but it can have disadvantages in relation to conservation, due to the standard wording and a lack of flexibility. This is most apparent where much of the condition of a building and the method of construction are unknown before work commences. Clearly under these conditions a builder needs to exercise extreme caution before making a contractual commitment, and it is this type of ambiguity which can make the application of the standard form of contract difficult to use and reconcile under such circumstances.

Design and build

This method is normally more suitable where standard components and routine methods of building are involved. It is not usually favoured by official organisations and public authorities, who mostly favour the leading involvement of an architect or consultant. The system can work well for conservation contracts, providing the builder has a reservoir of high quality expertise and skill, and an in-depth knowledge of the work in hand. The resource implications can also be considerable and for this reason the option is mostly available through the large contracting firms who operate specialist divisions for conservation works.

Management contracting

With management contracting, a project is run by a construction firm which undertakes all the work through sub-contractors, for a fee. When operated by a suitably experienced management, the system can work very well, especially when there are a large number of specialist sub-contractors to organise and coordinate. Particular care should be taken in the selection, ordering and control of materials and the main contractor needs to have a tried and tested management structure.

Construction management

This is similar to the system used before 1800, when the client would normally employ all the trades directly and be responsible for the whole project. In this situation the builder takes on the role of construction manager and becomes the client's representative. The system is liked by specialist sub-contractors, as they are employed directly by the client and this affords them full design and commercial involvement from the earliest stages of a scheme.

Investigative contracts

Investigative contracts can minimise the risk of uncertainty and avoid unexpected expense and delays, but there are circumstances where the additional cost can outweigh any merit in taking this course of action, especially where separate accessing involves major expenditure. At times the issue becomes a matter of fine judgement, but in most cases any initial intervention can be adequately justified on grounds of both cost and efficiency. It can be particularly beneficial in circumstances where the subsequent main works are carried out in accordance with the terms of the standard form of contract. In cases where a preliminary investigation cannot be undertaken, a suitable alternative is to put the client on notice giving a worst cost scenario. Effectively this means the submission of two estimates, one detailing the likely cost and another indicating a possible higher cost outcome.

1.10 CONSERVATION PROJECT MANAGEMENT

The operating and financial criteria used in modern construction planning and management are linked to one of the following production systems:

- *Mass production*: In which units and schemes are built in large numbers to the same design and constructional system.
- *Batch production*: Whereby standardisation is used but to a lesser degree, together with some variation.
- *Job production*: A single-purpose scheme operated to a particular specification and to individually stated requirements.

Over the past 50 years the building industry has been orientated more towards mass production, where standardisation and repetition are the key elements to efficiency and increased output. The growth of semi-skilled labour has been a feature of this change and this has also had an effect on the way batch production is operated. The criteria applied to job production are especially relevant to conservation work, which is a specialist function needing careful planning and much advance preparation.

1.10.1 Conservation contract evaluation

Although normal building management procedures apply, extra care has to be taken with all available information and in the documentation. A full site inspection is essential and the proposed work should be analysed and assessed from a different perspective when compared to modern-day building, particularly in relation to any likely uncertainties or potential problems. Assumptions cannot be made on the same day-to-day basis as for ordinary building work and adequate investigation is the only way to avoid a build-up of unwelcome complications at a later date. The contractor needs to have particular regard to the specification and be satisfied that every commitment to detail can be met. In the event of difficulties arising, never take for granted the notion that a variation is an easy way out of a problem. Altering the stated requirements may not be an option.

1.10.2   Work programming

The key factors in compiling a programme are to fully record the commitment and to accurately assess the detail. This also involves the provision of a timetable for implementing the various stages, which must show the sequences involved and how they are to be coordinated. It is at this stage that the differences between routine contracting and conservation operations become more apparent and special consideration should be given to the following items:

- Early confirmation that all necessary statutory consents and permissions have been granted is vital. (The extra approvals relating to listed buildings are likely to cause substantial delays.)
- The time allowance for recording warrants particular care, as this frequently takes longer than anticipated and can affect costings.
- As soon as practicable make sufficient time for the main operating team to become familiar with the programme and any specialist techniques. Consider any need for on-site induction sessions. Also ensure specialists such as painters and sculptors fully understand how they will be expected to integrate with the main team, as they are not always experienced in working on site with builders.
- Any special insurance risks require confirmation at the earliest opportunity. It is important for the insurance company to be made aware of any deviations or alterations in work procedures which do not accord with the terms of the standard form of contract.
- Ensure that adequate provision has been made for the protection of any sensitive areas, items or artefacts.
- Check that responsibilities under the Construction (Design and Management) Regulations 1994 have been clearly allocated, so that mistakes and misunderstandings are avoided.
- Ensure that satisfactory arrangements are in hand to plot and document trees on site. The condition of trees in the area of operation is best checked before, during and on completion of work.
- Full consideration must be given to environmental factors such as the care of bats, barn owls and other creatures which are legally protected.
- Ensure any legal issues such as ownership or access rights have been confirmed in writing.

- Particular attention should be given to the time of year when the work is to be carried out. This can be critical, as traditional materials are often more sensitive to weather conditions and additional precautions and protection may be essential.
- Check whether there is a need to obtain a HOT WORK PERMIT which is often required as a precaution against fire. A TOOLS PERMIT may also be necessary, as some contracts expressly exclude the use of power tools unless special permission is granted.
- The standard formats used in the preparation of method statements and risk assessments may not be appropriate. Some items may warrant being more fully recorded, especially any matters that are out of the ordinary.
- In difficult locations, allow for work breaks to evaluate and consider new information or circumstances that may have arisen during the course of building operations.
- Ensure that copies of the approvals covering listed building consent, planning permission and the building regulations form part any contract document.

1.10.3   Coordination and liaison (scheduling)

Materials

Blending new or replacement work with materials from the original source may not always be feasible. Many historic materials can no longer be obtained and substitution may be necessary. This situation often applies to certain types of stone, and other sources may need to be investigated. Suitability will involve taking samples for tests on strength and durability and checks are necessary to ensure the compatibility of a selected stone with the existing ones. If alternatives meet the correct requirements, samples should be worked to ensure they can be tooled to a quality and style similar to the original. Old brick sizes can vary significantly from the present day and matching work may call for a specialist order if salvaged equivalents cannot be obtained. Likewise, similar differences can apply to clay tiling, as many older tiles have a cross-camber which render later alternatives of the same size and texture unsuitable for repair work. For such reasons the supply element of a contract should be carefully investigated and checked. Delivery times are often longer and may need to be clearly defined and agreed with a supplier beforehand. In addition the following considerations will apply:

- The testing and analysis of existing mortars and renders to ensure all new work can be formulated to blend with the old. Newly compounded test mixes must be sampled for colour, texture and finish before orders are placed (see Section 2.2).
- The implications of manufacturing and installing non-standard joinery warrant full investigation. Additional overheads such as the provision of special tooling can occur.
- Many historic paints and colours and some wall coverings can only be supplied through special order. Ensure that samples are provided before confirmation of an order.
- Faulty timbers may need to be replaced by the same quality, colour, variety and condition. Replacement supplies will require adequate checking and testing. Traditional

timbers are often difficult to obtain and sources of supply should be contacted and the required quantities secured well in advance.

- Modern insulation and ventilation requirements installed in older buildings can have unfortunate consequences unless properly applied. Adequate provision will need to be made for items such as breather membranes and hidden vents.
- If repairs to timberwork call for metal strapping and similar solutions, ensure well in advance that a skilled blacksmith will be on hand. It is becoming increasingly difficult to find craftsmen for this type of work.
- Ensure that all site personnel understand the correct procedure for the slaking of quicklime, which can be a highly dangerous material. A metal tank should be filled to about one-third capacity with clean water. Add the quicklime gradually, ensuring that it is covered with a small amount of water at all times. On no account must water be added to quicklime. Slaking produces a violent reaction with a large amount of steam and heat being generated. For the best results, the material should be left to mature for three months before knocking-up as 'coarse stuff' or using as lime putty.
- Suitable replacement iron is now in short supply and arrangements will need to be adequate.

Labour

The selection of labour calls for meticulous care, particularly in relation to stone masonry where craft skills should be matched to the task in hand. The work of the stone mason divides into categories such as: banker, fixer, carver, pavier and waller and an individual craftsman is unlikely to be proficient in all of them. Appointments to the trades covering leadwork, roofing, glazing (including leaded lights and decorative glass) and plastering should be checked for their suitability for the work in hand. Many remedial treatment contractors are not adequately experienced in the additional precautions necessary for conservation contracts. To ensure labour with the necessary skills and experience is correctly employed, consider the following:

- Require craftsmen to provide samples of previous work and commission some exemplars before they are engaged. (Make arrangements for them to be fairly remunerated for this work within overall costings.)
- Make sure that they are fully aware of the true cost of the work, and have a thorough understanding of the needs and expectations of the final outcome.
- Issue a set of site rules to all engaged labour. Implement a system whereby everyone entering the works site is required to obtain a PERMIT TO WORK from the person in charge of the site.

1.11 PLANT AND EQUIPMENT

Extra protective work may be necessary for screening, masking or padding certain parts and components. The following additional items are likely to be required:

- The provision of mortar mills and gauge boxes, hoisting equipment, steeplejacking ladders, bosun seats, abseiling equipment and special cutters for wood moulding and turning. Similar allowances are required for the tooling and working of stone.
- A covered shelter for the mixing of mortar located near the area of operation, to prevent wind gusts dissipating or altering measured mix proportions.
- Suitable provision must be made for the control and prevention of dust, which can be a major on-site problem and a health hazard.
- Protection for sands and aggregates to prevent them from becoming contaminated or being washed out by heavy rainfall.
- Adequate allowance must be made for the disposal of waste and debris, including the ready availability of industrial vacuum cleaners. Health and safety and other statutory issues connected with this operation must not be overlooked.
- To minimise the risk of fire, portable electric tools should be restricted to low voltage appliances with earth linkage (110 V supply).
- Higher illumination levels may also be necessary in some operating areas.
- Provide a cluster of British Standard sieves for tests on existing mortar samples. Also have on site a 50 mm mesh sieve for screening lime putty.
- Ensure full protective clothing kits, together with all accessories, are available to anyone who is likely to be involved in the slaking of lime.

1.12   THE ASSESSMENT OF OLD BUILDINGS

At the earliest opportunity, certainly before making any contractual commitment, a contractor should fully survey and analyse an old building. The findings may be very different from those anticipated and could be critical to operational success or failure. Moreover, an investigation needs to allow enough time, much forethought, an inquisitive approach and an understanding of historic methods of construction. Few buildings remain in an original state and as a result later alterations or additions sometimes mask hidden faults. Assumptions cannot be made about quality, as standards can vary between phases. From the Georgian period onwards, much speculative building was poorly constructed, leaving a legacy of failures and problems to the present day. Many older structures have also undergone changes which conceal the true nature of the construction. Brick or stone facework or external rendering may mask a different method of building in the main structure such as timber frame. Later changes made in the same mode and style, as the original can frequently be deceptive and be difficult to recognise except through subtle and sometimes obscure indicators.

1.12.1   Looking for clues

However, informative clues are likely to emerge from a thorough and detailed examination when differences such as the texture and composition of the mortar and minor variations in other materials will be revealed. If these differences are plotted on a plan, valuable indicators will accumulate and give a clearer idea of the historical development of a structure. Often other signs, hidden as a result of weathering, can provide vital analytical evidence if the fabric is inspected with discernment. Items such as the filling-in of windows and the insertion of new door and window openings might otherwise be missed. Although not immediately apparent, slight scarring can usually be traced if an earlier addition or an original wing has been removed or rebuilt at a later date (Figure 1.1).

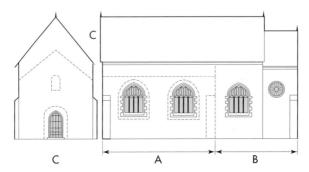

Fig. 1.1   The appearance of the above building gave the impression that the whole structure was original. A careful examination revealed slight differences in the wall texture along the dotted lines which led to the discovery that B was a later addition. It was also found that a buttress had been removed from A, with larger windows having been installed in the side elevations, together with an increase in the roof height. There was enough evidence to trace the original roof height at A from a close scrutiny of the elevation at C which also revealed the blocking-up of a small window and the insertion of a larger entrance door. These clues would have been missed without a painstaking examination

1.12.2   Some common causes of cracking

Shallow foundations increase the possibility of fractures from ground movement. If the cracks are of long standing and no serious damage has occurred, they are probably acting as expansion joints and are best left for that purpose. Intervention in such circumstances could upset an existing balance. Foundations which lack proper depth are also likely to have subsided in the early life of the structure to produce cracking and distortions which may be inactive and of long standing. Careful monitoring may, however, be necessary before an accurate analysis can be made. There is also a need to be alert to the possibility that foundations have been laid over underground water-ways. Much early culverting is now failing and in need of attention.

Cracks which appear in old buildings need to be evaluted by different criteria to those used in more modern structures. Cement/sand mortars will give a clear cracking pattern when they shear through tension, but in the softer, older lime/sand mortars the same signs may not be so apparent. This can mean the overall integrity of a building it not as secure as it may appear and a delicate stability could be upset by unsympathetic alterations or new additions.

1.12.3 Surveying

When conducting a survey, walls should be plumbed both internally and externally and floor levels need to be checked using a constant datum to enable a clear pattern of any movement to be determined. It is also important to keep in mind the possibility that signs of distortions and distress may be due to more than one defect and could result from an accumulation of circumstances. In the past, fair-faced masonry was not always adequately bonded into the backing and may have become detached. A useful, rough test is to lightly tap the facework with a club hammer, which emits a ring if the wall is solidly bonded and a dull thud if it is defective. Much of the very early cavity walling is prone to cavity wall-tie failure. Spine and party walls can frequently be discovered standing independently, without having been bonded into the other parts of the structure. This will often cause bulging, particularly in flank walls, but is a feature which can also be produced by thermal stresses. In some cases the inadequacy of the wall thickness may mean that the stability of the building is reliant on lateral support from the flooring and trussed partitioning. Overloading is likely to be clearly visible through deep vertical cracking in the external facing. The state of lime mortar in the inner parts of excessively thick masonry walling can be a potential source of weakness. If carbonation has failed to occur, the mortar remains in a plastic condition and is unable to combine the mass. In renewal work the problem is overcome by introducing a suitable proportion of white cement into the lime/sand mix in the vulnerable areas.

1.12.4 Structural interference

Interference with roof trussing to make space for extra accommodation and ill-conceived work to trussed partitions are frequent faults in later modifications (Figure 1.2). Changes to roof trussing can alter the stable balance of triangular forces in the truss design, causing a gradual creeping action, which can push the head of a supporting wall out of plumb. Another factor to consider is the undersizing of roof timbers in many of the speculative developments built in Georgian and Victorian times. Some of these roofs have insufficient restraint and inadequately sized roof members, which results in excessive deflection.

1.12.5 Problems with damp

The traditional solution to rising damp involved either masking, screening or increasing the rate of evaporation. Some builders opted to lay the first few courses of brick or stonework dry and open jointed, the object being to improve ventilation around the wall fabric at a sensitive point and to reduce capillary action by the omission of mortar. This form of construction may also be found in plinths taking cob or clunch and can be difficult to detect without a close examination. Over the years silt, debris and vegetation combine to give the impression of conventional mortar jointing and now act as a ready medium for the passage of moisture. An alternative approach was the formation of dry areas, which are frequently seen as an integral feature in later construction. Sometimes a special mortar was used in exposed locations. It contained wax, pitch

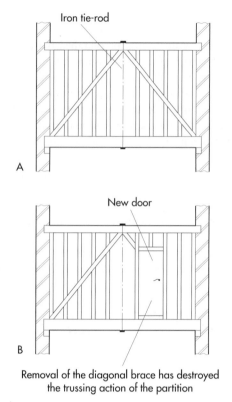

Fig. 1.2   Trussed partition

and resin applied in the molten state. Subsoil drainage strategically placed to lower the level of the water-table, and the use of air drains around the perimeter of a building, were further options. In some districts, it became the practice to char the feet of wooden posts in the belief that this would prevent fungal infestation if dampness occurred.

Under close examination, mystifying signs of rust staining can on occasions be detected on external wall surfaces. It is the residual evidence of a Victorian damp-proofing application made from fine iron dust mixed with sal-ammonia and water. The treatment worked on the principle that as the sal-ammonia corroded the iron the resultant rust caused the pores in the wall fabric to rust and become blocked. It was not a success. External renders can also be found laid on laths attached to vertical battening and while this can be an indication of timber frame it is not necessarily so. At around 1860 interwoven wire started to replace wood lathing and from about 1890 the use of expanded metal became the fashion.

1.12.6   Traditional solutions

In essence, the historic solution to internal dampness meant masking the defect and usually took the form of lath and plaster on vertical battening, but in better quality work independent studding was often introduced to create an isolated, intervening air space. The presence of this form of construction should not necessarily be taken as an indication of dampness and the reverse may be the case. Often it is part of the original construction. A cheap alternative involved the use of match boarding nailed to battens. In the fullness of time, pitch-paper sheeting became available for use as a waterproof lining. Hung as a wallpaper and fixed on the bituminous side, it tended to blister and peel away from the wall if trapped moisture could not evaporate freely. A later improvement came in the form of Willesden paper, which incorporated a copper film treated with ammonia, which has a water repelling effect.

1.12.7 Changes in construction

From the Victorian period onwards much attention was given to the prevention of dampness at the construction stage. The Public Health Act 1875 contained a requirement that all dwellings should be built with damp coursing. In the fight against damp, builders tried two or three courses of slate bedded in cement mortar, but problems arose if the slates cracked under load. This resulted in the use of either engineering bricks or the provision of damp courses in materials such as zinc, lead and copper. At around the same time, an innovation came with the production of perforated brown stoneware slabs designed to induce air movement at vulnerable points. From about 1850 onwards, hot asphalt poured to a thickness of 25 mm seems to have been the favoured option and eventually set the trend towards the commercial production of bituminous felt strips.

1.12.8 Trial and error

The foregoing illustrates some problems which are likely to be encountered in work on older buildings and is by no means exhaustive. The essential difference between old and new construction is the input that science and technology has been able to make in more recent times. The architects and builders of the past lacked, for example, the structural engineering knowledge of today, and in consequence operated through tradition which developed from trial and error. In quality work, this usually resulted in oversized components. The opposite occurred in many poorly built structures, which often lacked adequate safety margins.

FURTHER READING
See sections on Damp in old buildings, Structural aspects and Surveying in the References.

1.12.9 Non-destructive inspection techniques

The use of modern technology can now overcome the danger of important historic features or elements becoming damaged or harmed during the course of a survey. Special equipment is now available which offers a suitable range of options without the need to open up areas for examination. Advances in X-ray and gamma-ray applications have been of particular value in this respect and can reveal features which might not otherwise be easily traced. This type of equipment must, however, only be used by properly trained technicians and twenty-eight days notice needs to be served on the Factory Inspectorate which may stipulate certain conditions before filming can proceed. A possible alternative is the use of infra-red equipment which gives different coloured images according to the nature and state of the fabric under focus. Designed for thermographic purposes for heat loss monitoring, it can also be utilised to indicate other inconsistencies such as voids. The technique is particularly helpful in tracing masked timber framing. The application of impulse radar can produce similar results and ultrasonics have also been developed on the same theme. Impulse radar is also helpful in tracing underground drainage runs. The condition of chimney flues and drainage pipes may be viewed through portable closed-circuit television monitors. Metal detectors and magnetometers are suitable for tracing metal pipework and other metallic objects.

Intricate wall movements are more suitably observed with EDM (electronic distance meter) equipment which uses infra-red waves to record with extreme accuracy movements within a structure. Hand-held endoscopes and boroscopes are now available and are an effective site tool for certain forms of inspection. The system of using simple tell-tales has also been developed in a manner which can give more reliable recordings. Tell-tales made from calibrated perspex now enable measurements to be taken in either oblique, vertical or horizontal directions. They have, however, the disadvantage of being slightly distorted through thermal movement. An alternative is to insert, in a triangular pattern around the crack, specially prepared non-ferrous discs or pins. Regular measurements can then be taken using a calibrated vernier scale. A more advanced version of this system is the demec gauge, which displays changes on a calibrated dial. An accurate and ongoing system of monitoring is the LDVT (linear variable differential transducer) system, which measures voltage changes within a pre-arranged circuit. The transducers have a piston-type movement which accommodates and records wall movements as the voltage either increases or decreases according to circumstances. Although many of these systems require expert application others can be either purchased or hired (see Appendix B).

1.13   INSTALLATION OF SERVICES IN HISTORIC BUILDINGS

The highly sensitive nature of this work calls for a pervasive approach having due regard to all the services required and in a manner that allows adequate access, without causing harm to the historic elements of the interior or to the effectiveness of any fire barriers. As far as possible, all work should be hidden or screened within existing voids and spaces and the concept of reversibility needs to be considered at all stages of the operation. It is also more economic and practicable to consider the demand for services as a whole, including those which are likely to require renewal within the foreseeable future. If the delicate nature of this work requires a detailed investigation before proper planning and design issues can be put into effect, the contractor is advised to consider negotiating a separate INVESTIGATIVE CONTRACT before undertaking the main operation.

Extra precautions for the protection and safety of internal elements and features need also to be taken into account. These can entail the erection of screens to contain dust and the masking and padding of surrounding features. The historic value of existing installations such as sanitary appliances, old stoves and electrical fittings must also be recognised as they may have intrinsic historical significance and may be worthy of preservation or rescue. The disposal and transportation of waste and debris is often problematic. Full regard should be given to the sensitive nature of the working environment, including the need to use industrial vacuum cleaners regularly throughout the entire operation. Floors, openings and similar elements also call for extra care where they are to become part of the working thoroughfare.

Unless carefully controlled, the provision of new or updated services is likely to modify the internal environment in a manner which could cause serious damage. Additional heat may encourage joinery to draw through shrinkage and these conditions can propagate dry rot when associated with damp. A lower relative humidity may also harm historic furnishings and old wallpapers can become brittle and deteriorate. Expert advice is crucial in circumstances where this is likely to occur.

Adequate concealment in the fixing of electrical cabling and hardware is essential and can be achieved by judicious placing in hidden or unseen locations. Much can be achieved through the use of multi-core cables which avoids the prolific use of single cabling. The timbers in old buildings are often very dry and pedantic provision against the risk and containment of fire is essential.

FURTHER READING
See section on Services in the References.

1.13.1   Fire safety

The fire risk in work of this nature is significantly higher than in a more modern building, and for this reason additional precautions are necessary. Fire-fighting equipment should always be close to the areas of activity and operatives need to be instructed on how it can be effectively and speedily utilised in the event of an emergency. Smoking must be prohibited in danger areas and all combustible material needs to be removed from sensitive areas of operation before work commences. A wise precaution in vulnerable locations is to install temporary smoke detection equipment, which is left primed at the end of each working day.

Meticulous care is necessary in the use of any form of equipment involving a bare flame or the likelihood of sparking. Appliances such as hot air or arc welding and cutting equipment, and operations such as brazing, soldering, blow lamping and hot bitumen applications are a particular fire risk. Sometimes the requirement of a HOT WORK PERMIT is stipulated in the contract, which restricts the use of potentially fire hazardous equipment without specific approval being granted beforehand. A special risk assessment should also be made.

FURTHER READING
See section on Fire protection in References.

1.14 ACCESS PROVISION

1.14.1 Introduction

The provision of safe and secure working access often calls for purpose-designed systems that have been devised and erected by fully trained and experienced specialists. With historic structures, the appointment of a specialist contractor should only be made after taking up satisfactory references from a reliable source or from personal knowledge, particularly when accessing involves out-of-the-ordinary situations and extended heights, when the need to engage qualified and suitably experienced specialists is paramount. The services of a certified steeplejack not only ensures safer working access, but is also likely to result in the whole operation being more cost effective, especially at the pre-tender stage when inspections can reveal the full extent of any necessary work which could not otherwise be determined with confidence and accuracy. Steeplejack examinations provide valuable close contact information and photographs, which avoid items being misjudged when viewed from a distance. Adequate access in the early stages of a scheme also enables the costs to be more precisely determined at the outset, and allows an immediate opportunity to render safe items which are considered to be a danger or a potential hazard. Once as much information as possible has been gleaned from a preliminary examination, the extent and demands of the project can be assessed and the parameters decided on the type of accessing equipment needed. Under the Construction (Design and Management) Regulations 1994 this will also involve the 'principal contractor' being responsible for a method statement and risk assessment before work can commence.

1.14.2 Access equipment

Scaffolding

With historic properties, the use of scaffolding often requires the superintending officer and installer to consider the mode of construction, the condition and the nature of the building fabric before deciding on an accessing scheme. Meticulous care may be needed to prevent damage. It is advisable to remember that most older structures are not in modular form, and are unlikely to be fully compatible with some of the modern access systems. Normally scaffolding can be classified as being within one of the following broad classifications:

- Putlog.
- Independent. ⎫
- Independent tied. ⎬ also known as masons' scaffolding
- Suspended stage and working platforms (flying scaffolds).
- Cantilevered.
- Birdcage.

Within these groupings, the design considerations and methods of assembly provide for light, medium and heavy-duty use. It is vital therefore to make a correct assessment of need at the outset. For example, light-duty scaffolding erected for inspection purposes will become unsuitable and unsafe if heavy materials are imposed on the structure at a later stage.

With conservation contracts there will normally be a requirement for scaffolding to be of an independent type, but consideration will also need to be given to the following factors:

- Scaffolding must be founded on a firm footing and considerable care needs to be taken in assessing the bearing capacity of the ground. Historic properties and in particular churches and chapels often have undocumented cellars, crypts and other voids below ground which need to be traced and recorded. In consequence there may be an unseen danger of instability. If problems of this type are encountered, the provision of spreader and bridging timbers in addition to sole plates is essential.
- Determine the full extent of the works involved and the amount of equipment that will be required. Reference should be made to British Standard 5973: 1981.
- Bracing **must not** be attached to carved or slender sections of masonry.
- Particular care is necessary where scaffold attachments are likely to be affected by wind-loading factors.
- Expansion-type anchors should not be used, as they can exert a force on the stone and cause splitting of the masonry. If anchoring cannot be avoided, it needs to be fixed chemically and tested for 'pull out' resistance.
- If lateral support to the scaffolding is necessary, this can be achieved by tying braces to buttresses or inserting stainless steel anchors set chemically into the wall.
- Where scaffolding abuts masonry, capped ends must be provided, set at a minimum distance of 75 mm away from a wall. Additional protection should also include 50 mm polystyrene over fragile roof coverings.
- All masonry must be protected from direct contact with the scaffolding by packing with timber not less than 25 mm in thickness.
- If sheeting is to be used as a protection against inclement weather, the additional wind-loading factor needs to be calculated and additional strengthening provided. If this is overlooked it could result in a failure of the entire scaffold system. The effect of wind loading can be reduced by using 'debris' holed-type netting fixed around the immediate work area.
- As a precaution against a strike from lightning, all metal scaffolding erected against the side of a building should be connected to earth.

Steeplejack ladders

Laddering systems normally divide into either the Yorkshire or Lancashire classifications and both methods need to be erected in a particular manner and by experienced and properly qualified steeplejacks. Under no circumstances should inexperienced labour have involvement in or access to this type of work. Many of those registered within the industry articulate their skills into a specialism and it is important to ensure a contractor is selected who has the necessary experience and credentials in conservation work. The demands and skills needed for say an industrial chimney are very different to those required for laddering a historic spire. All work should be carried out in accordance with the code of practice issued by the National Federation of Master Steeplejacks and Lightning Conductor Engineers.

With the *Yorkshire system* the holes made for receiving the holdfasts and pins are cut at the top of the mortar 'T' joint in the masonry (the perpend/bed joint junction). In normal circumstances this needs to be not less than 50 mm in depth and is usually chased out with a cross-cut chisel. It is then plugged with straight-grained and knot-free soft wood.

The *Lancashire system* involves drilling, in suitable locations, holes to a diameter of up to 16 mm and to a depth of not less 100 mm into which the holdfasts, pins and other fittings are secured using straight-grained and knot-free soft wood plugs.

Before seeking quotations from a specialist contractor, consideration should be given to the following:

- Determine whether built-in ladder fixings have already been installed. If the answer is in the affirmative a survey will be required to establish the condition and safety of the fixings.
- If holdfasts and pins need to be fixed consider the placing and progression of the laddering with both the proposed and any likely future work in mind.
- Routes to the summit need to be selected to avoid damage to ornamental masonry and other components of a delicate nature.
- Make provision for all the surfaces adjoining the area of operation to be checked for stability and condition.
- Consider the possible options if laddering needs to be spliced and turned, so that priorities can be more effectively programmed.
- Allow for the possible provision of walkways over sensitive parts of the structure, including protective screening.
- Under **no** circumstances should laddering be fixed to a lightning conductor.
- All ladders **must** be on a firm base.
- Ladders and securement fittings must not be used as anchor points for hoisting loads unless they have been specifically designed for that puropose.
- Assess the condition of the building fabric. If either the bricks or stone are dense and difficult to tool, or the mortar has excessively hardened there will be a need to introduce deeper chases and drill holes for fixings. Otherwise the fixings may work loose as a result of vibration from repeated hammering.
- Fibre rope lashings must **never** be used where a heat source could be a danger to the strength and quality of the rope. The specialist contractor should be alerted to any known perils of this nature.

Bosun's seats

This form of accessing enables steeplejacks to reach all areas of a tall structure for inspection and remedial work, but it is an extremely dangerous function and should only be undertaken by fully trained and certified specialists. British Standard 2830 details the requirements for suspended access platforms and activities also need to be in accordance with the code of practice issued by the National Federation of Master Steeplejacks and Lightning Conductor Engineers.

Accessing in this manner divides into three main categories namely:

- The boatswain's chair, which is a backed plastic seat more often used for activities such as cleaning and painting.
- The bosun's seat which is a plywood board with rope lashings and is used by steeplejacks for unrestricted movement (Figure 1.3).
- Abseiling is a technique requiring special equipment and accessories which enable the operator to 'walk' the side of a structure. At times it can offer a greater measure of accessing flexibility. Certified steeplejacks must have completed additional training for this type of work.

It is also necessary to consider:

- Whether or not fixing points have to be provided. They can be fitted either by means of a purpose-made cantilever jib or with a counterweighted scaffold tube outrigger.
- Ensure that slings, chairs and ropes can be properly protected from friction and damage from resting on sharp edges. Suspect points will need protection using sacking, soft padding and timber.
- An adequate form of protective storage is essential for when the equipment is not in use.
- Storage facilities must also provide for ropes to be kept clear of the ground.
- Ropes should not be exposed to contamination by solvents or any substances that have an acid or alkaline content.
- There is a need to ensure the Health and Safety Directive is observed in every respect and that action is taken to remove fouling by pigeons and other animal droppings. The danger of slipping or sliding on a fouled surface can be minimised by thoroughly cleaning before, during and after operations.

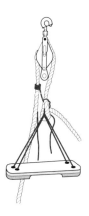

Fig. 1.3   Bosun's seat

Hoisting

Simple rope and block hoisting is usually the more suitable means of lifting materials where access is restricted to steeplejack laddering. Elsewhere, transporting materials to weak or sensitive parts of a building may require careful forethought if mechanical hoisting is contemplated. There is sometimes a danger of vibration, causing damage in weak and sensitive areas, but this can usually be minimised through the use of lightweight scaffold hoists. Checks also need to be made to ensure the movement of materials will not cause damage to any parts of the adjoining fabric of the building and additional protective measures may be necessary. The lifting of wrought stonework usually involves the need for mechanical assistance and may require the provision of devices such as a three-legged lewis or a chain lewis, lifting pins, sling chains and similar equipment.

FURTHER READING
See section on Accessing in the References.

1.15   LIGHTNING CONDUCTORS

In basic terms, lightning is no more than a massive electrical spark which occurs as a result of a natural build-up of positive and negative charges between clouds or between a cloud and earth. The effects of a strike cannot only kill living things but also cause extensive damage to property. Apart from the danger of falling masonry and similar hazards, the outbreak of fire is a likely occurrence, with the resultant fumes, smoke and flames creating additional risks and destruction. The installation of a lighting protection system is specialist work and should only be carried out by fully qualified engineers who are members of the National Federation of Master Steeplejacks and Lightning Conductor Engineers. There are, however, a number of factors in the early stages of a project which need to be determined in advance by the builder to ensure protection can be achieved satisfactorily in both operational and aesthetic terms.

1.15.1   Principles of protection

The essential components of a lightning conductor system are:

- The air terminations or finials which receive the strike.
- The bonding attachments which help prevent side flashing.
- The conductors which convey the current to earth.
- The earth termination that receives and dissipates the electrical discharge.

Air terminations need to be on the highest points to ensure adequate coverage is provided. Effective protection from each terminal is, in essence, a cone formation with the line of the apex at the highest point meeting the base at a point which gives a radius equal to the height at the apex (see Figure 1.4). When a single air termination cannot provide an overall protection, additional terminals will be needed, but this may

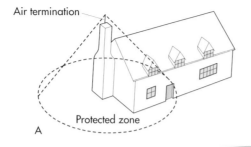

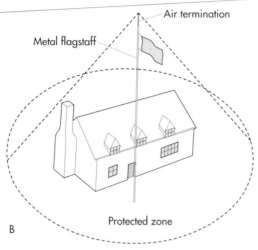

Fig. 1.4

not be sufficient to protect the sides of a tall structure and extra measures may be required. Protective coverage is not likely to be adequate without introducing a series of intervening down conductors. All principal towers, spires and similar high points need a minimum of two down conductors placed in diametrically opposite locations to each other. Moreover, large buildings are likely to need conductors fitted to a grid-form pattern with additional air terminations at projecting points such as pinnacles, fleches, vanes, finials and similar features.

1.15.2 Installation of conductors

The down conductors function as a low impedance path from the air termination to the earth termination. The conductor tape needs to be either high conductivity annealed copper or aluminium strip. For long runs, the introduction of expansion bends at suitable points is essential. All connections must be made with clamps, with a test clamp being fitted in an accessible position at the earth end of the down tape. High resistance throughout the entire lightning protection system can occur as a result of a faulty joint, which makes the building fabric more vulnerable to strike damage. All earth electrodes should be located as close as possible to the building. To ensure a lightning discharge can be suitably dissipated, there must be low electrical resistance between the electrodes and the earth. Soil conditions can have an important influence in this respect, with the moisture content of the ground, the chemical composition of the soil and the soil temperature all being relevant factors.

An important consideration is the problem of side flashing, which can occur if metal is in close proximity to the lightning conductor. If a lightning strike finds an impedance path to earth lower than that offered by the conductor system, the flash will divert to the lower impedance route. This will not normally occur if the design and workmanship of the installation is to the required standard. Most such strike incidents are the result of either incorrect fitting, bad routing of the conductors or a lack of regular maintenance.

1.15.3   Step potential

The immediate aftermath of a lightning strike creates a voltage build-up in the ground that can be fatal to anyone in the vicinity. It occurs through an instantaneous voltage accumulation at the point of discharge which produces a phenomenon known as step potential. After the strike has reached earth, the dissipation of the current in the soil can establish a difference in electrical potential between the feet of a person within the affected area which causes electrocution (Figure 1.5). It is a hazard that can be minimised by an analysis of the soil structure. A careful interpretation of the findings may enable more effective earth terminations to be constructed.

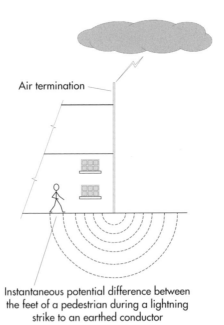

Air termination

Instantaneous potential difference between
the feet of a pedestrian during a lightning
strike to an earthed conductor

Fig. 1.5

1.15.4 Historic buildings: general considerations

With old buildings, a primary concern will be the selection of conductor routes which avoid the visual effect of unsightly attachments and other intrusions that detract from the historic appearance of the structure. In this the choice of materials is crucial and selection needs to ensure the installation blends with the whole. This can sometimes be achieved by using PVC-coated conductor strips which are obtainable in different colours. Careful planning of the conductor routes often enables much of the system to be placed behind buttresses and pinnacles or along the backs of parapets and similar features. The profile of a building can also be harnessed to good effect by avoiding points which attract the eye and by taking advantage of permanently shadowed areas. Care should be exercised when selecting unprotected copper and in locations where salt is present in the atmosphere, because verdigris can form and cause ugly staining which is difficult to remove.

- Lightning protection systems that have been fitted without regard to the visual appearance of a building can inflict immense aesthetic harm. It is imperative that a specialist contractor is selected who has adequate experience of working in this idiom. Always take up references and check past work before making an appointment.
- An installation should be tested on completion of works and then maintained and tested every twelve months.
- If a lightning strike has taken place, the system should be checked and retested.
- If feasible, metalwork (including metal windows) should be bonded into the lightning protection system to reduce the risk of a flash-over.
- Seek advice from the National Federation of Master Steeplejacks and Lightning Conductor Engineers before painting bare metal conductors, as some paints can impair the efficiency of the system.
- The earth termination should never be placed in an area which is likely to become a pedestrian walkway.
- Lightning conductors' systems should always be bonded to electrical earth to prevent side flash.
- When planning conductor routes, try to avoid sharp-angled bends in conductor runs as this can affect the efficiency of the system.
- Do not cover conductors with renders or similar coverings. If it is necessary to provide an external wall cladding such as vertical tiling or slate hanging, ensure there is a free flow of air around all conductor strips.

FURTHER READING
See section on Lightning conductors in the References.

1.16 GRANTS AND LOANS

Financial assistance in the form of grants or loans can sometimes be obtained for conservation works through sources such as English Heritage, private trusts and local authorities. Approved applications are, however, subject to compliance with strict rules and to be elegible building operations must normally be confined to:

> Structural works and repairs relating to the restoration of traditional features.
> Major repairs of a structural nature concerning roofs, brickwork and stonework.
> In addition, traditional materials and methods must be used to a required standard.

1.16.1   Conservation grants

It is important to understand that conservation grants are concessionary and are not intended to help finance ordinary repairs, alterations, modernisations, improvements, conversions and the renewal or installation of services. This does not, however, preclude other works from being undertaken at the same time as those accepted for conservation grant aid and local authority-approved grants under the Housing Acts remain applicable.

Grants or loans made by English Heritage on individual buildings are mostly confined to buildings of outstanding architectural or historic interest. No formal definition has been ascribed to this category although all Grade I and Grade II* listed buildings are almost certain to comply. Grants made by English Heritage seldom exceed 40 per cent of the total cost, and the work must be carried out to a high standard and be implemented under an approved supervisor. Assistance is primarily aimed at a structural works programme which an owner is unable to fund from private resources. Evidence of a commitment to the conservation cause is also needed and for this reason English Heritage is unlikely to respond favourably to an application if a property has not been in the same ownership for at least four years. However, an exception can be made if a listed building is on the at-risk register.

Conservation grants offered by local authorities are normally restricted to listed buildings, but they also have the power to give assistance for works to unlisted buildings where they form an integral part of a conservation theme or programme. This concession can be extended to the repair of non-residential buildings including structures such as historic walling, barns, dovecotes and workshops. Normally the maximum grant available is 50 per cent of the eligible costs, but loans can also be made and are mostly repayable over a four-year period. In addition some organisations and charitable trusts can sometimes obtain assistance through the National Heritage Memorial Fund and from the Heritage Lottery Fund.

An offer of grant is likely to be made subject to compliance with stated conditions and stipulations and these can vary between authorities. The undermentioned terms are usually imposed:

- A commitment to repay the grant monies if the property is sold within a prescribed time from the date of the grant (normally five years).
- The need to carry out works to a specified standard.
- English Heritage sometimes imposes a condition which requires the owner of an outstanding historical building to provide regulated access to the general public.

1.16.2 Action on default

English Heritage and all local authorities are empowered to recover all or part of any grant monies if the terms under which a grant has been made are contravened.

1.16.3 Conservation areas

Although some buildings in isolation do not merit listing, they may nevertheless contribute collectively to the historic charm and character of an area. These circumstances are recognised by both English Heritage and local authorities, which are sometimes prepared to allocate grants for works to unlisted properties within a conservation area. Situations can arise whereby English Heritage and the county and district councils concerned form conservation area partnership schemes for the implementation of structural repair works on selected structures, which can include unlisted buildings. Normally the limit of the assistance provided is 40 per cent of the approved works.

1.16.4 Additional sources of finance

Other sources of financial aid may also be available through local trusts, but this is usually restricted to charities and churches. The Historic Churches Preservation Trust can be an important source of grant assistance for churches and Grade II churches can also apply for grant monies from the Lottery Heritage Fund. Special provision has also been made for local preservation trusts and voluntary organisations which can apply for interest-free loans where other sources of finance need to be supplemented. In this respect the Architectural Heritage Fund is empowered to give assistance for the acquisition and restoration of historic buildings. If a property is to be retained by a trust or voluntary organisation, loans normally cover a period of two years at a low rate of interest (usually 5 per cent). If a revolving fund is in operation, no fixed rate of interest is charged when the property is to be sold on completion of works, providing any profit which has accrued is reserved for a future restoration project.

1.16.5 Making an application for a grant or loan

- Initiate this at the earliest possible opportunity after planning permission or listed building consent has been obtained.
- Do not commence works of any kind before an application has been submitted, as this will negate the submission.
- A good and reasoned presentation needs to be made which can justify the allocation of grant aid. In addition to the approved plans the use of photographs, perspective drawings, specialist reports and a clear, objective statement is likely to have an impact on the outcome.
- If an application is being made to English Heritage, first seek the support of the local authority, which can influence the result.
- Following an indication of approval, no works should begin until a formal notification has been received and any conditions or stipulations imposed checked to see what effect they may have.

■ If there is a need for any works to be put in hand urgently, it is sometimes possible to negotiate a 'without prejudice' start with the local authority. Always ensure this is confirmed in writing before entering on site.

FURTHER READING
See section on Finance and economics in the References.

1.17 FOUNDATIONS: REMEDIAL WORK MEASURES

Old walls tend to rest on shallow foundations, which may cause movement due to seasonal climatic changes. It was normal practice to excavate to a depth which did little more than expose the top of the subsoil. The base was then rammed and beaten and large stones were laid with the spaces between being filled with sand, gravel and small stones. Sometimes the filling was mixed with a lime/sand mortar. The likelihood of movement means that under these circumstances cracks often act as expansion joints and are usually best left for that purpose. Historic lime/sand mortars are able to absorb a proportion of movement without the appearance of cracking. If serious settlement has occurred, however, it may be necessary to consider underpinning, but part-underpinning is seldom a satisfactory remedy, as this is likely to result in differential settlement. Structural issues of this type require careful investigation and analysis and frequently warrant advice from an expert.

As brick entered into more general use, it became the practice to build upon brick footings with offsets. If the bearing capacity of the soil seemed suspect, stout elm piles were sometimes sunk into the ground in series to provide extra support to the brick footings (Figure 1.6). The introduction of Portland cement enabled concrete foundation strips to be used without causing excessive delay to the follow-on trades. Later concrete foundation strips were thickened and the use of brick footings was abandoned in favour of current practice. Many early Victorian artisan dwellings have been

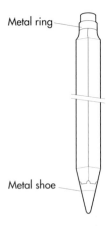

Metal ring

Metal shoe

Fig. 1.6 Timber pile

built without any proper foundations or footings. Another common fault was to build internal walls onto stone flags, which have eventually settled to cause cracking and distortion.

Walls built on shallow foundations are often prone to an outward lean, normally due to differential settlement between the rain soaked soil around the foundations and the relatively drier soil within the inner confines of the structure. It is a fault that can induce problems such as roof spread, which can be arrested through the use of either tie rods, additional roof collars or some other method of support.

The cause of cracking in older buildings calls for a wider perspective. The undermentioned possibilities may need to be considered and investigated in addition to those more likely to be the encountered in a modern structure:

- Thermal movement especially when a structure has evolved at different stages through different forms of construction.
- Cracking caused by the drying out of materials or the introduction of a heat source such as central heating.
- The action of creep (as a result of loading many historic materials can deform over a long period of time).
- Load pattern changes through either the redistribution or addition of loads.
- Vibration, which can exacerbate existing stresses within a structure.
- If shallow foundations are found, the possibility of landslip needs to be investigated.

1.18   INVESTIGATION AND ANALYSIS

- Do not undertake any work without a detailed analysis of the method of construction.
- All cracks and other signs of movement should be accurately plotted on a plan.
- On completion of the survey, analyse the crack patterns and identify the cause. In more serious cases seek the opinion of an expert if this has not already been done.
- Make provision for the adequate monitoring of cracking and other movements if this is considered necessary.
- Formulate possible remedies and consider alternative options, such as soil stabilisation.
- Submit the preferred solution to the appropriate source for approval.

FURTHER READING
See section on Structural aspects in References.

CHAPTER 2

USE AND APPLICATIONS OF MORTARS

2.1 MATCHING MORTARS

In conservation work careful mixing and batching of mortar is not sufficient. Considerable caution also needs to be exercised over the use of constituent sand and aggregates, otherwise the result may be an unsuitable or unsightly finish. Samples of the original mortar to be matched should be broken down and left to stand in a solution of hydrochloric acid, which reduces to a sand/aggregate residue only. After washing in clean water it is then dried, weighed and passed through a stack of BS sieves ranging in grading from 5.00 mm to 0.15 microns.

The deposits from each sieve then need to be weighed separately so that the readings can be converted into correct proportional terms against the gross sum. This information enables a specification to be drafted for a mortar comparable in texture and colour to that which is to be matched. At the appropriate stage, the supplier should be given the recorded sieve readings, together with small samples from each sieve. This is normally sufficient for the compounding of a purpose-made sand/aggregate mix that blends suitably with the old.

Before a specially compounded aggregate is used, however, a test mix should be prepared and moulded into a series of small biscuits. When dry, they need to be snapped in half, with the exposed edge being placed against the face of the original mortar to test whether there is a satisfactory match. Comparability may not always occur and can be due to a number of circumstances, including the presence of a calcareous aggregate that has digested out with the lime binder. When difficulties of this nature arise, a laboratory analysis will be necesary.

If during rebuilding work the original mortar can be salvaged and is found to be clean and untainted, it can be satisfactorily ground down for reuse as an aggregate (Figure 2.1).

2.2 LIME MORTAR MIXES

An essential consideration is the type of lime to be used and the ingredients of the aggregate, which affects not only appearance but also quality, strength and durability.

Fig. 2.1   The Lime Centre, Morestead, featuring old and new flintwork. The projection is new and due to an accurate analysis of the original mortar and to careful cleaning of the old flintwork, a near perfect match has been achieved

A non-hydraulic lime hardens through a slow process of carbonation, but a much overlooked option is the use of hydraulic lime. When in contact with water this has a combined setting action of carbonation and a chemical chain similar to that of Portland cement. Hydraulic limes divide into three groups, commencing with the eminently hydraulic, which has a setting action of one to four days, the moderately hydraulic, which ranges from five to fifteen days and the feebly hydraulic, from fifteen to twenty-one days. When selecting a hydraulic lime mortar always consider the strength and porosity of the brick or stone to be fixed. The more normal $1:2\frac{1}{2}$ to 1:3 (hydraulic lime/sand) mix can sometimes be too strong and may need to be weakened. Mixes should also be used within four hours of wetting and must not be 'knocked up'.

A non-hydraulic lime can be adapted to set more rapidly by gauging with a pozzolan such as finely crushed brick, PFA (pulverised fuel ash) or HTI (high temperature insulation). The addition of Portland cement has the same effect, but research undertaken by English Heritage through the Smeaton Project showed that many of the sampled lime mortar mixes containing small quantities of Portland cement were prone to segregation. This raises doubts over the efficacy and suitability of Portland cement as a pozzolanic additive and calls for caution. When specified, lime–cement mortar is often described as 'compo' and is mostly used in the ratio of 1:1:4 (Portland cement/ non-hydraulic lime/sand).

An excess of water in lime mortar mixes must also be avoided, as this creates undue porosity. Under normal working conditions additives such as PFA and HTI present a health hazard and should not be used without the protection of a mask. If quicklime is to be slaked on site, provide for the work to be undertaken as already described (see Section 1.10.3 (Materials)) and ensure that protective clothing and goggles are worn. The health and safety aspects of the operation cannot be overstressed.

FURTHER READING
See sections on Mortars and Aggregates and sands in the References.

2.3   JOINTING AND REPOINTING

There are two critical factors which must be carefully determined before commencing operations. The first concerns style and the other the suitability of the mortar mix. It is important that the shape and form of the jointing are correctly worked and conform with the period concerned. This may require some research. It is unwise to assume that any earlier repointing has met this requirement. The ravages of the weather usually mean that it is necessary to repoint periodically, so the original pointing is seldom found untouched in early masonry. With ancient structures, repointing requires discerning care and any deviation from the original can harm the intrinsic qualities of an earlier period.

The flush joint has long been the correct form of pointing in older work and has an established tradition, but other fashions have taken hold from time to time. From the Elizabethan period onwards, two alternative methods are sometimes found. One is the double struck joint which is slightly recessed into the brickwork and is half rounded with side margins. The other is the beak joint which is slightly recessed and has a triangular projection. Styles such as the weathered joint and the overhead struck joint and some projecting styles used in maintenance work are wholly inappropriate for conservation work (Figure 2.2).

Tuck pointing is intended to give the impression of rubbed and gauged brickwork and is achieved by forming a flush mortar joint which is coloured and textured to match the adjoining bricks. A thin line representing bed and perpend joints is scored into the pointing while still wet and later filled with white lime putty (Figures 2.3 and 2.4). Bastard tuck pointing is an imitation of tuck pointing and is formed entirely from one infilling of mortar.

During the nineteenth century, black ash mortars, prepared from a mixture of lime, ashes and sand, enjoyed a period of popularity. When they are in contact with wall-ties corrosion of the metal is likely to cause damage.

2.3.1   Repointing

- Power tools must never be used to chase out or remove existing mortar. Also avoid using a club hammer and bolster.
- When cutting out old mortar take great care to prevent damaging or bruising the arrises.
- Always work samples and have them approved beforehand.
- Dress out old mortar with a tool that is narrower than the joint to be repointed. The cutting should be to a depth of 25 to 38 mm and then brushed and flushed out with clean water. Avoid drenching, otherwise the mortar is likely to seep into the surrounding masonry.

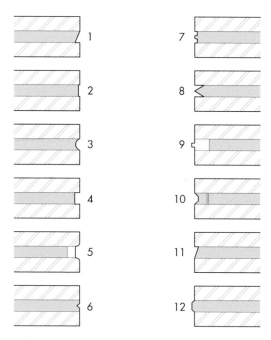

1. Struck jointing: this is bad practice and encourages water to lodge in the lower recess
2. Flush jointing: appropriate for most forms of historic brickwork
3. Keyed jointing: satisfactory but the arrises to the bricks should be left slightly exposed
4. Recessed jointing: only suited for high density bricks
5. Flush pointing to worn brickwork: when the arrises of the bricks have become chipped or eroded, the pointing needs to be set back as shown. Under no circumstances should mortar be feather-edged to run flush with the face of the brickwork
6. Vee jointing: not good practice and has mostly been used to give an impression of narrower joints
7. Double struck jointing ⎫
8. Beak jointing   ⎬ Note 7 and 8 are an occasional feature in Elizabethan brickwork
9. Bastard tuck pointing: an imitation of tuck pointing formed entirely from the bedding or pointing mortar. The projecting band forms part of the whole and although not so aesthetically acceptable it is more durable than tuck pointing
10. Hollow recessed pointing: as for 5
11. Weathered jointing: satisfactory in function but the style is not appropriate for most forms of historic brickwork. It is more suited for machine-made bricks of uniform appearance from the Victorian period onwards
12. Mason's vee joint: more usually found in rubble stone walls. Often selected with the intention of forming an even-looking joint with uneven thicknesses of bedding mortar

Fig. 2.2   Jointing and pointing

Fig. 2.3   Tuck pointing

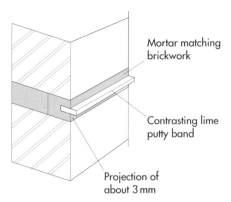

Fig. 2.4   Tuck pointing. This first appeared in the eighteenth century and involves the pointing mortar being coloured to match the brickwork. About 60 to 75 minutes after application, narrow lines are scored into the mortar to precise dimensions. When dry, contrasting lime putty is pressed and dressed into the recesses to give the appearance of gauged brickwork. Occasionally the tuck is found in black, being made from a mixture of Roman cement and lamp black

Fig. 2.5 Ugly ribbon pointing to brickwork. The mortar mix is too hard and has resulted in efflorescence in the brick which is beginning to deteriorate

- It is vital to select a mortar that is suitable for the existing fabric. If the mix is too strong and sets hard, it will create an impervious joint and cause moisture to dry out through the bricks or stone. The result is likely to be rapid deterioration through spalling, frost damage and decay (Figure 2.5).
- With historic structures most aggregates will be found to be coarser than those used today. The utmost care is necessary when selecting sand and aggregate if a texture similar to the original is to be achieved.
- Plasticisers and colouring additives should never be used.
- After mixing, bagged hydrated lime should be left for a few days before use.
- Hydraulic limes produce a more impervious mix.
- Pointing work must never be undertaken during periods of frost.
- The lime putty line in tuck pointing frequently deteriorates faster than the rest of the joint. Replacement is best achieved by cutting out with a hacksaw blade, followed by brushing and rinsing out with clean water. Fresh lime putty can be pressed in if it is held as a sandwich between two sheets of plastic and is then squeezed into the recess and dressed (Figure 2.6).
- Before new pointing is allowed to set, the whole should be lightly brushed to expose the aggregate.

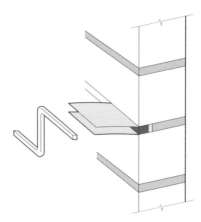

Fig. 2.6   Repointing gauged brickwork and finely jointed ashlar stonework. (Avoiding even the slightest damage to the arrises is essential. This is best achieved by carefully cutting out the old work with a hacksaw blade to a depth of about 25 to 30 mm. Then flush the joint clean with water using a small hand spray. Lime putty sandwiched between pieces of fairly stiff plastic to the thickness of the joint is then inserted into the joint. The lime putty must be firmed into position with a pointing iron. One sheet is then withdrawn and the lime putty dressed back and consolidated before removing the second sheet by holding the wet putty in position with the pointing iron)

- If there is a need to tone down the work and encourage natural weathering, the work can be safely dressed with a cow dung slurry.

FURTHER READING

See section on Pointing in the References.

CHAPTER 3

BRICKS AND BRICKWORK

Before the commencement of operations, the condition of historic brickwork should be carefully examined to determine the tolerances and characteristics of the material. Particular attention should be given to signs of cracking, leaning or deformation which are factors that may necessitate the involvement of a specialist structural engineer. The first English-made bricks appeared around the year 1200, but due to cost were not used in lesser buildings until well into the seventeenth century. Contrary to popular belief, brick size is not a positive guide to dating. A more reliable approach is the character and texture of the material, and the manner in which it has been laid and bonded. Due to irregularities in shape, the early bricks needed to be laid on thick beds of lime/sand mortar which give a different and distinctive appearance when compared to examples from later periods (Figures 3.1–3.4).

Fig. 3.1   A surviving example of Roman walling
© Brick Development Association

Fig. 3.2   Early Medieval brickwork
© Brick Development Association

When investigating brick deterioration, failure or decay, it is necessary to consider the following possible causes:

- Use of underfired or poorly made bricks, which tend to crumble and erode when exposed to moisture (green bricks that have dried too rapidly crack and warp during kilning).
- Prolonged saturation due to faulty construction or components.
- Shattering or surface disruption as a result of frost action.
- Formation of ice lenses between mortar joints which causes physical disruption of the brickwork.
- Presence of water-soluble salts which may cause efflorescence or cryptoflorescence. Repeated cycles of saturation and drying can cause blockage to the surface pores and induce exfoliation (Figure 3.5).

Fig. 3.3   Tudor brickwork

- Aggressive contamination from air pollution.
- The effect of blast cleaning, which can sometimes destroy the 'skin' or outer surface and leave the exposed under areas vulnerable to decay.
- Damage due to calcium deposits being washed into the pores of facework from nearby limestone walling or from limestone dressings which have been incorporated into the brickwork.
- Movement due to inadequate bearings, abutments or wall thickness, either from an original error or as the result of subsequent alterations and changes.
- Corrosion of iron and steel constructional components.
- Damage due to decaying timber embedded within the brickwork.
- Expansion of mortar due to calcium sulphate in solution reacting with Portland cement to form ettringite (calcium sulpho-aluminate) which generates an increase in mortar volume. This condition is usually confined to chimneys.
- A rare form of expansion can also be caused through the use of magnesium lime mortars. If the quicklime has been produced at the wrong temperature, slaking will not take place in the correct manner. There is likely to be a delayed reaction from the magnesium, which can cause an eventual expansion in volume.

Fig. 3.4   Elaborate Victorian brickwork in a house designed by Alfred Waterhouse

- Thermal movement in older brickwork is normally minimal due to lime mortars being softer and more able to absorb climatic differences. Nevertheless it is a condition which should not be overlooked, particularly where large areas of brickwork have been built in harder mortars containing a proportion of Portland cement.
- Although normally associated with the action of frost, spalling can also occur if the brickwork has been exposed to intense heat from fire at some point in the past.
- A deterioration of the binding properties in a mortar is detectable when large amounts of sand and lime can be picked out as single fragments. The bricks become individual components surrounded by a disengaged mortar mass. The structural integrity of a wall in this condition will have been depleted.
- Growing vegetation can be harmful and cause damage, especially ivy, which has roots that penetrate into the mortar to produce eventual expansion and dislodgement. Although Virginia creeper is less harmful it is liable to sustain a wall in a condition of perpetual dampness.

Fig. 3.5   Efflorescence to a brick wall

3.1   THE REPAIR AND MAINTENANCE OF BRICKWORK

Operations need to be undertaken in accordance with the undermentioned principles:

- An accurate written and pictorial record of both the original and completed work should be compiled for future reference and left in a place of safe keeping.
- As far as is practicable leave all authentic features untouched and preserved.
- Ensure all new work harmonises with the original.
- Check the site for any likely historic or archaeological revelations which could hinder or disrupt works when in progress. If in doubt, seek advice from an archaeologist or an appropriate organisation and delay any digging until an inspection has been completed.
- Execute work in a manner which is reversible so far as feasible.
- Areas which need to be rebuilt can be suitably strengthened using either stainless-steel ladder or helical bar reinforcement.

Brick making has passed through a number of different stages and the various fashions and styles need to be recognised and correctly interpreted. As far back as 1425, attempts made to standardise brick sizes never achieved uniformity due to a combination of circumstances, including variations in firing tolerances between different clays. The introduction of a brick tax in 1784 also meant a shift towards larger brick dimensions in an attempt to minimise the effect of the tax. The legacy has been a range of different sizes and textures which are likely to vary in size from those of the present day (Table 3.1). Before operations begin, it is essential to secure an adequate supply of suitable bricks obtainable from one or more of the following sources:

- Matching bricks that have been salvaged through a reputable source.
- Retrieving bricks that have been damaged and re-laying them in reverse on the clean or unmarked face.
- The manufacture of special bricks to the same size, colour and texture as the original (Figure 3.6).
- The application of brick slips that have either been purpose made or cut from bricks that are compatible with the existing ones.

Table 3.1   A chronological summary of variations in brick sizes

1200	About this time the first English bricks (then known as waltyles) were made. No set size established. Dimensions usually varied from $12''$ to $11'' \times 6'' \times 1\frac{3}{4}''$ to $2\frac{3}{4}''$ (306 mm $\times$ 279 mm $\times$ 70 mm). Brick lengths of up to $15''$–$20''$ (381–508 mm) have been discovered. All these sizes are now described as 'great bricks'.
	During the thirteenth century Flemish craftsmen settled in East Anglia and introduced smaller brick sizes. The dimensions varied from $9\frac{3}{4}''$ to $8'' \times 4\frac{3}{4}''$ to $3\frac{1}{4}'' \times 1\frac{3}{4}''$ to $2\frac{1}{2}''$ (230–203 mm $\times$ 103–77 mm $\times$ 44–52 mm).
1490	About this time a notable era in English brickwork began. Bricks moulded to various shapes including the replication of stone ornamentation. 'Tudor bricks' mainly sized $9'' \times 4\frac{3}{4}'' \times 2''$ (228 mm $\times$ 102 mm $\times$ 50 mm).
1571	Bricks sizes were determined by decree and were required to be $9'' \times 4\frac{1}{2}'' \times 1\frac{1}{4}''$ (228 mm $\times$ 103 mm $\times$ 57 mm). The ruling was not effectively enforced and some bricks from this period are likely to have different dimensions.
1700	From about this time, brick sizes tended to diminish to $8\frac{1}{2}'' \times 4\frac{1}{8}'' \times 2\frac{3}{8}''$ (204 mm $\times$ 101 mm $\times$ 51 mm). The trend towards reduced brick sizes resulted in the introduction of the frog.
1729	Size regulated by statute to $8\frac{3}{4}'' \times 4\frac{1}{8}'' \times 2\frac{1}{2}''$ (205 mm $\times$ 101 mm $\times$ 52 mm). These bricks became known as 'statute bricks'.
1784	Brick tax introduced.
1840	Imperial brick size introduced: $8\frac{3}{4}'' \times 4\frac{1}{8}'' \times 2\frac{1}{2}''$ (205 mm $\times$ 101 mm $\times$ 52 mm). In parts of the Midlands and the North of England the thickness was increased to $3''$ (75 mm).
1850	Brick tax abolished.
1965	A British Standard came into being under BS 3921: 1965 which stipulated dimensions as $8\frac{5}{8}'' \times 4\frac{1}{8}'' \times 2\frac{5}{8}''$.
1969	The British Standard size was metricated to 215 mm $\times$ 102.5 mm $\times$ 65 mm under BS 3921: Part 2.

Fig. 3.6 Polychrome brickwork. The projection to the right of the picture is a more recent addition and is constructed in purpose-made matching bricks. A perfect example of how new and old can be made to blend

If the original brickwork has weathered, it may be difficult to avoid a contrast between the old and the new, but the problem can be lessened by applying a soot wash or a tinted solution to the new areas (see also Section 2.2).

3.2 PLASTIC REPAIRS

Badly decayed bricks can be refaced with a specially compounded mortar that matches the original brick. This solution is not normally favoured, but if permitted the damaged areas must be cut back to a square and even face to a depth of not less than 25 mm. Use of clean sharp sand which blends to the situation is essential, together with a masonry cement binder and matching brick dust. Additives such as SBR (styrene butiadene rubber) can sometimes be suitably incorporated into a mix but the use of proprietary pigments should be avoided.

3.3   STRUCTURAL CRACKING AND DEFICIENCY

This will require detailed analysis and specialist advice should normally be sought. When assessing cracked walling it is well to consider if it has been caused through the alleviation of internal stresses, which may be best left unaltered. It is a condition which is frequently mistaken for a failure in the foundations. Any remedy will be influenced by the severity of the distress, but serious structural disorder could necessitate the dismantling and rebuilding of the wall concerned. In older buildings the action of roof thrust is another reason for distortion. Conventional repair systems for leaning or bulging walls can provide a satisfactory solution, subject to them not harming the visual appearance. To overcome this problem, internal buttressing using 'L' shaped cranked reinforced concrete can offer an unobtrusive remedy, provided the work is carried out in accordance with the recommendations issued by the SPAB (see also Figure 3.7 and SPAB Technical Pamphlet No.1).

Due to the softer nature of lime mortar and to the increased tolerances this allows, it is sometimes possible to jack a leaning wall back into a vertical or near vertical position. If failure is caused by inadequate bonding between brick skins, this can normally be rectified by the use of grouting or the insertion of stainless-steel ties. Detached facework is frequently found in properties built in the eighteenth and nineteenth centuries and arises from a failure to bond skins with an adequate proportion of headers. The appearance may be satisfactory, but in reality 'snap' headers have been inserted which have created an inherent weakness. Insufficient bonding at wall junctions is often an additional source of weakness in buildings of the same period. It usually happens because skilled labour was only used for the facework.

Impregnation with either epoxy or polyester resin has to be viewed with reluctance, but is a possible solution. Where the brick fabric is soft and has weakened substantially, the treatment combines and consolidates the bricks and the mortar into a solid mass. This effectively converts the whole into a new material with a different coefficient of expansion, which apart from being irreversible, can also cause new problems of an incremental nature.

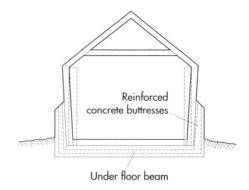

Reinforced
concrete buttresses

Under floor beam

Fig. 3.7   Methods of restraining outward movement. The introduction of reinforced concrete buttresses tied into a ground beam under the floor is an effective method of restraining outward movement. SPAB Technical Pamphlet No. 1 offers guidance on dealing with the problem

3.4 REPAIRING CRACKED BRICKWORK

A difficult and problematical condition occurs when movement has resulted in differential settlement and the pattern of continuous coursing falls out of common alignment at the points of fracture. The variation in joint levels can often be concealed by
cutting back the brickwork on either side of the fracture to a distance which will allow
the mortar jointing to be gradually adjusted to give an acceptable optical effect. In
more difficult cases, the remedy may require a complete rebuild or the introduction of
a feature which masks the scarring legacy of the remedial work. Replacement brickwork should normally be undertaken in lifts of not more than 1 m and should extend
at least 450 mm on either side of the fracture even when the adjoining bricks have
remained in alignment.

3.5 WALL-TIE FAILURE

The advent of cavity walling was accompanied by an array of materials used as wall-
ties. Slate strips and header bricks were a popular choice at one stage and a number of
unsatisfactory proprietary brands in other materials also appeared on the market
(Figure 3.8). When investigating original cavity work, it is well to remember that
some of this work lacks any form of tying between the skins.

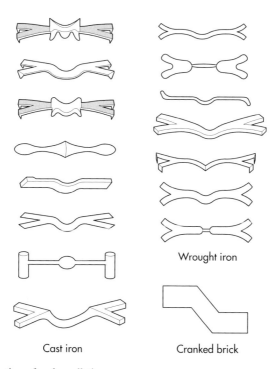

Cast iron   Cranked brick

Fig. 3.8 A selection of early wall-ties

Many of the mild steel 'fishtail' ties used after World War I are now corroding and are liable to cause considerable damage. The signs are lifting and sometimes bowing of the brickwork, together with rust staining in the mortar jointing. The wire 'butterfly' ties which became popular during and after the 1930s are also vulnerable to the same problem but the effects are normally less severe. While remedial action necessitates the insertion of mechanically fixed and corrosion-resistant replacements, all the offending ties must be completely removed otherwise the effects of rust expansion will continue to cause further damage.

3.6 RAIN PENETRATION IN BRICKWORK

Rain penetration in either the bricks or the mortar or both can induce serious decay. If bricks are of sufficient density, repointing may be adequate. But if the mortar and the bricks are unduly porous the application of a water-repellent solution may be a better remedy. The colourless proprietary liquids now available are mostly formulated from silicone resins, which alter the treated fabric from a hydrophillic to a hydrophobic condition. There is, however, a need to be cautious before deciding on a treatment, as spalling can occur if soluble salts are already present in the brickwork.

It is necessary to follow this routine before use:

- Have a chemical analysis made to check for the presence of soluble salts in either the bricks or the mortar.
- Follow the suppliers' instructions completely.
- Make a careful inspection of the general condition of the wall concerned and make sure that the source of any dampness has been accurately traced; otherwise treatment may exacerbate faults by increasing the rate of penetration at certain points. If points of water penetration have not been correctly identified, considerable damage can occur through restricted evaporation of the fabric after treatment.
- Applications should only be made to dry walls; otherwise trapped moisture may migrate to the interior surfaces and evaporate out.

3.7 USE OF CONSOLIDANTS

Normally alkoxy-silane-based systems are chosen, but there is some concern over the long-term effect that consolidants may have on older brickwork, and they are normally considered unsuitable for use on bricks with a high density. Any treatment of this type should not be used without taking expert advice.

3.8 REPAIRS TO GAUGED BRICKWORK

Gauged brickwork is produced by setting finely jointed and accurately formed bricks in lime putty to standards of extreme precision. This is achieved by rubbing soft outsized bricks down to a particular shape or size and considerable skill is required to produce slender joints to uniform dimensions (Figure 3.9). The close juxtaposition of gauged bricks makes repair or replacement work difficult and attempts to rake out and repoint joints are rarely successful. Good practice should:

■ Allow for careful dismantling and re-assembly when bricks need to be reset or replaced.
■ The surfaces surrounding the area of operation require adequate protection, such as the application of a latex solution which is peeled away upon completion.

It is normally possible to replace an individual brick by cutting it out with a hacksaw blade, especially in more accessible locations. The replacement brick can be set into position with the aid of wedges after which a lime putty slurry or a slurry of lime and HTI powder is injected into the joints using a hypodermic syringe.

Fig. 3.9 Arches in gauged brickwork

3.9 TERRACOTTA AND FAIENCE

There is no definitive demarcation between moulded bricks and terracotta; the practical difference is in the method of manufacture and the texture of the raw material, which for terracotta is more finely blended (Figure 3.10). The term faience is normally confined to glazed terracotta. Colour is influenced by the composition of the constituent clays, which are fired to very high temperatures. This has the effect of causing extensive shrinkage in the finished product and is a factor which makes the production of

Fig. 3.10   A fine example of intricate terracotta

replacement items difficult. It is the reason why alien materials such as fibreglass are on the market, but they are seldom permitted for use in buildings of architectural or historic importance.

All work to terracotta and faience should observe the following principles:

- Visual signs of surface decay do not always reveal the correct degree of deterioration, which may be more extensive in concealed and inaccessible locations within the body of the terracotta. Cellular units can be checked with an endoscope to determine the condition of the internal webbing, but this causes slight, permanent damage and demands caution.
- The preservation and protection of terracotta and faience is dependent upon the quality and weathering properties of the mortar joints. Jointing is highly vulnerable to water penetration due to the impermeable nature of the surface skin of the terracotta. If moisture is allowed to creep into the main body of the material, it cannot evaporate and incipient decay will take effect.
- Replacement units should be inspected and checked for quality before installation. Inadequate firing, which leaves the surface less resistant to moisture, is a likely fault. Badly fired products are prone to distortions, warping and cracking.

- Inadequately glazed faience surfaces will become pitted and eventually powder.
- Persistent water penetration under the surface skin can result in salt crystallisation either at or immediately below the fire skin and causes serious spalling.
- Metal fixings should be made of stainless steel.
- Defective parts can be cut out using a small diamond-tipped masonry saw lubricated during use with clean water.
- Extensive cracking can be a sign of overloading in the wall.
- A useful mix for repointing is 1:3 (hydraulic lime/finely graded sand and stone dust).
- Small areas of surface damage can be filled with a matching polyester or epoxy paste.
- More extensive plastic infill repairs are feasible using a suitably compounded mortar. This will require some experimentation and the use of experienced labour.

FURTHER READING
See sections on Bricks and Chimneys in the References.

CHAPTER 4

UNBAKED EARTH CONSTRUCTION

4.1 MONOLITHIC FORMS

The dictates of economics and difficulties in transporting building materials forced many communities in earlier times to utilise locally available materials such as unbaked earth. Light sandy soils are not suitable for this form of construction. Thus clay and earth building, commonly known as cob, is only found in certain locations within the British Isles. It should be noted that the term cob is more precisely used for unbaked earth work in the counties of Dorset and Devon (Figures 4.1 and 4.2). In other parts of the country many different local names are used, such as clam in Cornwall, clom in

Fig. 4.1   Building of a cob wall in progress

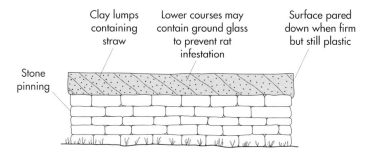

Fig. 4.2 Cob course. Cob is trodden in and consolidated to a diagonal pattern as shown

Wales, clay dabbins in Cumbria and wichert in Bedfordshire. Useful visual clues for identification purposes are deep window reveals, a well-raised plinth and the absence of a sharp arris at the quoins, which tend to be rounded or less defined than normal.

The mud strata used for unbaked earth work are mainly derived from chalk marls, sedimentary clays and drift deposits and most require tempering before being ready for use. When preparing mixes for repair work, it is essential to reduce to a minimum the natural tendency of clay to expand when wet and to shrink when dry. This can be achieved by balancing the clay with straw and a stone aggregate, the latter being suitably graded for particle size. There are many localised practices and preferences for tempering clay, including the use of a variety of additives. It is widely believed that cow dung was used extensively for this purpose. This is incorrect, although it is often found in repair mixes, especially those dating from Victorian times. The dried mix remains fast and cohesive because the clay content not only binds the aggregate but also acts as an agglutinant, while the straw functions as integrated reinforcement and reduces shrinkage. The presence of chalk, lime or iron carbonate also has a mild cementing action and an acid reaction between the clay and the straw has a similar effect. In following correct practice, it is important to understand that the material does not remain stable due to this action alone. Cohesion, suction and compaction play a vital part, in association with the essential presence of water in chemical combination and as moisture. When inspecting unbaked earth systems, particular attention should be given to the following:

- The quality of the brick or stone plinth (pinning) upon which the walling is built, which is critical to the durability of the entire structure.
- The condition of flat pieces of timber called stringers which are often found embedded in the cob at directional changes and act as reinforcement.
- As cob is highly vulnerable to damage from roof thrust, it was often the practice to tie-down roof timbers with a series of tie wires which need to be checked at regular intervals.
- Look at door and window frame openings which are normally fixed to wood blocks sunk into the jambs.
- Investigate beam and lintel bearings and check they are well tailed back into the wall. They should also be resting on wood pads usually described as trestle pieces.

4.2   CLAY LUMP WALLING

This is a method of using unbaked earth in block form and is mainly found in East Anglia with blocks being laid in a similar fashion to bricks using either a lime/sand mortar or a clay slurry (Figure 4.3). Variations in block dimensions can be found but 450 mm × 225 mm × 225 mm seems to be the more regular sizing. Clay was tempered in a similar way to cob, with straw being added prior to moulding. Once dry, the blocks were used in a conventional manner and had the advantage of minimal drying shrinkage which allowed for a stronger structure. This added stability and gave scope for use with brick and stone. In consequence, many clay lump buildings have facings in these materials which can give a very deceptive initial impression of the true method of construction (Figure 4.4). Signs which can alert the presence of clay lump are:

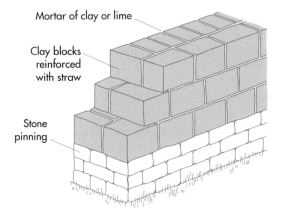

Mortar of clay or lime

Clay blocks reinforced with straw

Stone pinning

Fig. 4.3   Clay lump walling

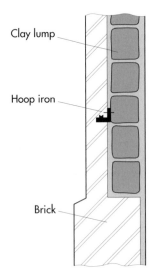

Clay lump

Hoop iron

Brick

Fig. 4.4   Clay lump and brick used in combination

- Unusual wall thicknesses.
- The presence of a brick plinth.
- Rendered walls with internal reveals.
- The pitch of the roof.
- Brick on edge facing.
- Rust stains in brick or stone facework which do not match wall-tie patterns are likely to be from hoop iron, which was used to tie the clay lump and brick or stone together and has rusted.

4.3   CAUSES OF DETERIORATION TO UNBAKED EARTH

- The infiltration of water.
- Excessive weight bearing.
- Failed timbers and beams.
- Inadequately tied roofing.
- Erosion of protective wall covering.
- Accumulations of foreign material against the structure.
- Lack of adequate maintenance.
- Damage from penetrating vegetation.
- Damage by animals and insects. Rats and bees can cause extensive damage by burrowing into the structure.
- Modern paints applied to the wall surface.
- Faulty foundations.
- The use of hard, impervious, cementitious renders which crack and allow moisture to penetrate into the wall and to become trapped.

4.4   REPAIRS TO EARTH STRUCTURES

The more usual failures found with this form of construction are:

- The erosion, displacement or collapse of earth.
- Severe cracking (Figure 4.5).
- Outward leaning walls.

Never attempt a repair until the exact reason for failure has been accurately traced and identified. If reclaimed material is used, it must be thoroughly broken down, sieved and tempered and will require the addition of fresh quantities of chopped straw. The addition of hydraulic lime or lime putty is not recommended, as it makes the mix too heavy and too strong. The increasing practice of adding a biocide to reconstituted cob causes an excess of acidity in the mix. If clay contains spores, vegetation or some other form of contamination, it should not be used. Under most circumstances, the application of a reconstituted material is preferable to infilling or indenting with brick or concrete blocks set in lime mortar. Special consideration needs to be given to the following:

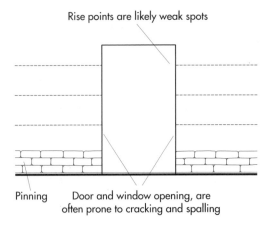

Rise points are likely weak spots

Pinning   Door and window opening, are
often prone to cracking and spalling

Fig. 4.5

- New clays used for repair work should preferably be derived from the original source or otherwise have a matching composition and binding content.
- Defective parts need to be cut to a clear profile with even surfaces and clearly defined edges with changes of direction set at right angles.
- Replacement often requires additional support, which can be achieved by laying clay tiles in lifts within the body of the work. The tiles need to be arranged in horizontal series not less than 300 mm apart, with the ends being set in lime mortar in chasings at the trimmed face. This provides an anchor between the new and the old work. With smaller patches the use of stainless-steel or bronze mesh can provide a satisfactory repair. The defective area must be chased out and filled with new or reconstituted cob, with the mesh being placed horizontally at suitable intervals.
- Cracks can normally be stitched using the mesh repair technique in horizontal series. In all cases where a wet cob mix is used, it needs to be dubbed out proud of the wall surface and trimmed back when in a semi-plastic state (Figure 4.6).
- Always apply cob mixes to a pre-wetted surface.
- The repair media must never be harder than the original material.
- If a large area needs to be rebuilt, it is usually better to infill with unburnt clay bats or bricks as they have the advantage of being pre-dried and can be laid on narrow mud mortar beds of the same material. This method eliminates the problems encountered with shrinkage and steel mesh can be incorporated into the courses for extra strength. The top course is best pinned with a dry packed mortar.
- The mortar jointing to clay lump buildings faced with brick needs to be maintained in good condition to prevent corrosion to the hoop iron ties.
- Renderings which contain Portland cement are prone to the effects of seasonal movements and should be checked regularly for cracking.

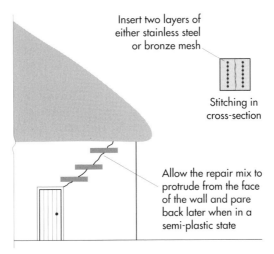

Insert two layers of
either stainless steel
or bronze mesh

Stitching in
cross-section

Allow the repair mix to
protrude from the face
of the wall and pare
back later when in a
semi-plastic state

Fig. 4.6   Stitching to an unbaked earth wall. If stitching is to be done in series, do not chase out all the stitching points in one operation. Work individually taking care to remove the cob with a clawing or scraping action. Serious damage can occur through hammering or by using power tools

4.5   THE REBUILDING OR ALTERATION OF WALLS

The following operational considerations apply. Freshly prepared cob should be obtained from the original source if possible. This is likely to involve some research and a laboratory analysis of the existing material. It is in order to reuse existing cob, provided that it is adequately broken down and any missing elements are reintroduced. It is vital to ensure the constituent materials are in the correct proportions and are distributed uniformly. This is achieved by ample mixing and foot treading until the correct plasticity is reached. In this regard local custom is a reliable yardstick. Building should be carried out in lifts of between 0.30 and 0.60 m in height, which need to be placed and then trodden down at a slight angle to the vertical with the material being allowed to protrude over the intended profile of the wall. The whole is then pared back when the cob is still in a semi-plastic state.

The following considerations are critical when undertaking work to structures built in this manner:

- A small moisture content is essential to prevent failure. However, an excess of moisture will cause the clay to swag or sag and eventually collapse.
- Wall coatings and renders must have the capacity to breathe to ensure the correct moisture balance is maintained.
- Constructional and design features require particular sensitivity to weathering and the exclusion of rain penetration by features such as a wide eaves overhang.
- Consideration needs to be given to natural features to avoid excessive ground dampness and to allow rain-water to drain away from the structure.

- The proper throating of all external joinery and other projections is essential to prevent surface erosion, wall saturation and damage by frost.
- External renderings must be thoroughly mixed and be uniform in texture to prevent uneven moisture and thermal movement, which can cause cracking and eventual deterioration.
- The presence of clinging vegetation and plant life is a likely source of water infiltration and may cause parts to become saturated and 'run'.
- Boundary walling or other structures in direct contact with an unbaked earth walling may have a similar effect and can cause extensive localised damage.
- Internal heating systems need to be designed to standards that will not disturb the equilibrium of the clay and cause an unacceptable fall in the critical moisture factor. Localised concentrations of heat from appliances such as radiators may also need to be shielded from direct contact with clay surfaces to prevent crumbling and cracking around the immediate areas of heat emission. For the same reason, hot pipes taken through walling must be sleeved and external runs should be blocked to stand proud from the wall surface.
- Always maintain a good eaves overhang.
- Replacement cob needs to be protected from rapid drying.
- The quality of the pinning (plinth) is important. If a site tends to be damp, the height of the pinning should be increased to improve the protection.
- Cob is a true masonry form and with repairs to irregular holes, the material must be cut back to give a proper horizontal bed for the repair media to sit on. A patch laid on a sloping bed will eventually slide out from the wall.
- New cob does not adhere properly to old. This may necessitate the provision of bonding points such as tile toothing.
- Cutting into existing cob requires particular care; otherwise unnecessary damage will occur. Do not use direct impact tools such as a bolster and hammer which cause cracking. Cob is best clawed away with an implement such as a scutch hammer.
- For door and window openings, needle and then cut out one side of the wall, insert a timber half lintel, pin and make good. Repeat the exercise for the other side of the wall and clamp the lintel sections together. Complete the cutting out of the opening and the finishing items. Special care is necessary for alterations of this nature.
- To reduce suction, the existing substrate needs to be thoroughly wetted to assist the mortars and renders used in repair work to become more effectively attached.

4.6 PROTECTIVE COATINGS AND RENDERS

The traditional use of limewashed sand/lime renders remains the more satisfactory system of protection though limewash can sometimes be found applied directly to the clay surface. To reduce porosity, additives such as tallow or linseed oil were often incorporated into limewashes, especially in exposed locations. Another form of protection was the application of hot coal tar, which was sanded before the tar had set. Limewashes were then continually applied until staining from the bleeding of the tar ceased.

Under no circumstances should coatings derived from emulsions or a cement base be used, but lime/casein formulated paints are likely to be acceptable if correctly applied.

From about 1850 onwards, renders are frequently found applied to a mechanical key such as expanded metal or chicken wire. As a result they are likely to be defective due to inadequate keying, although this may not always be fully apparent from a visual examination. Many of these renders have been prepared from Portland cement-based mixes which are too strong for use on unburnt clay. In Scotland walls built of monolithic clay are often found faced with an in situ external face of brick or stone to act as an additional weathering surface. Other critical factors to consider are:

- Poor adhesion of the render due to rapid drying.
- Badly proportioned mixes and over-trowelling cause segregation within the mix.
- Hard renders which have cracked result in rain penetration and a serious loss of cohesion within the surrounding areas of the clay (Figure 4.7).
- Over-moist cob walls have a tendency to collapse without warning.
- Renders which have become detached from the wall face can normally be detected by a hollow sound when tapped.
- Lime/sand renders should not be stronger than 1:3, with two-coat work usually being adequate. Animal hair added to the first coat will minimise the incidence of

Fig. 4.7   Clay lump. Moisture penetration from cracks in the rendering has caused erosion on the surface of the clay lump

shrinkage. A thickness of 9 to 16 mm is usually necessary for this coat. The final coat needs to be no more than 10 mm thick and should be worked to a smooth finish using a wood float.

■ Before 1925 it was not established practice to wash building sand. In consequence, most sands used in early building work contain clay and silt impurities, which generally produced better lime mortars and renders.

FURTHER READING
See sections on Unbaked earth construction and Chalk in the References.

CHAPTER 5

STONE AND STONEWORK

5.1 WALL CONSTRUCTION

There are two basic methods used in the construction of stone walling:

- Rubble work.
- Ashlar.

Ashlar is the term used to describe stonework that has been cut and dressed to precise dimensions and which uses narrow jointing. The high quality and regularity of ashlar means it is mostly found in buildings of substance, although features in this idiom are often seen in properties of lesser social importance. Ashlar stone may be worked and dressed to various decoratively tooled finishes. By contrast, rubble work has a much wider interpretation, ranging from many forms of dressed stone blocks to undressed stone of irregular shape and size. Variations in rubble work arise through the natural bed and cleavage of rock formations, the workability and texture of the stone and other characteristics. Included in this category are some miscellaneous forms, such as polygonal walling, flintwork and Lake District masonry.

Apart from the quality of the stone, the strength and stability of a wall depend on the method of construction and the degree of bonding between the stones. In rubble work, 'through' stones should be used at regular intervals and have sufficient length to bridge across the thickness spanning from face to face. A common type of rubble walling is formed from inner and outer skins of stone, with the core or hearting being filled with small, compacted stones or other inert material, including earth. Normally rubble stone walls should be not less than one and one-third the thickness of equivalent brick or squared blockwork to attain a similar degree of structural reliability. Under normal conditions, the allowance for stress should not exceed three-quarters of that permissible in conventional brick or blockwork.

Many stones break down slowly and disintegrate naturally over time through environmental and climatic effects which induce surface erosion, flaking and exfoliation. The more destructive defects occur through either chemical attack or physical disruption and both can be accelerated through biological activity. A clear distinction also needs to be made between weathering and decay. The term weathering relates to those changes which do not materially affect the durability of the stone and can bestow a pleasing aesthetic effect. Decay refers to undesirable changes and conditions which cause accrued harm.

5.2   NATURAL STONE DEFECTS

Many failures arise from the use of stone which is unsuited for the purpose and function to which is has been applied. It is important to be alert to the following natural defects when investigating or selecting material for walls built in sedimentary stone:

- The presence of vents, which are small fissures that permit the penetration of moisture, especially in exposed positions.
- The existence of shakes (sometimes known as snailcreep), which are minute cracks within the body of the stone containing calcite. They can be identified as hard veins which eventually become very pronounced if the stone erodes.
- Sand holes that occur when loosely bound sand has become trapped in the stone.
- Clay holes are formed in a similar way and both conditions cause early decomposition when exposed to extremes of weather.
- Shelly bars are shells and fossils embedded in the stone which can harbour unwanted moisture.
- Stone which has a high clay or iron-oxide content is likely to be disfigured by brown bands and marks, which also reduce durability.
- Sandstones consist mainly of quartz grains held in a matrix of either silica, calcite, magnesium carbonate or a similar substance. It is important that the nature of the matrix is correctly indentified, as this is likely to affect durability. Where the cementing material contains clay, the stone will have poor weathering qualities. A matrix with a high silica content makes for a good quality stone.

5.3   FORMS OF DECAY

The decay of all natural building stones has an association with moisture through:

Chemical attack: Arising from the presence of soluble salts which have either been absorbed or contained within the stone or from atmospheric pollutants. Salts in solution can lead to a build-up of the salt content in the surface areas, which eventually exerts pressure and causes internal stresses and rupturing. Evidence of this is usually seen as powdering and fragmentation. Some soluble salts gain entry through the capillary attraction of moisture in the soil. Damp soils contain ions of dissolved mineral salts, particularly nitrates and to a lesser extent chlorides. Nitrates are a sure indication of ground contamination, except where soil has accummulated as a result of plant life growing in unusual locations at higher levels.

Apart from carbon dioxide, there are other substances in polluted air, including sulphur dioxide and sulphur trioxide, which combine with water to form sulphurous compounds and sulphuric acid, respectively. Although exposed areas of limestone are gradually washed and eroded by rainfall, the more sheltered parts receive little direct cleaning in this way. The acids are carried into the pores of the stone to form calcium sulphate, which slowly builds up as a skin and eventually becomes a thick black encrustation. In the course of time this blisters and exfoliates to leave a severely weakened layer of limestone. It is a cycle which continues until the limestone has been eaten away (Figures 5.1 and 5.2).

Serious cumulative damage can also occur as a result of carbon dioxide, dissolved by rainfall, penetrating the stone in solution. This action is harmful to limestones and calcareous sandstones, as it gradually weakens the cementitious material within the stone to cause loss of cohesion and eventual disintegration.

Physical action: Action arising from penetrating frost, thermal stress or attrition by wind-borne action can be highly destructive. Susceptibility is linked to the size and nature of the pore structure, with limestones more likely to be affected than other stones. Moreover, if soluble salts have accumulated just under the surface, they block the pores and create a breakaway pattern which follows the contour of the surface rather than the bedding plane. It is normally caused by a difference in the coefficients of expansion

Fig. 5.1 Encrusted limestone showing how internal stresses have resulted in exfoliation

Fig. 5.2   Exfoliation of limestone surface

of the absorbed salts in the stone and the unadulterated parts of the same stone. In exposed locations, stonework can be harmed by rapid wetting and drying which drives salt-laden rain into the stone to cause excessive crystallisation.

Biological and biochemical activity: Occurs when algae, fungi, lichens and mosses grow on the face of the stone or from the deposition of animal waste. Organic growths tend to encourage the retention of water which promotes the process of decay. However, some forms of bacteria and algae only remain active in the presence of persistent moisture. Although these die if the offending source of moisture dries up, the residual humus can host other forms of plant life such as mosses, liverworts and grasses. Many of these growths release acids which etch marks on limestone surfaces. Slime fungi only occur in heavily shaded and excessively damp conditions.

5.4   INCOMPATIBLE STONES AND COMPOUNDS

Deleterious compounds originating in the mortar can be absorbed into the stone and cause decay. A destructive action will occur if limestone and sandstone are used in combination. Rain can induce calcium sulphate in the limestone to migrate into the sandstone, causing excessive deterioration. Similarly, limestone used in conjunction with magnesian limestone will decay through the absorption of magnesium sulphate. There have also been recent reports of some Scottish sandstones being adversely affected by the presence of lime in the fixing mortar.

Fig. 5.5 Concave bedding. The blocks were hollowed out to enable very fine joints to be formed at the facing. This causes unequal stressing and renders the stone vulnerable to spalling along the mortar lines of the bed joints

- The upper surfaces of projecting labels, mouldings, string courses and similar features tend to become saturated more readily than the surrounding stonework. As a result they need to be carefully checked, as they are prone to earlier decay.
- Iron embedded in stone masonry is a constant cause of damage from expansion due to rust. To minimise this risk, it has long been the practice to run fixing points in lead. Older iron which has been smelted in charcoal has less of a tendency to rust due to the absence of sulphurous compounds which are produced during the more modern coal-fired process. Tinning can also increase the risk of rusting as a result of electrolytic action between the metals.
- Face-bedded stones must be more thoroughly checked as they are prone to frost damage (Figure 5.6).
- Examine pointing to make sure it is not having a harmful effect. If it is too hard this can increase the rate of decay in the stone. Soft sandstone in particular can be affected in this way. If the mortar joints protrude slightly beyond the face of the stone, check for surface erosion.
- Check the surface of exposed and weathered surfaces of granite for granulation, which is caused through a build-up of soluble salts at the surface due to the low

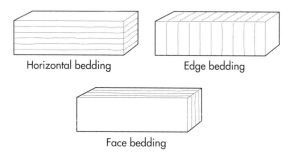

Horizontal bedding   Edge bedding

Face bedding

Fig. 5.6 Bedding of natural stone. Stone should normally be laid on its natural horizontal bed. When face-bedded, any weakness in the laminae may result in the layers separating and pinning may be needed

porosity of the stone. Also look for signs of flaking as this is a likely indicator of a deterioration of the mica content in the stone.
- Medieval stonework was sometimes painted in contrasting colours. If any remaining traces are found they must be properly recorded and brought to the immediate notice of an archaeologist.

5.8 REPAIRS AND MAINTENANCE

- As a general rule the mortar should be slightly weaker and softer than the stone.
- Where arch forms crack in a manner that indicates horizontal movement to the supports, either the load must be reduced, or remedial measures taken, such as the provision of buttressing, corsetting or the introduction of ties.
- Care should be taken to ensure bruising does not occur to replacement stone during the handling and placement stages. Heavy impacts can cause powdering and flaking at the point of contact.
- Unequally imposed forces can invariably be alleviated by reducing or removing them through techniques such as the provision of padstones, which provide a more uniform method of load distribution.
- Foundation failures and movements may be arrested by various forms of piling or underpinning. Likewise, leaning or unstable wall problems can be accommodated using measures such as reinforced concrete bands or buttresses, the fitting of mild steel rods and similar techniques (Figure 3.7).
- The redressing of an original stone face should only be contemplated if this is seen as the only suitable option. The practice is generally discouraged as being alien to conservation ideals, but can sometimes be condoned if the work is of a highly superficial or minor nature.
- Replacement stone needs to have characteristics which are compatible with and match the original. Always test for strength and check for durability. Samples should be worked to ensure they can be tooled to the same quality and style as the original.
- An alternative to complete replacement is indenting, whereby the defective face of the stone is cut back and a matching stone slip is fitted using either stainless steel, phosphor bronze cramps or epoxy resin and dowelling (Figures 5.7–5.9).
- Mortar mixes can often be made to replicate natural stone using finely ground reclaimed or matching natural stone together with lime and sometimes a hint of white cement. It is essential that the resultant material be weaker than the stone to be faced and that the plastic repair mix be built-up in a succession of layers if replacement goes much below surface level. An armature of phosphor bronze wire or other non-corrosive metal will also be necessary for deeper penetrations (Figure 5.10). Mixtures using epoxy resin as a binder are a possible alternative, but this creates an inappropriate substance and, when left unpainted, has the disadvantage of showing as a darker patch during periods of rainfall.
- Modern developments have resulted in the use of polymerised resins which impregnate the fabric in a manner that not only alters the nature of the stone, but also changes some essential characteristics such as porosity and the coefficient of thermal

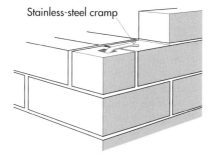

Fig. 5.7 Use of non-ferrous metal cramps. The stone indent should be bedded and consolidated in position using a matching mortar, with holes being left at strategic points to enable voids to be grouted in

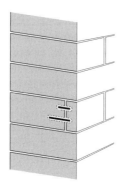

Fig. 5.8 Indenting stone with epoxy resin. The stone indent is secured by glass fibre-reinforced linking rods set in resin

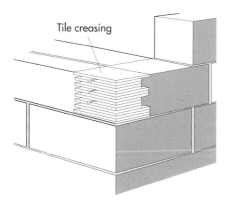

Fig. 5.9 Indenting with tiles. The tiles are set in a lime/sand mortar. This technique was developed by SPAB as a way of introducing an 'honest' repair

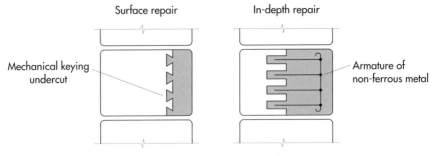

Fig. 5.10   Plastic repairs

expansion. Used as an alternative to grouting, the resin combines and consolidates the mortar and stone into a hardened cohesive mass. Both epoxy and polyester resins can be used, but the process is not reversible and for this reason is seldom acceptable for historic works. The changed nature of the stone means it may not be compatible with the remaining elements of the structure which have hitherto been in harmony. In the early aftermath of this treatment, there can be a problem with a lingering smell more particularly with polyester resins.

■ Resins can also be used for pinning layers of stone which are delaminating by injecting, either under pressure or by hypodermic syringe, a low viscosity resin which fixes and fills the fine fissures and cracks.

■ Considerable care must be exercised in the selection of sandstone for repair or replacement work. There can sometimes be a wide divergence in the strength and durability of sandstone from the same seam.

■ With granite walling, soft or decaying mortar often enables water to penetrate deeply into the joints. As a result, it cannot evaporate out properly due to the impervious nature of the stone. For this reason, replacement pointing mortar in granite walling needs to be stronger and denser than that normally used in other historic works in order that it can act as a moisture barrier. The use of additives in the mix will increase the bonding between the mortar and the stone.

5.9   GROUTING

Under suitable conditions, masonry walling can be consolidated and stabilised by grouting, especially if the walls are of a good thickness or have a rubble core, but allowance always needs to be made for possible redecoration of the internal walls as a result of the treatment. It is an operation which has to be undertaken with meticulous care, otherwise damage is likely to occur, particularly from hydrostatic pressure. If possible, injection by power pumping should be avoided, as it can be difficult to assess a safe pressure tolerance in the masonry. A number of mixes are in use, but those containing Portland cement are liable to cause a dark staining on stone through the formation of either calcium or sodium hydroxide. A cement content can also lead to surface damage through crystallisation. Such disadvantages have firmly established a preference for low sulphate pulverised fuel ash (PFA) which is increasingly being selected in conjunction with lime and other additives such as bentonite which aid mobility and suspension. A suitable mix is 1:1:$\frac{1}{2}$ lime (bagged)/ PFA/ bentonite. Grouting operations should be carried out in accordance with the procedures shown in Figure 5.11.

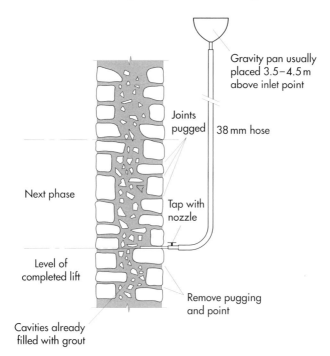

1. Any cracked areas together with loose or open joints need to be thoroughly raked out and cleared of debris.
2. Small holes are drilled about 1.2 m apart horizontally and 0.5 m apart vertically. The holes should alternate with those immediately above and below.
3. Wash out and thoroughly clean with water pouring into the core of the wall from the top.
4. Note where the water runs out and plug these weaknesses and the drilled holes with tightly fitting tow or well rammed clay to a depth of about 50 mm.
5. Operations should start at the base of the wall working upwards in lifts of about 0.5 m. Allow the grout to set before commencing the next lift.
6. When the grouting has set firmly the temporary jointing should be raked out and pointed in a matching mortar.
7. On no account should this work be undertaken during periods of frost

Fig. 5.11 Gravity grouting

5.10 WEATHER PROTECTION

5.10.1 Protective applications

Some success has been achieved with limestone by applying a solution of limewater (not limewash) to the point of saturation. Known as the Baker method, it relies on the lime in solution evaporating out as hard deposits of lime within the pores of the stone to create improved weathering. As a relatively recent innovation it has yet to withstand the test of time, but it does have the advantage of retaining the natural appearance of the stone. On the other hand, the use of limewash has long been a traditional method of protection but it conceals the distinctive features of the stone. Nevertheless, limewash gives proven protection and enables the stone to 'breathe' and if water penetration occurs moisture will evaporate out during dry periods.

5.10.2 Silicone water repellents

The use of silicone water repellents is seldom appropriate in conservation works as it can change the visual appearance of the stone and impart an uncharacteristic surface sheen. In addition it may alter the natural colouring. For this reason much care, forethought and discussion with those who are knowledgeable need to take place before embarking on such action. It is certainly not an acceptable treatment for sensitive stones surfaces or where the fabric is of special historic quality. If this form of treatment is approved, it is vital to thoroughly remove any vegetational matter or other growths, otherwise this will become affixed to the surface and appear as an unsightly stain.

When applied as a colourless solution, repellents have the ability to inhibit the ingress of water, but at the same time will allow water vapour to evaporate out when climatic conditions permit. Most treatments have a life of between five and ten years and can prevent the propagation of algae and unsightly moulds. They are available as either solvent-based silicone or aqueous formulated solutions. Normally silicone treatments are not so successful on limestones and the better results usually come from sandstones.

5.10.3 Consolidants

Consolidants can be used to protect delicate areas of stonework which have become soft and friable. The notion of treating stone in this way is not new, but modern chemistry has produced a range of products in the form of alkoxysilanes, acrylic polymers, epoxies and polyurethanes. The more promising results are from silanes, which offer improved penetration because they can be applied as a monomer. In chemical terms, the monomer molecules of silane eventually polymerise to form larger three-dimensional lattice structures which set rigidly and hold the stone particles firmly together. As it is a relatively new technique, the long-term effectiveness of this method has still to be proved. It is seldom favoured by conservators, as the changed condition of the stone cannot be altered. Before considering such treatment, there is a need to correctly identify the nature of the substrate and the extent of the decay. Small samples of the stone should be taken from a concealed point for laboratory examination so that the effectiveness of the treatment can be tested for suitability and strength, and whether or not it is likely to have any effect on the natural colour of the stone.

5.11 COADE STONE

Coade stone is an artificial product which enjoyed much popularity from the late Georgian period through to the Regency and mid-Victorian eras. Much of the ornamental detail which is perceived as stone from these periods is an artificial feature similar in composition to terracotta. The exact nature of the manufacturing process and the constituent materials were never revealed by the Coade family and the secret died with them. Subsequent investigation has indicated that Coade stone is derived from ball clay along with other ingredients such as ground flint, quartz sand and soda–lime–silica glass. Much of the success of the product is also thought to have been due to the skill and meticulous attention to detail exercised at the firing stage. Coade stone products were made to a variety of tastes and fashions and included classical details, reliefs and other forms of decorative embellishment (Figure 5.12).

Although Coade stone is chemically very different to natural stone, it nevertheless has an uncanny resemblance to the genuine material and is constantly mistaken for it. Even an experienced eye can find it difficult to differentiate. A useful indication is the

Fig. 5.12   Entrance dressed in Coade stone

presence of endless and identical repetition of a feature without even the slightest variation. Ironically, Coade stone also shows less signs of weathering and water staining than would be expected from natural stone. On the other hand, it seldom acquires the rich patina so frequently found on mature natural stone.

5.12   FLINT, CHERT, COBBLE AND PEBBLE WALLING

5.12.1   Flint

Flint is found as nodules in the upper and middle chalk formations but, as a result of erosion, there are locations where it appears at surface level. When exposed in this way, it is smooth to the touch, in contrast to quarried flints which have a coarser outer covering. Flat disc-shaped flints are sometimes found within the clusters of nodules. They were often collected separately and used to produce a distinctive feature known as tabular flintwork. Its appearance is not unlike rough-picked Kentish rag stonework. Flint is a near pure form of crypto-crystalline silica and though hard and almost imperishable, it can be difficult to work (Figure 5.13). The extemely dense nature of

Fig. 5.13   The flints in this wall have been carefully selected and are well placed in courses. It is also a rare example of flints being used at the quoins. The practical difficulties in dressing flints to the corners was more usually solved by building the quoins in either brick or stone. Flints quoins are a source of potential weakness

the material is accompanied by brittleness, a feature that has been exploited by generations of builders to good aesthetic efffect (see Section 5.12.6).

5.12.2   Chert

Flint must not be confused with chert which, although similar in form and make-up, is never present in chalk strata and is essentially a feature of other sedimentary rock formations. It is found mainly in the connecting border areas between Devon, Cornwall and Somerset and in parts of Yorkshire. It is derived from a silicious microcrystalline formation and has characteristics similar to flint, but is usually lighter in colour and is normally found in much larger nodules.

5.12.3   Cobbles, pebbles and boulders

Cobbles, pebbles and boulders differ in quality and strength from flint and come from a variety of rock fragments which have been worn to rounded irregular shapes by the eroding action of either glacial water or the sea. Those suitable for building occur in the beds of streams, esturies and on the seashore. Stones which are over 75 mm in diameter but do not exceed 300 mm are termed cobbles; those under 75 mm are called pebbles. It is a material which has been used extensively on the south coast of England in a similar fashion to flint (Figure 5.14). Boulder stones are those over 300 mm in size and are frequently set with smaller stones which sometimes function as positioning wedges. Stones of a gigantic size are sometimes described as cyclopean.

Fig. 5.14 Pebble walling similar in appearance to flint

5.12.4   Bedding and working

All these materials have highly amophous forms, making placing and jointing difficult. Due allowance needs to be made for much larger quantitites of mortar which under most circumstances is likely to be at least 30 per cent of the total volume. In this context, the quality of the mortar mix is a crucial factor when considering the strength and stability of a flint or chert wall. The impermeable nature of the material means that, unlike brick and most stones, there is practically no adhesion to the mortar, which results in the mortar functioning more as an encasing agent than as a binder.

All the foregoing materials can be laid coursed, roughly coursed or uncoursed, but the appearance and aesthetic effect is dependent on the thickness and quality of the mortar jointing. Walling is usually between 355 and 450 mm in depth with most outer facework being in flints selected to a particular size. The inner face is likely to be in random form, with the core or hearting taking small flints, stones and left-over chippings as well as chalk lumps and other rubble. The longer stones or flint nodules need to be used as 'through bits' to form a tie between the inner and outer skins. The early builders recognised the lack of an effective bond between flint and mortar and overcame the loss of structural strength through the use of either brick or stone at the quoins and by way of lacing courses and similar methods (see Figure 2.2).

5.12.5   Flushwork and chequer-work

The notion of using flint in combination with other materials resulted in the appearance of chequer-work at the beginning of the fourteenth century and the creation of a technique known as flushwork, which is indigenous to East Anglia. In essence, flushwork involves cutting hollows and cavities into ashlared stone to receive an infilling of knapped or undressed flint bedded in lime mortar (Figures 5.15 and 5.16).

5.12.6   Knapped flint

Knapping is a method of fracturing flint nodules to reveal a grey to black lustre surface which is often flecked with white. The technique of knapping requires practice and skill and is achieved by applying a short sharp blow with the aid of a tool. Craftsmen have their own preferences, but many work with a soft wrought-iron hammer while others follow an ancient tradition and use part of an antler. Exposed flint surfaces are sometimes described as polled but, if the nodules have also been dressed and squared, this is often called gauged work and is a later feature. From about 1760 onwards, gauged work became very popular in certain classes of construction and apart from producing a finely dressed surface created a finish which was more waterproof, owing to the fineness of the jointing (Figure 5.17).

Inspection and assessment

- Look for signs of bulging or leaning in the walling and pay particular attention to loading where an original structure has been adapted or altered.

Fig. 5.15 Flushwork (Photograph by kind permission of Brian Dawson and West Sussex County Council)

Fig. 5.16 Flint chequer-work (Photograph by kind permission of Brian Dawson and West Sussex County Council)

Fig. 5.17   Knapped and squared flintwork (Photograph by kind permission of Brian Dawson and West Sussex County Council)

- Cored walls have a tendency to weaken and can become unstable over a period of time due to the gradual consolidation of the hearting (Figure 5.3). The ravages of the weather can also be a contributing factor if rain has persistently penetrated the fabric and washed down the fines in the mortar.
- Knapped flint facework needs to be examined and checked with particular care due to the shallow nature of the bedding caused by the use of half flints, which can give rise to weakness in the facework.

Rebuilding and repairs

- When rebuilding, the outer face should be laid first in shallow lifts followed by the inner facework and hearting at the same level before commencing the next lift (Figure 5.18).
- At each stage ensure appreciable parts of the flint, cobble or pebble work are well defined and have a proud and matching outline, unless the existing work is at variance with this theme.
- The work is labour intensive and an experienced tradesman may average 1 to 1.25 m^2 per day at normal wall thickness, but more intricate work will reduce the work rate to 0.75 m^2 per day under acceptable weather conditions.

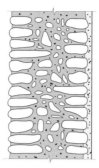

Fig. 5.18   The outer face is laid first, with the mortar joints being set back so that the flint profiles are well defined

- On average, one tonne of uncut flint is likely to yield around 2.7 to 3.25 m^2 of facework. The covering capacity of knapped flint ranges from 4 to 4.5 m^2.
- Old mortar mixes are generally found to be in the ratio of 1:3 to 1:4 lime putty to sand. Old jointing needs to be checked carefully, as in some Medieval flintwork, clay is often found to have been used as a mortar. The sands in old mortars are much coarser and generally contain impurities.
- Avoid embedding the flints or stones too deeply at the initial placing, as this can lead to mortar marks remaining on the nodules to cause permanent disfigurement.
- A successful repair is dependent upon an accurate perception of the method of mortar placement between the existing mortar and the flint or stone (Figure 5.19). To achieve uniformity, the earlier craftsmen often used the width of the thumb as a standard gauge for the thickness of the mortar joints.

Fig. 5.19   A demonstration wall at the Lime Centre, Morestead, showing how flint from the same source can be used to create different effects

- To avoid slippage and sinkage into the mortar, the flint or stone needs to be laid dry using a stiff mortar.
- Rebuilding is often an opportunity to bond back with reinforcement or insert stainless-steel cramps or ties, or alternatively provide a brick or block backing (Figure 5.20).
- In all situations it is essential to work in small areas at a time and to allow the mortar to harden before continuing with the next stage.
- When cutting into existing work, considerable care must be taken to operate in small sections otherwise the hearting may 'pour' or 'flow', a process which is extremely difficult to halt.
- When connecting new to old, always ensure the original surfaces are well wetted, otherwise there is a danger that the water will be sucked out of the fresh mortar.
- Work must not be undertaken in wet or frosty conditions. Too much wind is likely to cause early drying, which halts the carbonation process in the lime mortar.
- The modern practice is to build in flint or stone with a brick or block backing using headers at intervals to provide a system of bonding. Alternatively, stainless-steel ties can be used to link the two materials.
- Mortar joints trowelled to a finish will never blend with the original when left in that state. They need to be either brushed or rubbed with a damp cloth or sponge to bring the sand in the aggregate to the surface.

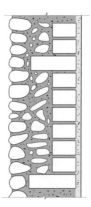

Fig. 5.20   Flintwork with brick or block backing using headers to provide bonding

5.12.7 Galleting

On occasions Medieval builders used a technique known as galleting (sometimes termed garnetting or garretting), which involved inserting small slivers of flint into the mortar jointing of facework before it had set. The exact purpose of the technique is not fully understood, but is more likely to have been conceived on grounds of aesthetics rather than function. From time to time, small stone fragments are also found worked into patterns in the wide joints of heavy block stonework. The technique could also have been devised to deter rain penetration and the erosion of mortar jointing, owing to the manner in which flint slivers were often set (Figure 5.21).

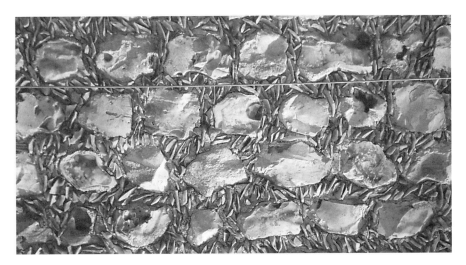

Fig. 5.21 An example of knapped and galleted flintwork

5.12.8 Chalk

In earlier times, chalk was widely used as a building material where it was readily accessible and could be transported at reasonable cost. In essence, chalk is a soft limestone
and in its purest form is 95 per cent calcium carbonate. Most chalks, however, contain
impurities such as quartz, glauconite, iron pyrites and other minerals which can produce slight coloration (Figure 5.22).

In the United Kingdom, the chalk strata vary considerably in composition and
quality, with the harder and more rock-like varieties often being described as clunch.
The term should, however, only be applied to a harder and denser form, found in certain strata in Cambridgeshire and Bedfordshire, which can be identified by a distinctive gritty texture due to the presence of silica. Another fairly coarse-grained chalk is
Beer stone, which is quarried in Devon. It has a distinctive cream colour and although
soft when freshly won, it becomes exceptionally hard on weathering.

Chalk from other parts of the British Isles was also used in block walling and many
well-preserved examples can be found in ashlar, roughly dressed or random rubble form.
It was often favoured as a complement to other materials. But where chalk blocks have
been used externally in isolation, they are mostly found with a protective render or
coating. This often took the form of a limewash or a chalk slurry which was built-up
by successive coatings to form a relatively thick coverage. Crushed chalk was sometimes
used in wet mass form, mixed with straw and clay and applied in a similar manner
to unbaked earth building methods. An alternative was the formation of chalk-mud
lumps which were made and used in a similar way to clay lump. A further variation
was the pise method of construction, which used broken down chalk.

Although most chalk walls are generally considered to be stronger than unbaked
earth, the material will deteriorate quickly and lose cohesion if an excess of water is
allowed to penetrate the structure. Chalk will readily crumble and disintegrate if it is
not properly protected against the weather. Thus all forms of chalk construction need

Fig. 5.22   External facing in roughly dressed chalk blockwork

to be built on a firm brick or stone plinth, together with a good roof covering which has a wide overhang at the eaves.

Repairs and maintenance

- Crushed chalk walling can be repaired with methods similar to those used for unbaked earth. All defective work needs to be cut out cleanly and replaced with a mix which is similar in composition to the original. Reclaimed chalk can be used subject to the addition of a small quantity of lime putty which acts as a binder.
- If repair mixes are kept to a stiff consistency, this will ensure a longer lasting mend.
- With chalk blockwork, the use of a weak mortar is vital, otherwise accelerated decay is likely to occur. Hard mortars cause moisture to evaporate out through the chalk instead of the jointing.
- Replacement blocks must have the same density and porosity as the original to prevent unequal drying and the trapping of moisture.
- Chalk blocks should be naturally bedded.
- All forms of building chalk are best left exposed to the winter weather before use.
- The suitability of chalk blocks for laying can normally be detected if they give a ringing tone when tapped.

FURTHER READING
See sections on Stone and Chalk in the References.

5.13 CLEANING STONE AND BRICKWORK

Cleaning any part of the fabric of an ancient building requires expert knowledge, meticulous investigation and skilled workmanship. The selection of a suitable process will depend on the condition and nature of the material, but immense damage and lasting harm can result from the application of an inappropriate treatment. A wide range of options are available, including water washing (some using high-pressure systems), ultrasonic vibration, air abrasion, micro-air abrasion, laser radiation and certain chemical applications, which may be suitable under expert supervision and monitoring.

Before undertaking any of these treatments, the following issues need to be considered:

- Decide whether cleaning is necessary and balance the differentials between weathering and soiling. The circumstances which cause soiling, such as air pollution and grime, bring about the need to clean, whereas weathering arises more from the formation of a harmless patina which can add charm and character to a building (Figures 5.23–5.25).

Fig. 5.23 All the walling shown has been built at the same time and in the same bricks. Note the contrast between the cleaned and uncleaned parts, the light bricks on the left are the same as the light bricks on the right.

Fig. 5.24   Iron staining on limestone can normally be removed or reduced using a poultice of attapulgite clay containing glycerine, sodium nitrate and water. The work needs to be undertaken by experienced operatives

- Before work commences, take coloured photographs of the areas to be treated and note any particular factors or circumstances. On satisfactory completion of the work, take a further pictorial record and date for future use.
- Thoroughly check the credentials and ability of the specialist contractor and take up references on operations elsewhere before entering into a commitment.
- Consult an independent authority, such as one of the heritage agencies, on the advisability of any recommended process.
- Insist on a trial patch being undertaken in an inconspicuous location, as some applications can remove or damage essential features.
- Ensure areas not to be treated are properly masked and protected. All cracks and joints should be temporarily stopped and window and door openings must be screened with plywood sheeting which is sealed at the edges. Paintwork and other features can be protected with a latex masking solution. Particular care is necessary in the protection of historic glass and knapped flint if a chemical application is to be used such as hydrofluoric acid, which can rapidly etch a surface to cause permanent scarring.

Fig. 5.25   Lime leaching out due to incomplete adhesion of the mortar to the stone

- If treatment involves the removal of graffiti, anticipate the likelihood of a shadow or residue remaining. If defilement has occurred on historically important or highly sensitive facework, it is advisable to take paint samples and have them analysed by an expert for guidance on a suitable remedy.
- If water-based cleaning methods are to be used, adequate provision must be made for the interception of run-off and the installation of temporary drainage and guttering to a suitable point of disposal. Also fully cater for the collection of silt to avoid creating serious problems in the work area, in addition to causing nuisance and interference to surrounding properties. Monitor the treatment to prevent excessive saturation, as this not only creates drying out problems but will also cause rust in ironwork and the migration of salts.
- Soft lime/sand mortars can sometimes be severely eroded by the action of water cleaning. It is advisable at the planning stage to allow for the possible need for repointing.

- Always plan for chemical treatments to commence at the base and work upwards, as this avoids streaking.
- Unless protective cover has been provided, do not allow work to continue during periods of excessive wind or rain.
- Ensure all those within the area of operation wear adequate protective clothing and safety equipment.
- If dangerous chemicals are to be used, make arrangements for warning notices to be displayed on site and notify the Health and Safety Executive.

FURTHER READING
See section on Cleaning in the References.

CHAPTER 6

TIMBER AND TIMBER WORKS

6.1 BUILDING TIMBERS

In the well-wooded areas of the British Isles the Romans, the Saxons and the Normans all used indigenous oak as a primary building material. The insatiable nature of this demand resulted in a scarcity of supplies during the Medieval period. In consequence other timbers such as willow, hornbeam, ash, pine, elm and Spanish chestnut were also used, but few properties built from these alternatives have survived, although other timbers are often found in oak-framed structures in secondary locations. It was customary to erect oak framing from green, unseasoned wood, which accounts for much of the warping and twisting now seen in many of the surviving buildings of that time. During the evolution of timber building, some fundamentally different methods of construction developed which need to be interpreted as being both technically and geographically separate, although some styles overlap in certain parts of the country.

6.2 TIMBER FRAME CONSTRUCTION

6.2.1 Cruck frame

The cruck system of framing is designed to transfer the entire load of the roof directly to the ground by a series of arch-shaped trusses spaced apart to form bays. The concept needs to be thoroughly understood before any attempts are made at structural change. There are also a number of subtle variations to the cruck theme which call for positive identification. The homeland of the cruck frame is essentially in the north of England and Wales. A different system of timber framing is found in the south east of England and East Anglia up to about the southern banks of the River Humber. In between are zones of mixed influence, with cruck being in the ascendency in much of the Midlands and the north east of England. In general, it is outnumbered in the south west and the mid-south of England (Figure 6.1).

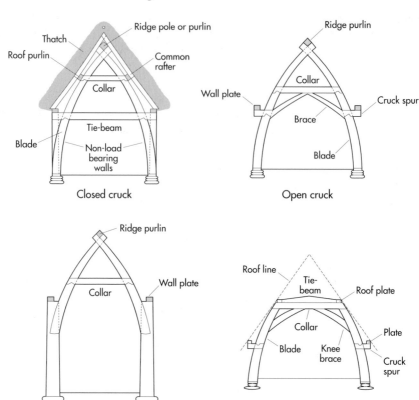

Fig. 6.1   Variations in cruck construction

6.2.2   Box frame and post and truss

The traditional alternatives to cruck are either post and truss or box framing. Both systems attained a high degree of sophistication in terms of inventiveness and craftsmanship, with joints being devised so that the placing of successive members locked into position previous elements. Thus alterations or repairs require much careful forethought, investigation and planning. Post and truss and box frame may appear similar in structural terms; however, they are entirely different. The post and truss system is basically a series of load-bearing frames spaced apart to form bays. In constructional terms, it is formed from a framework comprised of a roof truss resting on vertical posts between which run horizontal sills at ground level and wall plates at eaves level. The weight of the roof is taken mainly by purlins framed into the roof trusses, with the intervening common rafters taking very little direct loading, especially where wind braces have been introduced to direct as much weight as possible towards the trusses. In reality, the intervening timber walling between the trussed framework functions more in the way of infilling. Conversely, the concept of the box frame is derived from a series of timber uprights which share the roof load equally.

There are also some important variations in basic historic timber framing, the more notable being the distinctive appearance of jettying, the Wealden houses of the south east of England and the use of aisled continuations (Figures 6.2–6.5).

6.2.3 Roof construction

Some distinctive roof forms can be found in timber construction with local variations prevailing in some districts. In broad terms the classifications divide into:

- Tie-beam and king post.
- Collar beam and king post which gives increased head room.
- Arch-braced collar beam.
- Trussed rafter and crown post.

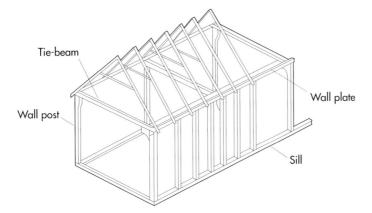

Fig. 6.2 Box frame system

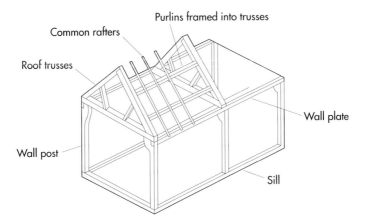

Fig. 6.3 Post and truss system

Fig. 6.4   The 'Bayleaf' house at the Weald and Downland Open Air Museum, Singleton, which is a timber-framed hall-house. Note the jettying to the front and the unglazed diamond-shaped window mullions spaced narrowly apart

King posts are a predominant feature of the north of England and consist of a heavy post supported on a tie-beam that connects directly to the ridge. The principal rafters either side of the tie-beam being tenoned into the king post while the purlins are trenched into the principal rafters. The east and south east of England are the home-land of the crown post system which consists of a heavy timber post resting on a tie-beam that connects to a collar to form a triangular void between the ridge and the upper face of the collar. Normally the favoured method of fixing the purlins is by the clasped method. In arch-braced roof forms, arch braces are used instead of tie-beams, the braces being connected to the collar and principal rafters (Figures 6.6 and 6.7).

An adequate understanding of all these methods is essential before undertaking structural repair or alteration work.

6.2.4   Inspection and assessment

Determine and record the original method of construction and trace any later alterations or additions. Throughout an investigation, accurately describe the existing state of the structure as, in addition to being good practice, this helps to avoid disputes or misunderstandings at a later date. Normally it is wiser to do this with

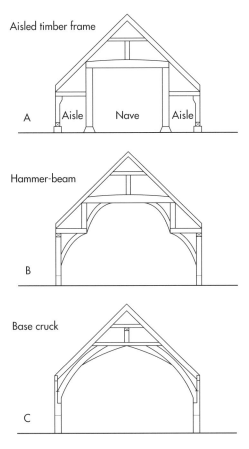

Fig. 6.5 Aisled, hammer-beam and base cruck construction. (The maximum lengths obtainable from home-grown timber imposed limits on building widths. To overcome this problem, some innovative ideas evolved in the form of aisles, hammer-beam roofs and base crucks. Aisles are basically side extensions and are regularly found in old barns and similar buildings. The composite nature of the base cruck, however, marked a significant deviation from a reliance on single-piece blades seen in other forms of cruck construction. Hammer-beam roofs and base crucks were only featured in prestigious buildings and the discovery of this form of construction is an indication of a past use of some importance)

evidence supported by photographs and drawings. The recording exercise should also take particular note of special items such as timber marks, stay notches and soot stains (Figure 6.8). Use a profile gauge to obtain accurate details of features such as mouldings.

Although some timber-framed buildings have been lathed and rendered at a later date, it is not generally realised that many were originally constructed in this fashion and the lathing was intended to act as a strengthener. Considerable damage from rot and general weakening has already been inflicted on a number of these buildings in the mistaken belief that the timbers should be exposed. Normally there is a discernable

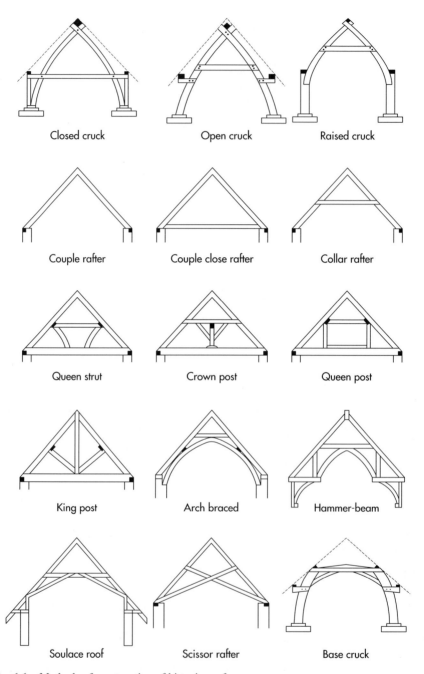

Closed cruck   Open cruck   Raised cruck

Couple rafter   Couple close rafter   Collar rafter

Queen strut   Crown post   Queen post

King post   Arch braced   Hammer-beam

Soulace roof   Scissor rafter   Base cruck

Fig. 6.6   Methods of construction of historic roofs

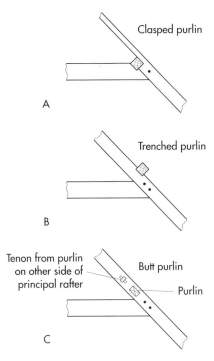

Clasped purlin

A

Trenched purlin

B

Tenon from purlin
on other side of
principal rafter

Butt purlin

Purlin

C

Fig. 6.7   Side purlins in historic roofs. (One of a number of fundamental differences between past and present roof construction is in the method of fixing purlins. Modern purlins are normally fixed strutted under the rafters. This differs in basic terms from earlier practice. The clasped purlin (A) is held between the principal rafter and the collar, the latter being cut to take the shape of the purlin as part of the housing. The trenched purlin (B) is trenched into the back of the principal rafter, but a common variation to this is the use of a through purlin seated on the back of the principal rafter and held by means of a cleat. The butt purlins (C) are tenoned into the principal rafter and are staggered to avoid two mortices at one point which could weaken the principal rafter)

difference in the quality and finish between structural timbers selected for external use and those worked to receive lathing.

- Check structural members for deformation, failed pegging, overloading, movement, slippage, physical damage and decay. Where there is evidence of mechanical failure or distortion, pay particular attention to the condition of the foundations, cill beams, main posts and bracing.
- Consider whether or not the functional and load-bearing demands on the structure can be adequately met.
- Check for any missing structural components which may have been removed as a result of ignorance or blind expediency. This is an important consideration because further operations without adequate safeguards could result in movement or instability in the structure.

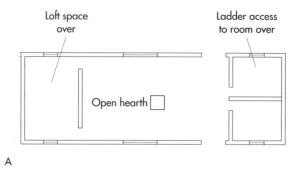

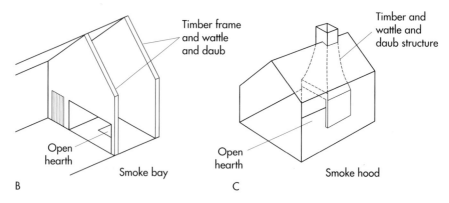

Fig. 6.8   Smoke disposal. It is not uncommon to find smoke-stained timbers in unexpected areas in old houses. This may appear to be evidence of past fire damage. In reality this can be an important legacy of what has gone before and needs to be recorded and protected as part of the historical development of a building. When the central hall was the focal point of domestic life, smoke from the fire (see A) simply drifted up into the roof space and escaped through ventilated openings in the ridge. As domestic living patterns changed, house layouts were adapted accordingly which resulted in the introduction of the smoke bay (see B). The large volume of space occupied by many of these bays can be a misleading indication as to the cause of smoke-laden timbers. Smoke bays were mostly superseded by smoke hoods of wattle and daub (see C) which were the forerunners to the now traditional brick and stone fireplaces and chimneys

- Test the moisture content of timbers at strategic locations. Note that, apart from the vulnerability to fungal or insect infestation, some timbers are liable to weaken and bend if subjected to heavy saturation for a prolonged period of time.
- Thoroughly examine all timbers which are close to or are in contact with the ground.
- Carefully check the ends of timbers embedded in masonry.
- Check for water penetration through defective rain-water goods, valleys, soakers, flashing and similar items.
- Check voids, underfloor areas, spaces behind panelling and similar features for adequate ventilation.

- Look for water stains and any signs of mould, fungal or vegetational growth.
- Examine timber joints and joins for soundness and the condition of any pegging.
- Check for any signs of roof-thrust or other active sources of failure or distortion.
- Pay particular attention to timbers composed or part composed of sapwood. Such wood is more prone to infestation from wood-destroying insects and is likely to have a higher moisture content.
- Check whether any metals are in direct contact with timber. As an example, tannic acid in oak can destroy lead. Also look for signs of wood 'charring' which arises from electrochemical corrosion when moist timber has been in direct contact with metal. This is often found around bolting. Although damage is always confined to the immediate area concerned, it can nevertheless result in the loosening of a joint or a connection.
- Thoroughly check the state of timbers which have been exposed to abnormally high temperatures such as those next to high temperature flues and boilers. Some timbers can split and degrade if exposed to such conditions for prolonged periods of time.
- Timbers of large dimensions, particularly oak and elm, are highly vulnerable to infestation from the death watch beetle, especially if they have been attacked by a wood-destroying fungus such as *Coniophora puteana* (cellar fungus). The beetle prefers damp and unventilated locations and under these conditions infestations tend to be localised. Damage cannot be accurately judged by the number of flight holes, as the life-cycle of the insect can take place entirely within the confines of the timber, leaving no reliable visual evidence as to the extent of the damage. For this reason, large timbers embedded in walling and in similar positions require a meticulous and in-depth check for soundness.

6.3 PRINCIPLES OF REPAIR

The primary aim should be to preserve the antiquity of a building and to keep it weathertight and in a structurally sound condition. Remember, the greater the intervention, the more the intrinsic value of a structure is likely to be impaired. The operating criteria must therefore have full regard to such issues and ensure as much as possible of the original work is retained. Any form of replacement needs to be undertaken in accordance with the principles of honest intervention and in a manner that does not detract from the significance or value of the original. While there is usually a preference for new work to be compatible with the old, the two phases should differ to some discernable degree to prevent any possibility of confusion. The need for replacement must not be interpreted as a licence for replication. Because oak was used in the green state, a technique was devised to pull mortice and tenon joints together so that the shoulder of the tenon rested hard on the mortice member. This was achieved by drawboring, whereby the hole in the mortice member was drilled slightly off-centre so that the final pegging action had the effect of pulling the joints firmly into place.

Certain features such as marks, scores or indentations on historic timber surfaces may be significant and should not be obliterated or removed. They can be important indicators and a means of identifying the history, age and development of a structure. It was the practice of carpenters to mark preformed timbers when ready for assembly with a system of identification resembling Roman numerals. Similar marks were made for setting out, compass arcs and suchlike. Hewing marks used for the conversion of logs into timber baulks and plumb and level marks follow a similar theme. Timber imported from the Baltic was similarly marked by the merchants. The practice was perpetuated into this century (Figure 6.9). Saw marks also provide helpful information from the past. The techniques of circular sawing, band sawing and pit sawing all leave distinctive patterns on the sawn face which can assist in the dating process and should be left untouched.

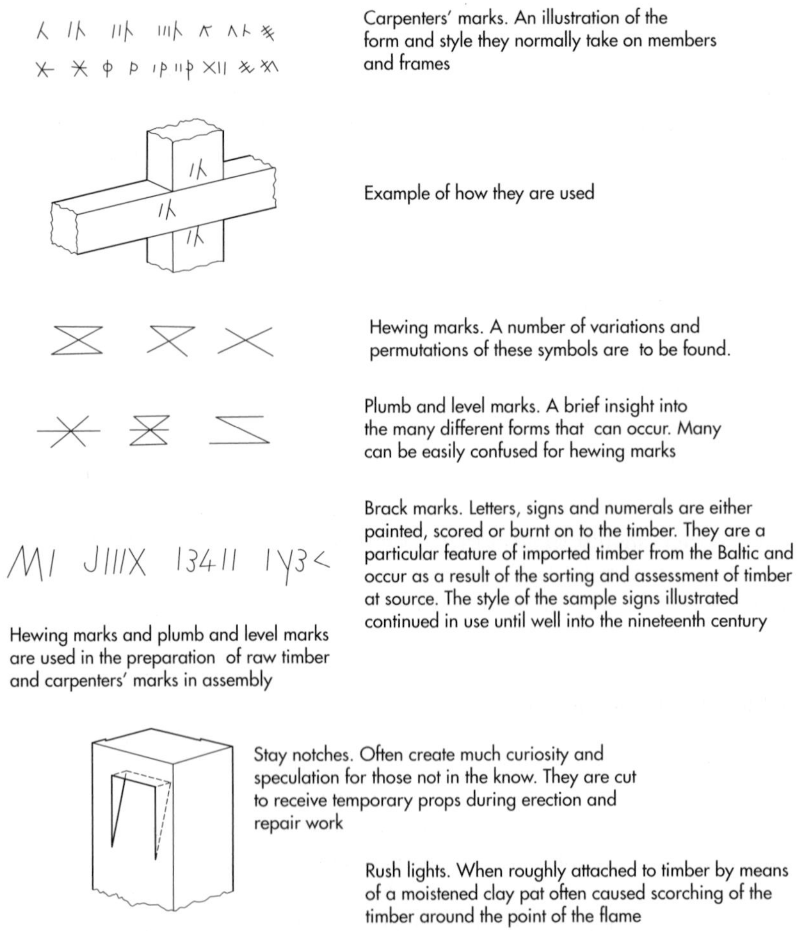

Carpenters' marks. An illustration of the form and style they normally take on members and frames

Example of how they are used

Hewing marks. A number of variations and permutations of these symbols are to be found.

Plumb and level marks. A brief insight into the many different forms that can occur. Many can be easily confused for hewing marks

Brack marks. Letters, signs and numerals are either painted, scored or burnt on to the timber. They are a particular feature of imported timber from the Baltic and occur as a result of the sorting and assessment of timber at source. The style of the sample signs illustrated continued in use until well into the nineteenth century

Hewing marks and plumb and level marks are used in the preparation of raw timber and carpenters' marks in assembly

Stay notches. Often create much curiosity and speculation for those not in the know. They are cut to receive temporary props during erection and repair work

Rush lights. When roughly attached to timber by means of a moistened clay pat often caused scorching of the timber around the point of the flame

Fig. 6.9   Timber marks. None of these marks should be obliterated, removed or tampered with in any way as they are important historical features

6.3.1 Methods of repair

Selection of replacement timber

- Identify the species of timber to be replaced.
- Determine the direction of the grain and the colour.
- Consider the method of cutting needed and whether it should be boxed, halved, slabbed, quarter sawn etc.
- Enquire how long the timber stock has been in the yard and hand pick the timber for the job concerned. Remember, a piece with knots will distort rapidly on drying as the grain changes direction.
- Previously used timbers should not be adapted or reused for structural purposes.
- Establish whether or not supplies will be seasoned when delivered.
- The visual impact of a repair is likely to become less apparent if the moisture content in the new timber is comparable to that in the existing timber.
- Determine the method of the original worked finish. Do not attempt to simulate historic techniques such as an adze finish with modern tooling.
- Replacement timber in sensitive locations should, as far as possible, match the existing timber in terms of quality, colour, the nature of the heartwood and the tree ring widths and numbers.

Repair techniques and practice

(See also Figures 6.10 and 6.11.)

- Ensure the cause of any defect has been correctly traced and made good.
- As much as possible of the original work should be retained.
- The integrity of a historic framed structure depends substantially on the soundness of the jointing and for this reason replacement jointing demands meticulous care especially in new pegging.
- Defective parts of timber lengths such as rafters and similar components can normally be repaired by splicing in new timber (see SPAB Pamphlet No. 12).
- Plan operations to minimise any disturbance to the structure.
- Always consider the repair and strengthening of existing timbers in preference to renewal.
- Before commencing operations check whether adequate protection has been provided for any surrounding features.
- Take measures to ensure work will not alter any existing equilibrium or structural balance in the building.
- Non-structural timbers which have original features and mouldings of historic value, but are suffering inner decay, can usually be saved by cutting out the infected areas and embedding wood inserts in either an epoxy resin or a suitable adhesive.
- Distortions in framed structures can sometimes be rectified by moving or jacking back into position. It may, however, be harmful to reposition timbers, particularly if they have 'set' to a different profile. Work of this nature should not be undertaken without the aid of a structural report.

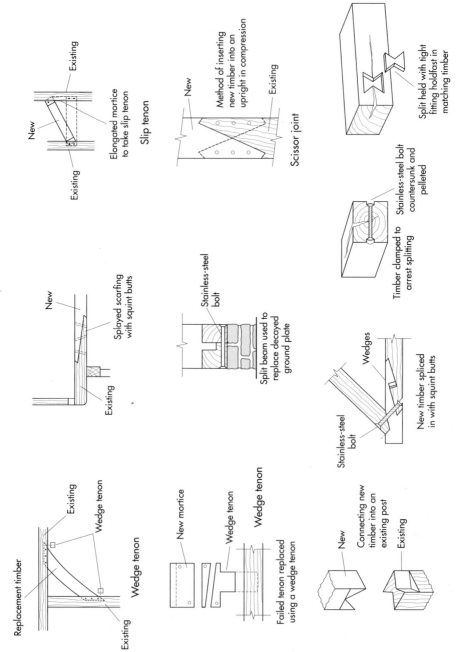

Fig. 6.10   Methods for timber repairs

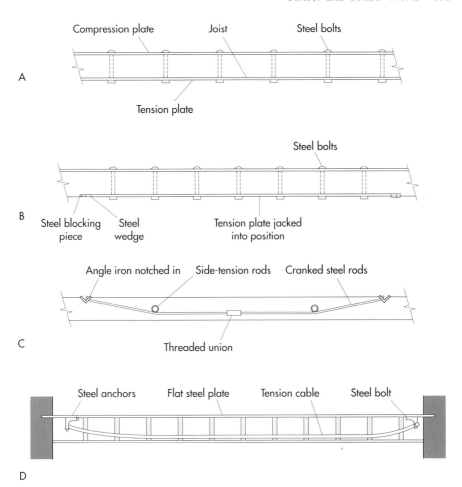

Fig. 6.11 Methods for strengthening timber floors. Methods A–D have been devised by SPAB to halt or reduce sagging and to avoid the need for renewal or undue disturbance (see also SPAB Technical Pamphlet No. 2)

- To ensure the integrity and balance of the framework is not altered inadvertently, always determine whether structural timbers in the area of operation are in a state of compression or tension and act accordingly.
- Weakened beams can often be restored in situ by providing temporary support and cutting a continuous slot along the length of the upper face and inserting steel flitchplates or 'T' sections secured by stainless-steel bolts. This can sometimes be a less disruptive alternative and avoids the need to remove and cut into two complete sections with a steel flitch plate sandwiched between the inner faces using stainless-steel bolts (see SPAB Leaflet No. 12).
- Scarf joints are an effective method of piecing in new timber, with the technique being adaptable for use in a number of ways. Splayed scarf joints with folding wedges are able to resist hogging and sagging as well as sideways movements. However

it is often necessary to strap edge half scarfs (see also SPAB Technical Leaflet No. 12).

- A range of tried and tested systems have been devised by the SPAB (see SPAB Technical Leaflet No. 12) for repairs to posts and studs. Failure usually occurs at the feet due to decay and can be repaired by cutting back to sound timber and inserting new wood by means of slip or fish tenons. Load-bearing posts and studs require a more substantial and intricate system such as the scissor scarf. Ample time needs to be allowed for making scissor scarfs. The process frequently take longer than estimated.
- SPAB Leaflet No.12 decribes some well-contrived methods of repair for use with sill beams, plates, ground beams etc.
- If metalwork is to be used in timber repair work it should, for preference, be of stainless steel. Mild steel plates need to be either galvanised or protected with a red-oxide paint.
- Timber floors in many old buildings weaken with age and are liable to sag or 'spring' from moving loads. The SPAB have developed a range of in situ strengthening techniques which have been designed to overcome the need for renewal. The systems provide a range of useful options, including the use of compression and tension plates, side tension rods and tension cables (see SPAB Technical Pamphlet No. 2).
- The use of flitch plates should be a final resort, as they are a deception and in reality violate basic conservation philosophy. A more acceptable alternative is the use of external plates fixed by bolts.
- A useful technique is splinting, whereby the load on a deteriorated member is transferred to newly fixed timbers using fish plates, gusset plates and similar methods. This may not, however, be an acceptable option if appearance is a sensitive issue.
- Pulled or distorted joints can be re-engaged by means of metal straps, plates or preformed connectors.
- If the existing joint pegs need to be replaced due to age or damage, extreme care must be taken in removing the original pegs. This should only be undertaken by boring a smaller dimension hole from each side and carefully removing the remainder of the defective peg. This ensures the off-centre line of the hole in the tenon remains intact and can still draw the tenon into the mortice. When re-pegging, use timber that has a low moisture content but is not completely dry. The pegs need to be tapered and longer than the section being jointed. After an initial driving-in, the pegs should be left and then re-driven after the timber has dried and shrunk.
- When undertaking repairs or alterations, take into consideration a possible need for dendrochronology (tree ring dating). It has become an accurate and precise method of dating and costs much less than radio-carbon dating. The latter involves laboratory testing which in essence measures the decay of a radioactive element in terms of a percentage decrease in the number of atoms per unit in time, which in the case of timber has a known constant. The following practice is advisable for buildings under alteration or repair until recording by an expert has been concluded:
  – Ensure all in situ sapwood is left untouched and do not defrass.
  – Do not discard or dump any timbers that have already been removed. Fully record and label them together with a note of the original location.

■ On completion of operations, all repairs should be permanently dated at source. A detailed record of work undertaken also needs to be lodged at a permanent place of keeping such as the county archives office.

6.4 INFILL PANELLING

6.4.1 Wattle and daub

The intervening panels between the timber frame members are mostly filled with wattle and daub. The wattle work is built-up by inserting staves of either riven oak or chestnut into each panel space. Auger holes were made in the underside of the upper timbers and a channel in the topside of the lower timbers (Figure 6.12). The staves were then cut, pointed and sprung into position. Sometimes the background for the daub was made from laths fitted into slots. The infilling started with pliable hazel withies being woven around and between the staves to form a basket-weave ground for the daub. Daub is a clay plaster containing fine aggregate or sand, chopped straw and cow dung. However, the proportions and constituents often vary according to local practice and custom. Some mixes were also gauged with lime putty. The daub is applied by throwing lumps onto the wattle work. It is then pressed in hard and trowelled. When dry, a limewash coating was applied and repeated until a dense coverage had been achieved. At vernacular level, the use of daub continued into the latter part of the eighteenth century and during the early part of the nineteenth century.

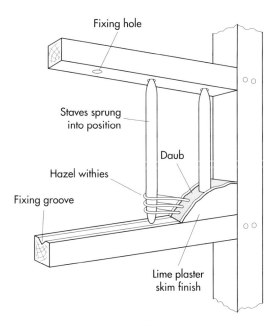

Fig. 6.12 External face of wattle and daub infill panel

6.4.2 Inspection and assessment

- Always fully record the method of construction and the condition before the commencement of any work.
- Cracking in the daub is a likely indication of decay or movement in the timbers.
- Check the strength and firmness of the panelling and look for signs of bulging caused by a loss of key.
- Look for signs of surface powdering.
- Cracks in daubing can also be caused by an insect infestation which depletes the wattle work. Normally this is the result of an attack by the common furniture beetle (*Anobium punctatum*), but if oak is in place it often attracts the Lyctus powderpost beetle (*Lyctus brunneus* and *Lyctus linearis*).

6.4.3 Repairs to wattle and daub

If instructions require replication of the original, it is necessary to become familiar with local practice and to apply the same constituents, materials and techniques as before. However, there may be a need to comply with a specified U value under the Building Regulations, which will necessitate an alteration to the original method of construction. The technique devised by the architect F.W.B. Charles (see References) is a good solution to this problem (Figure 6.13).

- If insulation board is used as infill, this should be cut slightly over size so that it can be pushed and held in position without further attachment.
- If the panel is to be slightly recessed, a lead tray needs to be provided and dressed down at the front and upturned at the back.

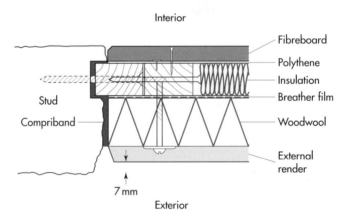

Fig. 6.13 Detail of infill sandwich panel (Diagram reproduced by kind permission of F.W.B. Charles). (Note the provision of a double sub-frame which is designed to overcome the problem of shrinkage, each frame having four separate pieces, the first being grooved into the original timber. It is important the fixing screws are left to protrude as shown. The edges of the woodwool must be dipped and sealed in a cement slurry. The back and edges are then wrapped in a 500 gauge polythene)

- Do not work the lime plaster in the external panelling so that it protrudes in front of the timbering.
- Always ensure any paint used to decorate the lime plaster will enable the material to 'breathe'.
- A suitable repair mix for daub is one part clay, one part hydrated lime and one part fresh cow dung, to which is added chopped straw or animal hair which needs to be well mixed in.

6.5 BRICK NOGGING

As brick manufacturing increased and costs fell brick nogging became a common alternative to wattle and daub, being mostly used in replacement work (Figure 6.14). Although it is now generally regarded as a later addition to an early timber frame, this is not necessarily the case. The use of brick as an original panel filling can be traced back to the early part of the eighteenth century. The bricks were usually set to either a herringbone or diaper pattern using a lime mortar, with whitewash sometimes being applied to the external facework (Figure 6.15).

Where brick nogging has been used, the structural factors relating to the timber frame need to be scrutinised more closely. If the timber members are in a sound

Fig. 6.14 Brick nogging

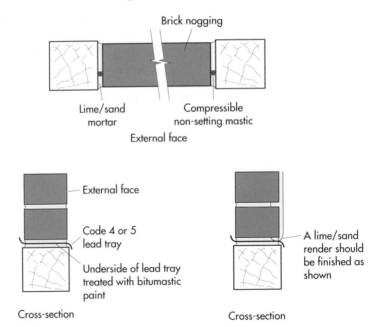

Brick nogging

Lime/sand mortar

Compressible non-setting mastic

External face

External face

Code 4 or 5 lead tray

Underside of lead tray treated with bitumastic paint

A lime/sand render should be finished as shown

Cross-section

Cross-section

Fig. 6.15 Brick nogging replacement

condition and the brick nogging has been well placed and properly pinned into each panel, there is likely to be a satisfactory distribution of loading between the bricks and the timber. On the other hand, the bricks can readily overburden the timbers if they are ill-fitting and rest on decayed or deteriorating wood beams.

6.5.1 Inspection and assessment

- Check the supporting timbers for stability and condition.
- Look for any signs of movement, shrinkage or overburdening in the timbers.
- Pay particular attention to the state of the external timber ledges and arrises and test for rot and beetle infestation at these points.
- Look for auger holes and fixing slots in the panel timbers. They are a sign of earlier wattle and daub which needs to be recorded.
- Check for any signs of rain penetration between the bricks and the timber.
- The likely installation date of the bricks used can normally be determined by their size, shape and texture. Note and record.

6.6 RESIN REPAIRS

Resin applications can be a useful option where an alternative solution may necessitate the removal and reinstatement of the surrounding fabric or where large amounts of the original timber would otherwise be lost. The basic objection to treatment with resin, however, is that the process effectively converts the wood into another material which cannot revert to the natural state.

Resin formulations are now available using a range of different techniques which offer a high degree of flexibility and most mixes can be gauged to a desired level of viscosity. Before recourse to this technique, the conservation officer of the local planning authority should be consulted if the use of resin has not already been approved. The implications of the treatment also require explanation and acceptance from those having a legal interest in a property. While there is a need to exercise discernment and caution before selecting resin as a suitable remedy, there are circumstances where it is acceptable in the conservation process. The following items require particular attention:

- Ensure that the specialist contractor has the necessary credentials and experience to undertake work to historic structures.
- Treatment to load-bearing members should not be undertaken unless there is evidence to indicate movement has remained static.
- Works should not proceed during periods of frost unless temperature levels can be constantly maintained above freezing point.
- Timber which has been subjected to excessive dampness must be dried to an acceptable level and the moisture content stabilised, otherwise loss of adhesion may occur at the interface.
- Resin applications must not be used with green timbers which have a high sap content.
- Resin mortars should be applied to external timbers in a manner which will not cause water pockets to form under and around the treated parts.
- Provision needs to be made for copious ventilation around the points of operation.
- Resin treatments must not be applied in a manner which destroys, fuses or alters conventional timber jointing. A failure to observe this rule is liable to cause new stresses in a structure, thereby altering the equilibrium in other components.
- Immediately after treatment, solvent and other gases emitted during the chemistry of the process may need to be dispelled by prolonged ventilation before a building is ready for occupation.

6.7 SURFACE TREATMENTS

Oak should normally be left in the natural state, particularly where there is evidence to indicate this was the original intention. Unpainted surfaces require to be cleared of any dust and debris and can be washed or scrubbed with clean water using a neutral pH soap. The whole should then be well washed with clean water. Timbers that have been blackened by smoke may be an important indicator of the original planform, age and use. Such evidence should be left and subjected to no more than a brushing unless expert opinion has deemed otherwise.

The following considerations also apply:

- Old varnish is best removed using a solution of American turpentine and acetone. After treatment the surface must be well washed.

- Replacement timbers should not be coloured artificially.
- Do not treat wood surfaces with linseed oil, as this is slow drying and harbours dust.
- Tar marks are best removed by using a specially compounded poultice (see SPAB Information Sheet 2).
- Never sandblast or blow lamp a historic wood surface.
- Internal surfaces in the natural state are best treated with a preparation made from beeswax dissolved in turpentine, which is gently rubbed onto the surface and then worked with a cloth.

6.8   REMEDIAL TREATMENTS

The primary aim should be to retain as much as possible of the historic fabric and to halt further decay. Ensure intervention is kept to the minimum necessary to contain the problem in a manner which preserves the essential authenticity and historic value of a structure. In essence this means that the standard remedial methods in general use are more likely to be inappropriate and unsuitable in the conservation context. Curative measures often call for innovative thinking and a need to view operations in a holistic way by accepting that limited treatments may necessitate regular checking and monitoring. This effectively recognises that the complete eradication of fungal spores and insect pests is often unnecessarily disruptive and impracticable, and that operations must be directed more towards containment and localised eradication.

6.8.1   Dampness

It is possible to eliminate and control fungal activity if the extent of the problem is accurately traced, identified and assessed and the sources of moisture penetration halted. With this course of action, the drying process relating to damp masonry warrants proper understanding. Once the source of the penetrating damp has been stopped, large amounts of water evaporate out in the initial stages, the rate being dependent on the porosity of the fabric and prevailing environmental conditions. There is, however, a critical phase when the rate of evaporation becomes retarded and gradually diminishes to a point whereby residual moisture can only be eliminated through adequate vapour flow. This, in turn, is influenced by air movement and temperature and is critical in preventing and controlling a fungal attack. At this stage the moisture level should be kept exceptionally low for an adequate period of time.

6.8.2   Monitoring

To ensure the sources of dampness have been permanently eliminated, this approach is likely to require the installation of an electrically controlled moisture sensory system. It provides constant monitoring of moisture levels and will trigger early warning at any sensor point where there is an indication of increased dampness. The strategic placing of sensors enables vulnerable areas to be observed closely and an accurate and reliable moisture profile to be compiled.

6.8.3   Assessment and action

- It is vital to undertake a survey at the earliest opportunity, but not before the form of construction has been identified and recorded fully.
- The main contractor needs to cure all known sources of water penetration as soon as practicable and to allow adequate time for drying out.
- Seek independent expert advice and commission a detailed report and specification as a basis for tendering. The investigation may involve laboratory tests and the use of expensive equipment. The standard free survey and general guarantee of work offered by remedial treatment contractors is seldom suitable for conservation projects and individual terms should be negotiated.
- When undertaking an assessment a complete overview is required, having regard to any likely changes in the use and the environmental conditions in the building.
- No work should be undertaken until a reliable pattern of moisture movement has been formulated. Also make provision for mortar samples to be taken and for the strategic placing of sacrificial dowels and bait rods.
- Pay particular attention to any internal joinery that has been assembled with animal glue, which is especially attractive to wood-boring beetles.
- Avoid wall irrigation treatments, as masonry can be seriously damaged by salt crystallisation. Never authorise this form of treatment without taking authoritative advice.
- Recent technological advancements now enable more accurate assessments to be made without the need for unacceptable disruption. Ultrasonic testing can detect hidden or suspect areas and determine the extent of an infestation in known locations, without any need for opening up. Another valuable diagnostic tool is the micro-drill, which has a high-speed probe linked to a recorder which gives an instant reading of gravimetric density. Sudden or unexpected changes indicate the presence of decay. The drill hole is barely perceptible. The micro-drill should only be used by trained operators.

6.9   STAIRS AND STAIRWAYS

During the early Medieval period, upper-level access in domestic property was normally by ladder. Even in the more prestigous houses the link between the ground and overhead areas was likely to be by ladder and trap door. The transition from ladder to stairs was especially slow at vernacular level. When the idea of fixed stairs did take hold, however, scant regard seems to have been paid to ease of use. Seemingly this was due to a reluctance to sacrifice space and many original staircases were housed in cupboards with the first few treads being set in a vertical position (Figure 6.16).

Shallow treads

The development of the staircase to present-day standards was slow and at first treads were shallow, being set on strings without risers. Moreover, the 'going' had only a

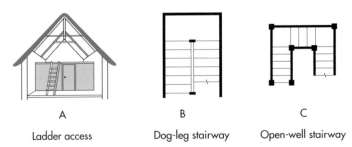

A
Ladder access

B
Dog-leg stairway

C
Open-well stairway

Fig. 6.16   Stairs. Use of a ladder as at A is sometimes described as a 'stee' access. (Security at night was improved by allowing dogs to roam freely around the ground-floor area. They were prevented from gaining access to upper levels by the provision of a small gate usually placed at the foot of the stairs. Many of these gates have survived and should be retained as a historical feature)

slight relationship with ergonomics. Spiral staircases are a particular feature of Medieval architecture and probably derive from the pattern used by the Normans in castle building.

Location

When fireplaces started to be constructed in the open hall with the overhead area being floored, this triggered a dramatic change in the design of internal domestic layouts. Most houses built in this new phase have fireplaces built into the gable end, thereby providing more space for general circulation and a central stairway. This practice was not universal however, as there was also a trend towards staircases that were either formed within the thickness of a wall or built around the chimney breast. In some properties they can also be found housed in an independent turret or tower, often described as a vise.

Dog-leg stairway

In the late sixteenth century the 'dog-leg' stairway appeared and became popular in more confined accommodation owing to the compact nature of the design. Again, this had little impact on artisan dwellings and cottages until the eighteenth century and in some areas as late as the nineteenth century. Use of the first-floor areas meant additional security was necessary at night. This was solved by allowing dogs to roam free. They were prevented from gaining access to the upper levels by a small gate, usually placed at the foot of the stairs. Many of these gates have survived to the present day and as a feature should remain unaltered.

Jacobean

After significant developments during the Elizabethan period, the staircase became an even more prominent feature in the following Jacobean period, especially the framed newel form. The surviving examples from this period have closed strings, a style which continued well into the eighteenth century in the smaller houses. At this phase it was normal for the newel posts to project above the handrail and they were visible below the strings, together with moulded, carved and capped features.

Open-well staircase

The middle of the seventeenth century witnessed the appearance of the open-well staircase, which separated flights with quarter landings to give a more spacious effect. They remained popular in the larger houses until the late eighteenth century.

Cut-string staircase

This superseded the open-well design in the larger houses and involved a change whereby the string was cut away to allow the tread to project slightly, with the nosing being returned to the side to act as a capping to the string. The appearance of the balusters also changed and they became lighter in form, with the handrails being continued along the top of the newel and finished at the ends with either a scroll or carved feature with panelled spandrils.

The classicism started by Inigo Jones and continued by Christopher Wren gave limitless opportunities to designers in the use of height, proportion and space, particularly in the presentation of the piano nobile (a Renaissance term for a reception room raised above ground level and resting over a basement or podium). The use of the staircase as an imposing artistic feature continued during the English Baroque period through to the Georgian and Regency phases, but the speed of industrialisation during the early part of the nineteenth century established different attitudes and a new ethos in favour of mass-produced components. The inspection of an old staircase needs to be approached in the following way:

- Check the condition of the timbers.
- Examine and record the method of construction and take particular note of the jointing and fixing.
- Identify the timbers used and compare them with other timbers elsewhere in the property. Comparisons can assist in the dating process.
- Record whether or not the staircase is a later improvement and indicate any signs of an earlier form of upper access.
- Try to date and categorise the work accurately. If in doubt seek expert advice.

FURTHER READING
See section on Timber in References.

CHAPTER 7

HISTORIC FLOORING

7.1 EARTH FLOORS

It is not unusual to find an old building where the original earth-bound flooring has survived. Earth floors were formed from a clay slurry mixed into the earth to a state of plasticity and then beaten down, levelled and allowed to dry to a smooth finish. Clay was not always the only constituent material and sometimes either lime or gypsum were worked into the mix, which hardened into a more wearable screed. Floors made from these materials should not be regarded as being primitive and expendable. In reality, they may form an essential feature that is critical to the correct interpretation of the history and development of a structure. Vital evidence can be lost if these areas are covered or altered prior to an archaeological survey being carried out. Often such floors are found, buried under later forms of flooring, during building operations.

The natural porosity of the material meant that it was prone to absorb foreign matter and to overcome this many local practices evolved, including washing down with a mixture of water and soot, which helped to build-up and harden the surface. Small animal bones were also driven into the surface and then either cut or rubbed level, often with varying sizes of bone being arranged into different patterns and designs. Sometimes small animal bones can be discovered mixed into the earth as an aggregate to help bind and strengthen the base material. An essential consideration is the likely presence of historic artefacts and relics buried within the body of the floor. Tangible evidence of this nature can be of exceptional importance from an archaeological point of view.

7.1.1 Inspection and assessment

The following items need to be taken into account as a matter of good practice and procedure:

- Before becoming engaged in any repair works, determine the composition and nature of the material by taking a small sample for analysis. A rough guide to the presence of clay can be obtained by breaking down a sample and mixing it with clean water. Allow it to settle in a glass jar. The clay will appear as a separate sediment.

- Examine for signs of staining. Normally this is caused by soluble salts migrating to the surface and is an indication of damp.
- Powdering or crumbling of the surface may also be caused by damp but should not be confused with 'dusting' which can result from normal wear and tear.
- Check for any ingress of moisture in the building fabric. Make provision for good drainage near the floor and around the site.
- Consider the type of traffic the floor will be expected to bear. It may be necessary to provide for moveable protective coverings especially during building operations.
- Check for the effect any heavy imposed loads are likely to have.
- Ensure repair mixes are compatible with the original and take expert advice if modifications or variations in the repair mix have been requested without proof of effectiveness.
- Take care not to introduce excessive heat into the environmental climate of the floor area. Overheating can draw moisture through the floor to cause damage and staining on the surface.
- Heated pipes and appliances located close to the floor surface may need to be lagged to prevent localised crazing and cracking.
- Carefully consider the likely effects of any nearby damp-proofing proposals which could encourage moisture to migrate towards the earth flooring and evaporate out to create additional problems.
- If permission has been granted for the laying of a cement/sand concrete overlay or screed, check for the presence of gypsum in the original floor.
- Before selecting a mix containing ordinary Portland cement, also test for the presence of sulphates and use a sulphate-resisting cement if the result is positive.

7.1.2 Repairs and maintenance

If the surface is worn or damaged lightly, break up and completely crush the spoil to a fine powder. Check the amount of clay present in the original mix using a sedimentation test. Much of the firmness and cohesion in this type of floor is due to the presence of clay. If necessary more clay should be added and the whole mixed and applied in the manner already described. If a harder wearing surface is desired, hydrated lime can be added in the proportion of 10 per cent by volume. The lime in the mix needs to be thoroughly worked in and the texture made uniform throughout before being either beaten down manually or consolidated by mechanical means. Other repair options include soil stabilisation using Portland cement and/or pulverised fuel ash (PFA) for a more durable and faster setting surface, but always check for the presence of either soluble salts or gypsum beforehand. Where it is necessary to substantially alter the composition of an earlier floor, it is probably better to opt for a suitable covering or a floating false floor placed over the original.

7.2 HAEMATIC FLOORS AND SCREEDS

Animal blood was sometimes added to earth/clay and lime concrete floors to improve the workability of the mix, which also induced quicker setting as a result of the natural congealing of the blood. In addition, it helped to bind and substantially harden the material. Used either in the main mix or as a screed, the compound could be trowelled to a smooth finish and be polished with an oil to produce a hard and shiny surface similar in appearance to black marble.

7.2.1 Earth-bound haematic floors

■ If instructions stipulate that an original mix be used, always advise on the hygiene implications and the unpleasantness involved before starting.
■ Cut out damaged areas to a square profile and clear away the debris.
■ Before applying the repair mix, wet the substrate to prevent the drawing out of moisture from the mix.
■ Add fresh animal blood to some prepared earth/clay and work to a plastic state.
■ Apply and level out the mix and finish with a wood float.
■ If the surface is to be polished, float and lightly scour the surface with a little water when the mix begins to set.

7.2.2 Haematic lime concrete floors

■ Prepare as before.
■ Make up a mix of one part lime to two and a half to three parts of finely graded clean sand and grit. Water slightly, turn over and then add fresh animal blood and mix to a 'fatty' consistency.
■ Apply by levelling out, tamping and finishing with a wood float.

7.2.3 Lime ash floors (including gypsum floors)

Lime ash floors, sometimes known as grip floors, are an ancient form of upper-floor construction that provided good sound insulation and hardened to give high strength and durability. The practice has been traced back to the fifteenth century and continued as a feature in some parts of the British Isles until the eighteenth century. The technique involved laying and fixing either reeds, straw, laths or thin boarding across joists to form a bed for a mixture of lime and ash, plus other constituents such as residues from the lime-making process. Local customs and individual idiosyncracies have produced a range of variations in the composition of a mix, with some containing gypsum in varying proportions. In some districts gypsum became the base material. Lime ash floors have sometimes been polished to a fine finish. These are normally found in the limestone regions of the British Isles (Figure 7.1).

7.2.4 Inspection and assessment

■ Be alert to this form of construction if the underside of a floor has a reed or straw bedding or is of some other unusual material.
■ Check that the discovery has not been confused with sound deadening, a feature more commonly found in the prestigous buildings of the eighteenth and nineteenth centuries.

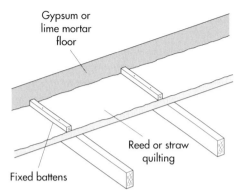

Fig. 7.1 A form of suspended flooring which developed in the Midlands during the eighteenth century

- Look for deficiencies such as minor cracking, crazing and spalling.
- Examine the bedding material for any signs of deterioration.
- Check for overloading.
- Pay particular attention to damage such as fracturing caused by the later introduction of services which results in a loss of strength.
- Take a small sample for analysis so that repair mixes can be proportioned for compatibility with the original.
- Do not dismiss the strength and insulating properties of the material as necessarily inferior to modern practices.

7.2.5 Repairs

All cracks should be raked out, the edges undercut and the debris removed. In the case of gypsum, repairs use a retardant such as natural keratin or sodium citrate to provide sufficient laying and levelling time before setting takes place. Lime ash produced from the traditional method of lime-burning is seldom obtainable. A suitable alternative is a pozzolanic pulverised fuel ash (PFA) mixed with ordinary Portland cement. Normally this should be in the proportions of 1:4 (cement:PFA) laid to a thickness of between 100 and 150 mm.

7.3 LIME CONCRETE FLOORS

Lime concrete is derived mainly from disused or surplus bricks and clay tiles crushed to form an aggregate plus the addition of lime putty mixed with brick dust. The basic criteria for inspection and assessment should follow the key stipulations in Section 7.2.3. White cement or lime can be used for repair work, with lime being mixed in the ratio of 2:4:1 (lime/PFA/clean sharp sand). White cement should be in the proportions of 1:2 or $2\frac{1}{2}$:5 (white cement/lime/finely crushed brick and brick dust).

7.4   STONE FLOORING

The use of stone has a long tradition and can be traced back to prehistory. If it is confined to a particular area of a house without any obvious reason, it probably indicates a different layout in earlier times. It was regular practice to floor the kitchen, scullery, pantry and hall in either slate or stone, with a different material being selected for the remainder of the accommodation. In many parts of the country, it was also the custom to raise the floor level of the kitchen and pantry a step higher than the hall.

Slate

A hard, impervious and fissile material favoured for flooring in the slate-bearing regions. It was usually laid directly onto soil, being used mostly in riven form until the introduction of mechanised sawing. Replacement slate should be from the same quarry or from a source which has proven wearing qualities. Many of the imported slates are not suitable for flooring.

Sedimentary stones

Certain limestones and sandstones are ideal for cutting into stone flags for flooring, but not all possess durability. Some stones rely on case hardening for surface strength, which occurs when the green sap migrates to the external face and evaporates out to form a protective skin. Before this action is complete, wear can set in causing surface erosion. Bath stone flooring exemplifies this problem. Replacement stone should, as far as possible, be of the same classification and type and on no account must an alternative stone be introduced without checking for compatibility. From the Georgian period onwards, kitchen, scullery and pantry areas were frequently located over basement accommodation, with the floors being constructed of stone flags laid over timber joists. The sub-floor was usually rough boarding covered by a thick lime ash overlay which had to be carefully levelled to take a thin screed into which the stone was set.

Inspection and assessment

- Determine whether there are any factors or circumstances which are likely to incur dampness.
- Check the level of the floor for any sinking or rising of individual flags and for any general undulations. Such conditions are a likely indication of a failing sub-floor.
- Assess any surface wear or damage and whether this has any health and safety implications.
- Stone laid on a direct-to-earth sub-floor is likely to deteriorate more rapidly if the ground conditions are unfavourable. For this reason, the state of the sub-floor should always be examined in depth, even if surface conditions indicate that this appears unnecessary.
- Be alert to the deceptive properties of some open-textured stones. Under damp conditions, the porosity can encourage rapid evaporation at the surface which may

not be visually obvious. The presence of efflorescence is an indication of underlying dampness. The action of sub-florescence within the inner fabric of the stone can result in excessive exfoliation, powdering and decay, which is not likely to be apparent until the final stages of deterioration.

- If stone flags are laid over a suspended timber floor, check the condition of the under-boarding and the joist ends. Also check for overloading and any signs of deflection.

Repairs

- Repair anything which may have contributed to floor dampness or decay.
- If sub-floor conditions are satisfactory, moist sand is suitable for levelling and packing when laying or re-laying. A hint of cement helps to firm the sand after the set.
- A defective sub-floor will entail lifting and carefully storing the stone and excavating as necessary. It should be followed by the provision of a clean hardcore base which needs to be well blinded with clean sand. Allow for the inclusion of insulation and incorporate a damp-proof membrane into the concrete slab. Relay and level using a cement/sand screed.
- A neat cement grout should not be poured between the joints, as it is likely to cause staining.
- If the lime ash base of a suspended floor is defective this can be satisfactorily replaced with a 1:4 lime and PFA mix.

7.4.1 Granite

In the granite regions roughly hewn flagstones are found in very old floors, but elsewhere granite was seldom used until the advent of mechanisation due to the difficulties of splitting and breaking by hand. It was something of a rarity until mechanisation in the nineteenth century speeded production and reduced costs.

7.4.2 Cobbles and pebbles

Although more usually seen in courtyards and streets, cobbles and pebbles are sometimes a feature of internal flooring. They were often collected as rejects from gravel pits, set in clay and made even by gently tamping down with a wide board. Later examples are usually set in lime/sand mortar.

7.4.3 Pitched stone

In some districts, particularly in certain areas of Wales, floors were formed from 'pitched' stones. Using a 'pitchin' and pitching hammer, stone was 'pitched off' from a large block to form a wedge shape. Pieces were then rammed edgewise into the ground side by side using a tool termed a beetle (a large wooden hammer). Replacement work involves a repeat of this process and requires masonry skills for the 'pitching off' of the stone and an ability to 'pitch in' new stones in the correct manner using a measured amount of physical power. Sometimes this form of flooring is found mixed with cobbles and pebbles.

7.4.4   Chalk

Chalk was often utilised as a low-cost flooring material in the chalk, bearing regions. It was broken down into small pieces and then rammed and compacted until firm, followed by a light watering-in which enabled the natural action of compaction to continue and the particles to gradually re-cement together. The process should be repeated if there is a need to replace or repair this type of flooring.

7.4.5   Brick and pamment flooring

With the exception of buildings of importance, beaten earth/clay floors remained the more usual feature until baked earth started to appear as a flooring material in the eastern counties of England. Formed into tiles known as pamments, they became a localised feature in brick and tile producing districts and in consequence the texture and colours vary according to the composition of local clays. The sizes normally ranged from 305 mm square to 229 mm square and between 38 and 50 mm in thickness. In Ulster, pamments became popular in the nineteenth century. From the eighteenth century onwards, as a result of improved transportation, bricks started to be used in areas where stone was not available. This speeded delivery, reduced costs and resulted in bricks being widely used throughout the British Isles for floors required for utility purposes.

Inspection and assessment

- Many of the basic issues concerning the assessment of stone floors will apply.
- Most defects arise through the porosity of the bricks and the leaching of salts and moisture from the soil.
- The colour, size and texture will normally enable an expert to identify the age and source of the brick.

Repairs

- Replacement bricks and pamments from the original source are likely to be unobtainable. It is usually necessary to investigate the possibility of obtaining supplies from either architectural salvage or for replacements to be commissioned.
- Individual replacements can often be satisfactorily set in clean sand containing a very small quantity of cement.
- If the original flooring is to be relaid, this is best achieved by excavating the sub-base and laying a bed of fine gravel concrete gauged at 1:6 to a thickness of about 50 mm, with the bricks or pamments being set in a lime/sand mortar.
- Most older floors are likely to be stained if a cement/sand grout is used, in which case lime putty is the more suitable option.

7.5 TILES

Decorated floor tiles first appeared around the tenth century when they became a prestigious feature in royal palaces, ecclesiastical and monastic buildings and in the homes of wealthy merchants and the gentry. Encaustic tiles made from different clays are an essential item of Gothic architectural decoration, which continued into the mid-sixteenth century when a preference emerged for black and white quarry tiles. The term encaustic applies to tiles which have an inlaid pattern of coloured clay. The inlay is fused into the body of the tile during firing. The glazed tiles of the Medieval period contain iron impurities which produced a yellow tinge with white clays, brown on red clays and olive green on grey. In addition they can usually be identified from the shape, lack of fine definition and sharp arrises found in later periods. If tiles are believed to be Medieval, they should be left untouched until expert opinion has been obtained as they may have particular historic significance.

Plain clay tiles are more usually known as quarry tiles and, with the exception of those laid during past 50 years, are mostly found on a thick lime mortar base. The usual sizes are: 101 mm × 101 mm (4″ × 4″), 152 mm × 152 mm (6″ × 6″), 228 mm × 228 mm (9″ × 9″). Coloured tiles were marketed in the following sizes: 152 mm × 152 mm (6″ × 6″), 107 mm × 107 mm ($4\frac{1}{4}$″ × $4\frac{1}{4}$″), 76 mm × 76 mm (3″ × 3″) plus half sizes in this range. The precision-made encaustic tiles in Victorian times were used predominantly for decorative effect in entrance halls and porches and are very difficult to replace.

Inspection and assessment

- Examine for abrasion.
- Look for signs of wear on the coloured inlays of encaustic tiles.
- The presence of loose and damaged tiling is an indication of a sub-floor problem.
- Tile failure can normally be detected by tapping the surface. A dull sound is evidence of deterioration in the sub-floor, while a higher sounding ring indicates the reverse.

Repairs

- Tiles which have become detached need to be thoroughly cleaned with any original mortar being completely removed.
- If a new concrete base is necessary extra care should be taken to ensure the finished surface is level and free of protrusions. One way of achieving this is to carefully re-adjust the mix and 'float-in' some additional fines when the pour is near the required level.
- Thick screeds should be avoided and is the reason why extra care is needed when finishing the base concrete.
- Do not soak quarry tiles, but make sure there is sufficient moisture in the bed for the screed to adhere.

Mosaic

Following the departure of the Romans, the use of mosaic work lapsed and did not re-appear until the early Medieval period when it was seen only in churches, cathedrals, monasteries and important buildings. Mosaic flooring is a technique used for making pictures and patterns set within the integral fabric of the floor. It is achieved by laying small pieces of marble and ceramic cubes ranging from 6 mm ($\frac{1}{4}''$) square to 25 mm (1″) square bedded on a screed. Until the advent of Portland cement, a lime/sand screed was standard practice, but this changed to a mix of one part cement and two parts sand, with a quantity of hydrated lime being added in sufficient amounts to make the mortar suitably plastic. This enabled the mosaic to be more accurately embedded in the screed. Once set, the surface is then worked to a smooth finish using stone or carborundum rubbers. The analysis, restoration and repair of historic mosaic requires the services of a skilled craftsman.

FURTHER READING
See section on Floors and flooring in the References.

CHAPTER 8

INTERIOR WALL DECORATION

Mural decoration is one of the oldest art forms and dates back as far as the cave dwellers. It was much in vogue with the ancient Greeks, Egyptians and Romans, but the practice lapsed in the British Isles when the Romans departed. The arrival of the Normans resulted in a significant revival of mural art and is a legacy which can reveal a great deal about the life and culture of both Norman and later periods. Many paintings of significance have been discovered buried under thick layers of wallpaper or have been hidden by various coatings of whitewash. As a result, they may easily be missed; nevertheless a failure to recognise the significance or historic worth of an ancient mural or an original wallpaper can have unfortunate repercussions, and is the reason why meticulous care is necessary when stripping and cleaning old wall coverings and coatings. Wall paintings can be found in ecclesiastical, domestic and secular buildings and prior to the Reformation featured either decorative, moral or biblical presentations. In earlier times the clergy used mural scenes to illustrate biblical teachings to a generally illiterate populace. Many ecclesiastical paintings were obliterated by order during the Reformation and Commonwealth periods and further destruction occurred in Victorian times when plaster was stripped from the walls of churches in pursuit of a fashion to expose the natural stone.

8.1 WALL PAINTINGS

If ancient artwork is found in a decayed and failed condition, never assume that it cannot be restored. In skilled hands most deficiencies such as flaking, blistering, crazing and detachment can be rectified. When a wall covering is believed to be of an historic nature, the following action should be taken:

- Halt any works which are likely to cause damage to the artwork or substrate. If the find is unknown to the authorities, it should be reported to the local conservation officer.
- Notify the instructing source and seek expert guidance.
- Take a photographic record of the painting as found. Also date and note any relevant factors.

- Provide protective screening which must be prevented from abraiding the surface.
- Do not create any significant changes in existing environmental conditions relating to light, humidity and temperature until authorised to do so by an art conservator.
- Make an assessment of the nature and composition of the substrate and issue a report. Ensure that this report is seen by an appointed art conservator.
- Inspect the condition of the general fabric of the building and advise the instructing source of any findings. If an art conservator is appointed, issue formal notification relating to any building or repair operations which need to be undertaken before art restoration work can be commenced.
- Do not brush or otherwise attempt to clean the surface of the painting, unless authorised to do so by an experienced art conservator.

The interior decor of many of the smaller and medium-sized houses was often more appealing than is generally believed and could feature whitewashed walls with simple decorative treatments such as imitation stone, which sometimes included designs within each painted block (Figure 8.1). The cathedrals, royal palaces and those with the means to indulge regularly supported extravagant mural work and similar enrichment. Elaborate scenes frequently involved the use of fresco, gesso and secco techniques.

Fig. 8.1   Sixteenth-century domestic mural

Gesso is made from a mixture of glue and linseed oil, stiffened with either plaster or whiting, and is used to produce images in relief either by hand moulding or by imprinting with a carved wooden mould. Fresco work is a method of painting newly applied lime plaster so that the paint combines with the plaster. By contrast, secco is a process of painting on dry plaster using colours mixed from a water base. High-class work often entailed gilding and in the late Middle Ages it became the custom to create scenes using the fresco and secco techniques in combination. Work of this nature is of the utmost historic and artistic value and it is a mistake to assume that paintings on walls with a gypsum finish are of more recent origin. The use of gypsum has early origins, but it was seldom selected due to a reliance on imported supplies from France. Later alternative sources became available including localised deposits in parts of the British Isles.

Many of the earlier coatings applied over historic wall paintings have formed a protective layer that has preserved the original work. As a result most discoveries have the potential for cleaning and restoration, as the overlying coatings are likely to be of either whitewash or limewash. Whitewash is a simple mixture of powdered chalk and water to which starch was sometimes added. The early limewashes were mainly compounded from slaked lime mixed with a small quantity of rock alum. Distemper is not, as generally supposed, a more recent innovation. The origins of distemper go back to the tenth century. It was made from whitening, size, water and natural pigments.

8.2 WALLPAPERS

The transition from mural painting to wallpapering began as an established fashion during the eighteenth century and by the end of the century the use of painted Japanese paper had become popular for those with means. It was not, however, an innovation as the earliest known example of wallpaper dates from 1509 and is believed to have been used as a substitute for woven or needlework wall hangings. In the mid-seventeenth century, expensive flock papers, produced by applying varnish to a stencil design sheet, were already on the market. Finely chopped wool or serge was then sprinkled over the wet varnish to give a raised surface. Another fashion involved the use of Chinese or 'India' paper, brought to Europe by the ships of the East India Company, which depicted complete scenes of either bird, plant or wildlife. The hanging technique used a wooden frame covered with linen or hessian to which a heavy cartridge paper was pasted. The wallpaper was then fixed to this ground and the framing was tacked to the wall. Many of these framings are still in existence.

The mass production of wallpaper started in 1841 and sales later received an enormous boost through the Great Exhibition of 1851. The outcome was to create a greater awareness of the effect that design, contrast and colour could have on the environment, but it was William Morris in the 1860s who established Britain as the centre for decorative quality. Morris's patterns continue to be fashionable and many are still obtainable from Sandersons. An important change occurred in 1877 with the appearance of an embossed, decorative sheeting called Lincrusta Walton. Made from a highly complex mixture of compressed gum, shredded fibres and resin, it was highly durable and impervious to water. The product enjoyed enormous popularity and Frederick Walton dominated the market until 1886 when Thomas Parker produced an embossed alternative known as Anaglypta. This was less durable than Lincrusta Walton but was washable if coated with paint or varnish. Both companies produced a phenomenal range of patterns and many are still available from Crown Decorative Products, Crown House, Hollins Road, Darwen, Lancashire BB3 0BG.

8.3   INSPECTION AND ASSESSMENT

- Wallpapers which have been tacked to the wall are likely to be of particular historic significance. It was the original practice to attach them in this manner.
- Note the method by which papers have been fixed. From the beginning of the eighteenth century it was customary to paste papers after sizing the wall surface. The paste was compounded from flour, water and alum mixed and boiled to a thick consistency.
- Check generally for dampness and look for any signs of mould growth on the wallpaper surface.
- If a stretched screen framework has been used to support the wallpaper check for the following:
  - Rust stains in the nails.
  - Signs of any fungal or insect attack in the timbers.
  - An adequate flow of air behind the screening.
  - The condition of the hessian or cartridge paper backing.
  - Gently tap the surface for oscillation which could be a sign of underlying damp. A taut wallpaper surface is a likely indication of a drier environment.
- Look for the presence of booklice between layers of wallpaper. They are evidence of high humidity in the immediate micro-environment.
- Check for any infestation from cockroaches or silverfish which are attracted to the starch in the wallpaper paste.
- Assess the composition and condition of the underlying substrate.
- Determine the number of overlying burdens of wallpaper and paint (if any).

8.4   CARE AND PROTECTION

- Make a photographic record of the wallpaper as found. Also date and note any important factors and notify the instructing or supervising source.
- Do not allow historic wallpapers to be subjected to periods of sustained high heat. This is likely to result in the dessication of the fixing paste and will cause a corresponding loss of attachment.
- The re-attachment of old wallpaper should only be carried out with a wheat starch-based paste. This will not normally harm the paper and will allow it to be removed more easily if this later proves to be necessary.

- Make sure old papers are protected from direct sunlight.
- In order to maintain historic wallpapers in good condition, room temperatures should be kept at about 65°F (18°C) with a relative humidity of not more than 50 per cent.
- If pieces of matching wallpaper are found elsewhere, such as in cupboards and suchlike, record this and notify the conservator or the instructing source.
- Historic wallpapers must not be lacquered, varnished or treated with a clear protective coating.
- Where there is a need to match original designs with replacement paper this can usually be achieved through purpose-made silk screen commissions.
- Do not undertake any cleaning or removal of old wallpaper without expert guidance.

FURTHER READING
See section on Wall coverings in the References.

CHAPTER 9

METALS

9.1 LEAD

In Medieval times, lead was the only available material suitable for flat roof coverings and it remained the most used metal in the building process until the Industrial Revolution. Prior to this it was also the only viable option for gutters, downpipes, rain-water heads and similar items of external plumbing. The crude forms of internal plumbing which began to appear from around the middle of the Tudor period were also fashioned in lead. Due to natural weathering, the anticipated lifespan of leadwork is about 100 years, though it may exceed 150 years. With some locally mined British lead ores this longevity can be attributed to the presence of impurities such as silver. Lead usage is classified in terms of mass rather than thickness, with metric code numbers approximating to the original imperial method of measurement which referred to weight in pounds per square foot. To assist in visual identification, the classifications are also colour coded as follows:

Code 3 – green. Code 4 – blue. Code 5 – red. Code 6 – black.
Code 7 – white. Code 8 – orange.

9.1.1 Sheet-cast lead

Until the latter part of the seventeenth century, all sheet lead used in building was cast by pouring molten lead over prepared moist sand beds. This had the effect of producing a rather attractive stippled surface finish and is a distinctive feature of this form of manufacture. Local tradition seems to have determined whether the sheeting was used sand face up or down. Sand-cast lead sheeting is thicker and less uniform than sheeting produced by later methods of production, and can be prone to flaws from air bubbles and sand holes.

9.1.2 Milled sheet lead

First produced towards the end of the seventeenth century, this is manufactured mechanically by passing cast lead slugs between large steel or cast-iron rollers that forge the metal into lead sheets. The finished product is nominally free from defects and of uniform size and thickness. The pressure exerted on the metal results in a different molecular structure to cast lead.

9.1.3 Direct manufacture lead sheet

Direct manufacture (DM) lead sheet is manufactured from an entirely different process to milled sheet lead. An internally cooled steel roller is rotated on the surface of a bath of molten lead. As the lead is picked up by the roller, it solidifies at the point of contact to produce long continuous sheets very similar in appearance to milled sheet lead. However, as the operation is chill cast, this produces a different crystalline structure to ordinary milled lead sheet and while it is still molten a small quantity of copper is introduced to enhance ductibility.

9.1.4 Environmental influences on lead

The bright metallic lustre seen on freshly cut or scraped lead quickly tarnishes to form either a dull grey, near black or white protective coating of lead carbonate. Acid rainfall can quickly wash this away to cause staining on other nearby materials. Eventually a permanent patina of lead sulphate will develop as a result of a reaction with carbon dioxide and sulphur dioxide in the atmosphere. However, the underside of lead sheeting is not exposed to the same environment, making it vulnerable to damage from corrosion. Patination cannot occur in the same way as on the exposed side and a protective coating is slow or unable to form.

Unoxidised lead is attacked by pure water, which can collect between the underside of the lead and the decking as a result of condensation. The likelihood of destructive corrosion taking place is therefore greatly increased in this type of environment. It is a problem which needs to be given most careful consideration, plus a dedication to correct detail at the repair or replacement stage. Apart from the presence of condensed moisture, another warning sign of decay is 'sugaring' which is the formation of a white (sometimes tinted) crystalline powder (lead hydroxide) that causes eventual thinning and pitting in the lead sheeting.

Lead is also liable to attack from organic acids in wet peat soils, but it is not appreciably affected when in direct contact with lime mortar. On the other hand, serious decay can arise under damp conditions from the effects of Portland cement mortar. Resistance to inorganic acids varies according to the levels of concentration and the temperature. Lead can be severely attacked by acetic acids found in timber, especially oak, chestnut and western red cedar, and by the organic acids in lichens.

9.1.5 Inspection and analysis of leadwork

- When examining lead sheeting look for signs of pitting, ridging, benching or ripples in the exposed surface and mark any visible signs of failure.
- Look for signs of fatigue in the metal. Lead has a relatively high coefficient of linear expansion, which results in dimensional changes under varying temperatures. Unless

the metal is allowed to expand and contract freely, ridges will form. Excessive fatigue stressing at the top of these ridges results in cracking. Bulges are indicative of a restriction in thermal movement and lead to eventual cracking.

- Lead can slowly stretch under its own weight due to oversizing or incorrect fixing. This will eventually result in cracking due to fatigue.
- Test for any depressions or unevenness. These are an indication of a faulty sub-base.
- Check for adequate roof falls for rain-water run-off and look for any signs of ponding.
- Try to examine the condition of the underside of the leadwork and look for signs of dampness in the ceiling area below.
- Check roof timbers for any signs of movement or deflection.
- Water test the functional efficiency of all gutters, downpipes and other rain-water appliances and fittings.
- Check the condition of the welts, drips or rolls and record any items which are not in accordance with good practice.
- Check soakers and flashings for adequate depth, lap and correct fixing. A lack of proper fixing will cause slippage and buckling (which is not the same as creep).
- Examine the gutters, parapets, box gutters, cesspools, outlets and similar items for condition and adequate functional capacity.
- Consider whether any overfixing has taken place. This can retard movement of the lead, so causing fine fractures.
- Check for contact with any incompatible metals.
- Look for any likelihood of acid rain-water run-off from vegetation such as lichens.
- Look for signs of faulty construction and poor detailing which is very prevalent in Georgian and Regency lead roofing.
- Examine vulnerable areas for impact damage.
- Be alert to the phenonmenon known as thermal pumping which can occur in the enclosed voids of the leadwork.
- Lead soil pipes were in general use up to the end of the nineteenth century. When found check for the following:
  - Distortion and impact damage.
  - Sleeving where pipes pass through masonry, plaster and mortars.
  - Examine the condition of the jointing. This is especially important where Astragal jointing has been used. It may need to be renewed to accord with modern standards.
- Where original lead piping is still used for supplying drinking water, it will need to be replaced in accordance with the standards specified by the Water Supply Byelaws.

9.1.6   Repairs and maintenance

- Determine the cause of any failure.
- All new work should be undertaken in accordance with approved practice (see Lead Sheet Association Manuals and English Heritage Lead Advice Notes).

- Be especially careful that the fixing and jointing is correct. Ensure adequate allowance has been made for thermal expansion.
- To accord with the principles of conservation policy, old leadwork should as far as practicable be retained and repaired. Complete renewal should only be considered when it is deemed necessary.
- A patination oil needs to be applied immediately after the fitting of new sheeting or where the existing patina has been removed or damaged by tooling during operations. Areas must be treated within seven hours.
- Do not apply mastic, bituminous or silicone compounds as a remedy for leaks. Bitumen in particular is extremely difficult to remove after application. The use of proprietary repair tapes and bandages should also be avoided. All cracks need to be sealed by lead burning.
- The use of lead burning techniques may require a HOT WORK PERMIT under the terms of the contract.
- Solders should never be used for lead sheet repairs.
- If dirt and animal droppings have accumulated, they should be removed and the area cleaned by using a bristle brush and water with a neutral pH soap.
- Where there is a need to minimise the contrast between new and old work, a special lead cleaning gel can be used on the original parts. Most proprietary cleaners are unsuitable for the removal of ordinary dirt and grime.
- If lichens and mosses are to be removed, the work should only be undertaken with approved materials marketed for that purpose.
- Where small patch repairs are acceptable, the old lead needs to be well shaved back to a bright unoxidised surface, with the new lead being set with a lap of not less than 25 mm.
- Underlays must be allowed to move freely over the roof decking. The best types are those with a geotextile structure, as they provide better ventilation to the underside of the lead. Bituminous-based forms should never be introduced as they bond with the lead and restrict thermal movement.
- Always avoid lead having direct contact with mortar containing Portland cement by coating with bitumen where the two materials meet.
- Never use galvanised steel nails or fixings.

9.2   THE USE OF IRON

9.2.1   The historical background

In the British Isles the use of iron as a building material dates from the Roman occupation and for a considerable time after their departure the metal could only be produced in small quantities by smelting local ores in a clay furnace. The process was costly and laborious and output remained low and the cost high. The practical constraints on manufacture confined output to the production of wrought iron and its scarcity value meant it was used sparingly for accessories such as locks, hinges and catches. The fashion for decorative architectural ironwork, which is a feature of many historic buildings, originated in the seventeenth century but was followed by a period of decline in the use of iron for artistic purposes. However, wrought iron enjoyed a revival around 1820, only to be largely displaced by the mass production of cast iron. From about 1850 onwards wrought iron made a remarkable return to favour which lasted for about 40 years.

The structural use of iron between the fourteenth and eighteenth century was limited to the fabrication of items such as stirrups, strapping and bolts, or as additional reinforcement to tie-beams and similar members. The situation rapidly changed as improvements in manufacturing techniques altered the scale of production from small localised furnaces to mass output in the major industrial locations. From 1845 onwards, rolled beams entered the scene and wrought iron steadily became established as being ideal for both beam and frame work. In 1774 the development of Wilkinson's cupola blast furnace enabled cast iron to be produced on a highly competitive basis and resulted in a major change in design applications. The switch to cast iron escalated between 1810 and 1840, by which time the material was considered to be superior to wrought iron. It was used for both beam and column work with the latter being cast in distinctive circular, octagonal and hexagonal shapes. Most columns had a hollow central core which helped to alleviate the differential stresses which occurred during cooling. Many of these units interfixed using spigot and socket joints. There were many different views about the structural applications of iron. These divergencies of opinion can be witnessed in a legacy of varied beam configurations which are to be found in old buildings (Figure 9.1). Much of the thinking behind structural theory was misconceived and some faulty ideas were put into practice. When making an analysis of an old building it is essential to identify and classify correctly the iron components and fixings, and to be alert to the possibility that wrought and cast iron have been used in combination.

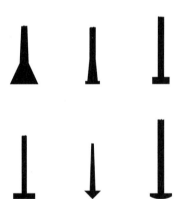

Fig. 9.1   Some sectional shapes used in cast-iron beams between 1796 and 1804

9.2.2   Wrought iron

Wrought iron is the purest form of iron and has a very low carbon content, being prepared for use by a repetitive process of heating, hammering and rolling which expels most of the silicon slag content. The finished product has a laminated, fibrous structure, as distinct from the crystalline forms of other types of iron. These laminations are a positive means of identification, but they also have a tendency to separate especially if the metal has been incorrectly rolled during production. Wrought iron is ductile and malleable and can be worked either hot or cold. Other means of recognition are a smooth surface and an absence of blow holes and although it is relatively soft and workable, it is also resistant to fatigue and is less prone to corrode than other forms of iron. It can also be satisfactorily welded (Figure 9.2).

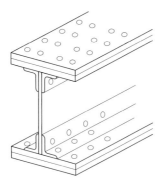

Fig. 9.2 Wrought iron girder made up from various sized plates and flange angles rivetted together

9.2.3 Cast iron

When in the molten state, iron can take into solution a level of carbon approximating to 3.5 per cent, but this will increase if substances such as manganese are also present. Variations in the ingredients of the iron determine the properties of the end product. If the correct carbon content is retained within the composition of the metal on cooling, a white iron will be formed. Conversely, if the carbon content separates out as free carbon during the production process, a grey iron is produced. If part of the carbon separates out as graphite, the cooled metal becomes mottled iron. The presence of sulphur makes the iron whiter, whereas a higher silicon content has a softening effect on the metal. Manganese has the opposite effect, making the metal harder. Fine castings are possible if phosphorous is present in the correct proportions. Malleable cast irons are produced by annealing white cast iron.

9.2.4 Inspection and analysis

To distinguish between wrought and cast iron, look for the following:

- The pattern of riveting can be a useful indicator of the type of iron used. Wrought iron members are more often built-up and assembled from a range of riveted sections.
- The nature of the surface finish. Wrought iron has a rolled and beaten surface, whereas cast iron is likely to reveal blow holes and pits.

- Wrought iron has a fibrous structure, in contrast to cast iron which is crystalline in form.
- Mould lines are often clearly visible in cast iron.
- The brittle nature of cast iron means that it can fracture more readily. Wrought iron has a greater degree of elasticity and can deform before ultimate failure.
- Delamination only occurs in wrought iron.
- Cast iron is prone to embrittlement with age.
- Cast-iron stanchions are likely to be either hollow or cruciform in shape, with end plates being finished in decorative detail.
- Many of the early cast-iron beams can be readily identified from curious shaping, and although later examples are to an accustomed form, the bottom flanges are often larger than the top.
- Slight surface cracking, which occurs during cooling, can be present in cast iron.
- An unusual form of anaerobic corrosion, known as graphitisation, can occur in cast iron. It occurs when the iron is in contact with acidic waters and soils and can be very difficult to detect. The reaction has little effect on the surface condition of the metal although slight blistering may sometimes be present. Probing with a sharp instrument will break the surface skin and reveal an underlying soft and friable structure.
- Determine the degree of any corrosion and look for places where water can be trapped.
- Although similar in appearance to steel, the corners and edges to wrought iron members tend to be more rounded.

9.2.5   Repair and maintenance

- When undertaking any form of metallic repair the danger of bi-metallic corrosion always needs to be considered.
- Most grades of wrought iron are suitable for welding. Welding cast iron can be difficult and is not normally favoured. The need for a repair must be accurately determined beforehand and the work should only be undertaken by skilled craftsmen.
- With wrought-iron repairs welding should not be used in lieu of riveting, which may cause localised forms of stress and molecular disturbance.
- Cold repair techniques are often a suitable option particularly in the case of cast iron. This can involve the use of straps, dowels, pins and metal stitching.
- Epoxy resins containing metallic fillers are suitable for patching and void filling when structural issues are not involved.

9.3   COPPER

The original methods used in the fixing of copper sheeting vary little from the present day but substantial changes have occurred in the method of production. Originally sheets were made by smelting ore into ingots which were first annealed and finally beaten into sheet form using heavy hammers. From the early eighteenth century onwards, the beating process was replaced by machine rolling. At around 1870 improved rolling techniques enabled sheets to be worked to exact and thinner dimensions. Until this development, sheets were smaller and it was standard practice to use standing seams at the joins. The use of larger sheets saw the more general adoption of the conical roll as a suitable connection. However, in the course of time the conical roll was found to have an induced weakness at junctions and abutments and this encouraged a general shift to the use of the batten roll system. These differences are a probable indicator of the date and origin of the sheeting, but are by no means positive or conclusive.

When inspecting historic copper sheeting, the following issues need to be considered:

- The nature and thickness of any patina. This usually forms as copper carbonate and is green in colour. In highly polluted atmospheres, however, the colour will vary from darker shades of green through to blue/green, brown or black.
- Look for any signs of verdigris which has a distinctive grey/green colouration. It is water-soluble and is caused by a chemical reaction between the copper and acetic acid and has a destructive effect.
- Examine to determine whether run-off from the copper surface is likely to affect other parts of the building fabric. This can cause corrosion in other metals and disfigures stone and brickwork.
- Look for any signs of cracking or slight fissures in the sheeting, which are likely to be due to fatigue. This can be caused by the alternating action of wind pressure and suction.
- Examine the effects of thermal movements which may result in deformation or splitting in the sheeting. With older sheeting that has become 'tired' this can also be accompanied by powdering on the outer surface.
- The acidity of rain-water run-off will increase when passing over surfaces covered with lichens, moss and algae to cause corrosion in the copper, which is usually evidenced by a series of holes and grooves on the surface. This can also cause the patina to dissolve resulting in the formation of a rust-coloured powder that comes away with rubbing to reveal a bright and shiny copper under-surface.
- Remember that fresh mortar can be aggressive and can attack copper.
- Iron products can cause severe staining of copper.
- Ensure cleaning compounds containing either ammonia, sodium or potassium hydroxide are not applied to copper surfaces.

The repair, maintenance and replacement of copper work should be undertaken in accordance with established practice and to current standards.

FURTHER READING
See section on Metals in the References.

CHAPTER 10

WINDOWS AND DOORS

10.1 THE HISTORICAL BACKGROUND

The original design and shape of the window arrangements to an ancient building represent an intrinsic feature of the past and any changes which alter this balance result in a dilution of the historic worth of a structure. For this reason all original window features should, as far as practicable, be retained, with any necessary intervention being kept to a minimum level.

In the Middle Ages window sizes were influenced by defensive considerations, in addition to the effect unglazed openings had on the warmth and comfort of occupancy. Unglazed orifices were first known as 'wind eyes' or 'wind holes', the origin of the term window. They often featured diamond-shaped mullions spaced narrowly apart, which are thought by some to have been contrived to act aerodynamically to reduce penetrating draughts (see Figure 6.4). To overcome the extremes of the weather, openings were sometimes screened with an assortment of materials, including parchment, greased linen or undaubed wattle, which diminished much of the incoming light. It was more usual therefore to leave the openings uncovered and to rely on the protection provided by shutters fixed internally on side, top or bottom hung hinges or on slides. Any surviving evidence of this nature should not be altered or obliterated unless expert guidance has been taken (Figures 10.1 and 10.2).

10.1.1 Progress and development

The emergence of the sash window in around 1670 was at first confined to larger buildings when they were known as 'shassis' windows. At this stage some of the earliest sashes were held by pegs with the upper lights being fixed. The counterbalancing weights were first housed in timber baulks hollowed out to take each weight, but it was not long before sash boxes appeared, which were similar in design to those which date from Victorian times. The earliest sash windows produced during the seventeenth century had thick glazing bars with very small glass panes. This design eventually developed into a twelve-pane window which was later reduced to eight panes. At the start of the Victorian period, this further reduced to four panes

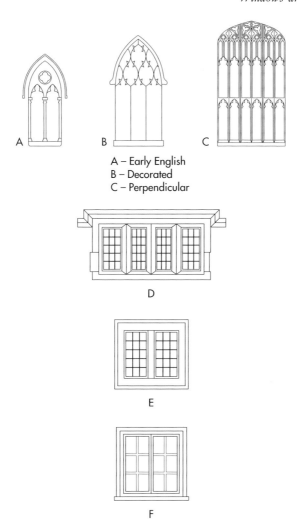

A – Early English
B – Decorated
C – Perpendicular

Fig. 10.1 History of window design – 1 Historic window shapes are best classified into Medieval, Interim and Renaissance phases, with fenestration being an important factor in the gradual changes which took place in the vernacular, polite and formal architectural styles. Nowhere is this more apparent than in the Gothic style, where progressive changes are clearly evident in window design between the beginning and ending of the Gothic phase. In the Early English period, the narrow lancet windows with heavy plate tracery contrast with the wider and more refined arched windows of the Decorated period. By the Perpendicular period, window design had altered to even wider and taller openings with an emphasis on the admission of light (see A–C). Vernacular windows in the Medieval phase were mainly in horizontal proportions, the length being greater than the depth, a notable exception being the window in the central hall which was to a vertical form. As the halls became floored over, newly installed windows followed the horizontal theme. In stone buildings, window relationships also pursued the horizontal trend as small lancet-type lights set in series (see D). At vernacular and polite levels, the Interim phase was marked by a general trend towards window shapes that were either square or slightly elongated in the vertical dimension (see E and F)

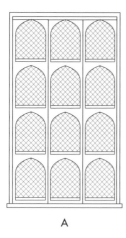

A

B

At first the Renaissance had no more than an adaptive influence on English architecture, which lacked the essential characteristics of correct classicism. In architectural terms the Tudor period is normally regarded as a transitional time with key features remaining Gothic in substance. This is clearly apparent in the large country mansions built around this time, particularly in the fenestration which continued to be in sympathy with the basic elements of Gothic design (see A)

The move to classicism in England is more correctly dated from the Elizabethan period, particularly in the architecture of the great houses. Although designers considered their work to be in the Italian Renaissance style, in truth it fell far short of that objective. B indicates how window proportions started to assume and identity with classicism but the wider qualities and features of classical design are absent

The predominance of the vertical cross window (C) during the peak of the Inigo Jones period was the culmination of a progressive shift from the horizontal mullion and transom window to the vertical style of the Renaissance

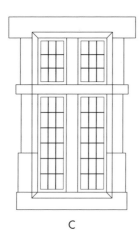

C

Fig. 10.2   History of window design – 2

and later to one pane to each sash (Figure 10.3). The absence of glazing bars placed considerable stress on the sash frame, which had to be strengthened by the introduction of the now familiar sash horn (sometimes termed a joggle) (Figure 10.4). The sliding horizontal Yorkshire sash was popular during the eighteenth century and the early part of the nineteenth century, and often provided a convenient solution where restricted headroom prevented the installation of sashes sliding vertically (Figure 10.5).

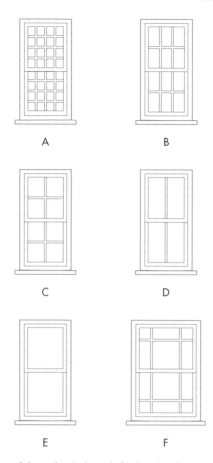

Fig. 10.3 Development of the sash window. A further development during this phase was the appearance of margin light windows (see F), which began in the early part of the nineteenth century and remained a popular feature until the beginning of this century. A particular characteristic of this phase is the use of either decorative or deeply coloured glass. Another representation of the time was the use of internally fixed folding shutters installed for security and extra warmth

10.1.2   Recent legislation

New or replacement work should be a correct representation of the original, but there are circumstances where different legislative aims can conflict in meeting this objective with planning requirements, being at variance with the Building Regulations. The Standard Assessment Procedure for energy consumption is now required for all newly constructed dwellings and for buildings which have been converted into dwellings.

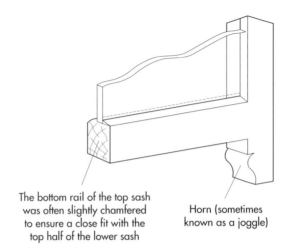

The bottom rail of the top sash was often slightly chamfered to ensure a close fit with the top half of the lower sash

Horn (sometimes known as a joggle)

Fig. 10.4   Victorian sash

Fig. 10.5   Yorkshire-style side sliding sash window

The assessment is calculated on the energy required for space and water heating and is generally perceived to be a requirement, which can only be met through the installation of double glazed units. In reality this may not be the case and satisfactory alternatives can often be negotiated with the local authority which enable the original windows to be retained. Approved Document L allows for a variation from the stated standard if compensatory provisions can be made. By increasing the amount of insulation elsewhere and through a restriction of the window, door and rooflight areas, it may be possible to meet the necessary U-value requirements subject to the submission of heat loss calculations. Where there is a requirement to introduce permanent ventilation, this may be difficult if historic glass has to be cut and altered. In that case an alternative means of providing a satisfactory air-flow will need to be improvised. In cases involving low-level glazing, it is likely that a demand will be made for the installation of safety glass or if the panes are small, the provision of 6 mm float glass.

Other measures which can be used to the same effect include the influence of solar gain and the installation of a heating system that can be shown to directly improve the heat efficiency and saving. In terms of thermal efficiency, the original components can be adapted by fitting patent draught-proofing systems and the installation of secondary glazing. Some categories of buildings are not, however, affected by Part L of the Building Regulations (in Scotland Part J of the Scottish Building Regulations). These exemptions cover all existing buildings where no building or alteration work is proposed. There is also an exemption for existing dwellings where any new floor area is increased by not more than 10 m², and for buildings where a low level of heat is acceptable such as those used for storage. Certain other industrial uses and activities are also included in this exemption.

10.1.3   Planning

- Changes or alterations of any kind to windows of a listed building require listed building consent.
- In conservation areas, the requirement to obtain permission to alter or change windows will normally apply to any building within a designated area which is subject to an Article 4 Direction (see also Section 1.5.3).
- Where the Permitted Development Regulations apply, planning permission is not needed for the installation of replacement windows. It is important to note that this exemption only relates to a single, private dwelling house.

10.1.4   Replacement systems

A wide variety of replacement windows are now available and many are made from alternative materials such as aluminium and PVCu. They are often marketed under brand names such as the Georgian or Victorian range, which by implication suggests they are acceptable for use in buildings of those periods. Apart from the alien nature of the material, most replica products do not match the essential detail of the original and are unsuitable where correct historic detail is important. However, a number of specialist companies now manufacture new made-to-measure windows in accordance with traditional methods, materials and fashion.

10.1.5   Wood windows

Inspection and assessment

- Check for signs of wood deterioration, distortion or decay. The bottom rails of sashes and casements and the ends of cills are particularly vulnerable to rot.

- Note features such as evidence of internal condensation and dampness to adjoining masonry or brickwork.
- Look for any jamming or binding in opening lights. Test for easy movement particularly for ventilation and cleaning access.
- Examine frames for signs of deformation as a result of movement in the main structure of the building.
- Check glazing putties for soundness, adhesion and correct application.
- Test for excessive accumulations of paint.

When inspecting sash windows check:

- The condition and fixing of the sash weights, cords or chains.
- The existence of a pocket piece for maintenance access to the sash weights.
- The state of the pulley stiles and parting beads.
- Ensure the stop beads are not jamming the sash frame. It should be possible to insert two thicknesses of newspaper between them.
- Determine the method of construction of the case framing. Some early forms do not have a back lining or parting slip, which can cause the sash weights to jam and the cords to fray.

NOTE: The pink-tinted filling found between window and door frames and the wall is an early mastic. It was made from finely powdered stone or sand and red lead, with linseed oil being added and mixed in to the required consistency.

Repairs and maintenance

- Eliminate any surrounding sources of dampness.
- Bed all new frames on an approved mastic.
- Accurately record the condition and design of the windows before implementing renewal or change.
- Aim for the minimum replacement of the existing wood.
- Replacement wood must be well seasoned and from the same species as the original, excepting cills and the bottom rails of sashes which are best renewed with timber containing natural oils.
- Allow any existing wood that is damp to dry out before fixing or splicing in new.
- Do not perpetuate any unsuitable or failed practices used in the original work. In those circumstances undertake replacement to an amended and well-tested design.
- Pre-treat or coat new and replacement timbers with an approved preservative.
- If removal of the window framing is necessary particular care is needed to avoid damage to the surrounding fabric, especially where the orginal work has been tosh nailed (nails driven at an angle).
- The fitting and movement of sash windows can be improved through the replacement of worn parting and stop beads.
- Loose wedges and tenons should be either removed or drilled out and replaced. Pegged slip or false tenon techniques are suitable for replacing weak or failed tenons.

- Maintain the original profiling for all renewed mouldings and astragals.
- Spliced inserts are best set at the top and bottom interfaces with an incline running down to the outer face. Fixing screws need to be of brass or other non-ferrous metal.
- Set Yorkshire sliding sashes on mature oak strips that have been waxed.
- Replacement window frames need to be fixed in the exact position of the original.
- In locations where access for cleaning and maintaining sash windows is difficult, the installation of the *Simplex* system can provide the solution. Already used extensively in Scotland, it enables sash windows to be inward opening when required, and is achieved by fitting specially made hinges and other parts. Simplex hinges are devised to slot onto pins which enable the sash window to open inwards in a similar action to a casement window. Some alteration to the joinery is necessary with sash cords being restrained with cord clutches before the opening action can be operated. Further information is obtainable from Historic Scotland.
- Where work involves compliance with the Building Regulations, the undermentioned Approved Documents stand to have an influence on window designs for historic buildings:
  - Approved Document B: Means of escape.
  - Approved Document F: Ventilation.
  - Approved Document L: Thermal insulation
  - Approved Document N: Safety glazing.

10.1.6 Metal windows

Throughout the seventeenth century, wrought iron was the more widely used material, with casements being set either directly in stone or in oak frames or sub-frames. Opening casements were of the lift-off type set on hinges known as gudgeon pins. The early eighteenth century saw a decline in the use of metal, but the advent of more sophisticated metal casting in the mid-eighteenth century set the scene for an improved market which for the first time included the use of other metals. Production methods also started to alter, as hand crafting was gradually replaced by an industrialised form of manufacture. Cast-iron windows became popular in the Victorian Gothic period and are distinguishable by thicker, indelicate profiles. In the middle of the nineteenth century hot rolled steel windows first appeared and in the wake of a number of gradual improvements, including galvanising, remained in general use until the 1970s.

Inspection and assessment

Wrought iron

- Examine for distortion.
- Check for an excessive build-up of paint.
- Look for signs of rust.
- Test the hinges and fastenings for correct and easy working.
- Record precisely the condition of the windows before commencement of work.

- Take photographs and prepare detailed working drawings of items which need to be either renewed or repaired.

Cast iron

- Look for fractures and determine the cause. Consider the possibility of damage through vibration or impact, and movement in the building structure and brittleness due to age.
- If parts are missing, take plaster casts of the remainder to assist in the creation of a composite replacement.
- Record accurately all existing cast-iron work with photographs, including close-ups.
- Check for an excessive build-up of paint.
- Examine for corrosion.
- Look for signs of flaws in the casting.
- If grey cast iron has been used check for graphitisation.

Galvanised steel

- If the metal has become exposed, check the condition of the galvanising.
- Check for distortion.
- Test all moving parts.

FURTHER READING
See section on Windows in the References.

10.2   GLASS AND GLAZING

10.2.1   Recording

The comprehensive listing and recording of historic glass is a vital prerequisite before work of any kind is commenced. This should take the form of a detailed plan with each pane or segment being separately referenced in sequence. This information needs to be enhanced and supported with coloured explanatory photographs, drawings and a detailed statement giving full information on the condition, nature and historical features of the material. It is of paramount importance that this work is supervised by a suitably accredited expert. If glass in an historic window is either missing or badly damaged, the Royal Commission on Historic Mounuments and records in local archives can often provide useful information.

10.2.2   Deterioration of ancient glass

Historic glass is vulnerable to chemical and physical changes as a result of environmental conditions, including a reaction with rain-water and water-laden solutions. Over a period of time the alkali content in many earlier glasses can be leached out, resulting in a loss of transparency and a tendency towards iridescence. Moreover, some lichens cause minute flaking, which occasionally penetrates into the body of the glass to create microscopic perforations. Damage can also occur from nutrients in some algae and fungi, which are capable of permanently disfiguring or etching the surface.

A wide range of pollutants also react with glass and many become bonded chemically to the surface. The natural weathering of lead is liable to cause salts in solution to be deposited on the outer surface to form a dull grey film. In built-up areas partially unburnt or unburnt particles of acidic hydrocarbon particles from vehicle exhaust emissions also attack glass surfaces. However, faults sometimes derive from the method and ingredients used in production. Some Medieval glasses have an unduly high proportion of lime to silica which results in a breakdown of the silica under very wet conditions. Eventually a fine crust can develop which holds moisture and encourages deterioration and exfoliation.

10.2.3 Inspection and assessment

- An inspection needs to include a general assessment of local climatic and environmental conditions and the effects that this is likely to have had on the glass.
- First determine the nature of the glass involved, such as whether it has been made from the crown or cylinder process. If the glass is pock marked, this is an indication that it has been produced by the cylinder process. Crown glass is normally clearer. Until the nineteenth century, most glass was manufactured in this manner.
- Look carefully at coloured and painted glasses and the likely techniques involved. Where glass painting has been incorporated into the design, check the condition of the paintwork for cohesion and bonding to the glass. Check for any loss of colour, detail or other features (Figure 10.6).
- Always include a detailed inspection of the lead cames and provide a condition report.
- Where ferramenta supports areas of leaded glass, check the condition of the iron framework, saddle and vertical bars. Unattended rust will eventually lead to serious cracking, distortion and staining of the glass.
- Check for buckling and bowing which occurs from 'creep' occurring in leadwork exposed to strong heat from the sun or from inadequate support (much nineteenth century work lacks sufficient support and 'T' bars are often needed to relieve the weight on the saddle bars).
- Check for any signs of organic or vegetational growths on the glass.
- Look for cracking or fissuring within the body of the glass.
- Examine for signs of water penetration and check whether the presence of moisture on the inside is due to condensation. Sometimes glass can 'sweat' due to an excess of lime in the original mix.
- Record any evidence of 'crizzling', which is recognisable from the development of a network of minute cracks. Glass in this condition is liable to weep and eventually disintegrate.
- Examine for surface pitting and crusting and for any indications of spalling and flaking.

Fig. 10.6   When viewed at a distance, the glass in this window appeared to be sound but a close examination revealed deterioration

- Historic glass can shrink and crack with, age which results in loose fitting quarries and panes in the frames and lead cames.

10.2.4   Repairs and maintenance

It is important to observe the concept of reversibility in relation to any treatments and to aim for minimum intervention. In addition, it is vital to ensure that work is only undertaken by specialists who have a thorough knowledge and understanding of the complicated nature of historic glass and the out-of-the-ordinary problems which can occur.

- Treatments such as re-painting in lost features and back plating, edge bonding and copper foil techniques are essentially an expert task requiring a particular skill.
- Replacement glass must be comparable with the original. Modern glass is flat and even in form, which produces a different and unacceptable contrast with earlier forms. Handmade glasses are uneven and distinctive and impart a multiplicity of reflections to give a more pleasing effect which does not blend with modern alternatives.

- Always ensure that replacement work is historically accurate. The existing installation may be the result of later work and could be out of keeping. Do not make assumptions but check first and seek expert advice.
- Always re-lead with matching lead cames using the original width. Before mass production started, lead cames were produced locally in the plumber's workshop. Matching lead cames may therefore need to be purpose-made (Figure 10.7).
- In the past, quarries were not cut to precise sizes. Allowance needs to be made for this when replacing lead cames.
- Traditional putty made from whiting and linseed oil can become exceptionally hard after the linseed oil has become fully oxidised. Do not attempt to chip or hack out by hand. Valuable glass should only be cleaned of putty using an infra-red lamp. On no account must a blow lamp or chemical stripper be used.
- When replacing glass in old sliding sash windows, check the weight of the replacement glass with the original. If the new glass is different in thickness, an adjustment to the counterbalancing will be needed. Any increase in weight can be made by threading nuts or washers onto the sash cord.
- Regular cleaning and maintenance of historic glass may not be sufficient to prevent gradual deterioration and additional protective measures may be necessary. Effective screening from the elements is a more acceptable remedy and can be achieved using either acrylic or polycarbonate sheeting. This has the disadvantage, however, of detracting from the historic appearance and a more suitable option is the installation of isothermal double glazing. This involves the careful removal of the original glass, with the frame being adapted to take a plate of modern glass that is leaded to follow the exact contour of the existing glass. When that has been fitted to the

Fig. 10.7   Historic glass being cleaned and set in new lead cames

external face, the original is replaced to the internal face and is fully protected from the weather.

- Only use distilled or de-ionised water for cleaning. Heavy soiling and corrosion can be removed with either ultrasonic equipment, laser beams, reagents, fine mechanical rubbing, fibreglass brushes or abrasive pencils. Any of these techniques must only be applied by specialists after full consultation with the authorities and others.
- When selecting a method of cleaning, always insist on a small test trial before use and examine the result under a microscope. This is especially necessary in the cleaning of painted surfaces.

FURTHER READING
See section on Glass in the References.

10.3   DOORS

10.3.1   Early side hung doors

Many of the earliest doors are fixed on 'harrs', a legacy from the Romans that endured in parts of the British Isles until the end of the nineteenth century. Most surviving harr hung doors are found fixed into a wood housing at the head and to an iron shoe at the base with the hanging stile thickened to take the harr pegs. This form of fixing has a long tradition in the northern and western regions of the country and enabled doors to be housed directly into masonry without the need for a timber frame or lining. The exception was properties constructed entirely of timber, where heavy wood framing can be found with hinges distinctive to the Medieval period (Figure 10.8).

10.3.2   Door frames and hinges

The absence of door framing caused excessive draughts and this led to the development of the purpose-made timber frame which, in turn, gave scope for the gradual improvement of hinging more akin to the patterns used today. Nevertheless, door framing did not come into general use until the sixteenth century. Framing in the form of a Gothic arch is sometimes described as a durn. The term should only be applied to naturally curved timber which has been split to form matching pieces.

10.3.3   Batten and plank doors

Original batten doors typically consist of vertical boards fixed to four horizontal ledges, except where more substantial protection was needed, which involved the marrying of two solid layers of boarding. One layer was fixed in vertical lengths and the other horizontally, the vertical fixing being featured externally to encourage the shedding of rain-water. In early work, the boards were mostly butt jointed against each other, although the jointing was often covered with either a chamfered or moulded strip.

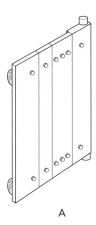 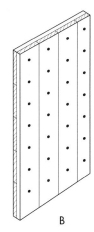

Doors which have exactly the same features, colour and style as the walls of a room are known as jib doors. They are blended into the overall design and decor without any form of visual interruption by being set flush with the wall. It is important they remain in this form if they are an original feature

Old doors are mostly wider than those made today and they also vary considerably in height Panel doors should not be stripped and featured in bare wood unless there is clear evidence this was the original intention

Some early plank doors have an adzed finish and should only be attended by an expert

Many of the door accessories which are taken for granted are relatively late features. The concealed mortice lock appeared in the nineteenth century, as did the letter box. Door knockers and pull handles were introduced in the eighteenth century and during the nineteenth century the increased use of carpeting saw the arrival of the rising butt hinge

Fig. 10.8 Historic doors. A, door on harr hinges. B, pegged plank and batten door

In some higher-class work, rebating and counter-rebating techniques can be found in the jointing between the boards.

10.3.4 Half doors and folding doors

Half doors (more accurately described as **heck doors**) and folding doors, together with larger doors containing an integral pedestrian door, are thought to have originated in gatehouses as a means to more effectively control entry. Heck means hatch and although now perceived to be a feature of farm architecture, it may well have an origin more closely associated with security. Occasionally large doors are found split vertically, these can normally be dated to the fifteenth century.

10.3.5 Framed and panelled doors

As a result of better tooling, joinery skills improved during the seventeenth century, and framed and panelled doors became more of a general feature. 'H' hinges first appeared at this stage, but the now familiar cast-iron butt hinge was a product of the eighteenth century. Glazed doors are a feature of the nineteenth century when either coloured or obscured glazing within the upper panels started to come into fashion. Towards the end of the seventeenth century, the influence of the Renaissance began to have a preceptable effect on overall design. Some distinctive features appeared at this stage such as raised and fielded panels and bolection mouldings.

10.3.6   Inspection and assessment

- Test the moisture content of the timber and look for any signs of fungal or insect decay.
- Examine the construction joints for shrinkage or expansion.
- Note any splits or cracks in the timber.
- Look for signs of distortion in the door.
- Check for the blurring of detail due to the build-up of successive layers of paint.
- Record the method of assembly, jointing and fixing.
- Check whether listed building consent needs to be obtained before any work can be undertaken.
- If replacement is necessary seek expert guidance if in doubt about the correct type and style of door to be installed.
- If alterations are required to the door frame, allow for the original size, shape and profile to be maintained.
- Make sure any colour scheme accords with the period to which the building relates.
- Aim for careful renovation and repair in preference to replacement.
- Check the ironmongery for compliance with correct historical detail.
- Take a photographic record of scarring from earlier fittings if this is likely to be removed or obliterated. This avoids the possibility of any loss of evidence hindering research at a later date.

10.3.7   Repairs and maintenance

The requirements for planning permission and listed building consent are the same as those described in Section 10.1.

- The replacement or splicing-in of new timber should be carried out in accordance with the techniques and recommendations described in Chapter 6.
- Do not fix planted mouldings where stuck mouldings have been used in the original work.
- Matching mature wood can be carefully pieced-in to hide old mortice holes and similar redundant features.
- Do not alter or introduce glazing that is likely to alter or harm the historic quality of a door.
- Ensure replacement door furniture and fittings are historically correct in every respect.

- Avoid removing paint by immersion in a caustic solution. Chemical applications are best applied using an approved paint stripper in accordance with recommended practice.
- In the past, carpentry joints to external doors were slightly reduced to cater for a coating of red lead primer before fixing. This needs to be taken into account when making replacement components.

10.3.8 Fire precaution doors

Where there is a need to provide fire protection, some existing doors can be adapted to comply with the requirements of half-hour fire resistance. An existing panelled door of suitable thickness can normally be upgraded to FIRE CHECK STANDARD by the application of an intumescent paint. Two coats are usually applied to the stiles, muntins and rails and three coats to the panelling. The whole is then treated with a sealer coat. This work should not, however, be undertaken without the agreement of the local authority and it is a wise precaution to obtain a statement from the manufacturers, confirming the suitability of the product for the purpose specified.

If the upgrading needs to be to the basic FIRE RESISTANCE standard, the following adaptations will be the minimum necessary before local authority approval is likely to be granted. The door thickness should be at least 50 mm and in correct alignment and flush fitting to the stopping. The following will also apply:

- The door stopping should be not less than 25 mm in depth taken from all dimensions (the use of intumescent strips and smoke seals is sometimes accepted as an alternative to stopping).
- Panelling to the door must be securely faced on the risk side with single-sheet fire resistant boarding approved by the local authority.
- Hinges are required to be of non-combustible metal and have a melting point of not less than 800°C.
- A self-closing device with a firm and positive action has to be fitted.
- The gap between the door edge and the frame needs to be not less than 3 mm.
- Glass lights over a door will require alteration to comply with the Fire Regulations. Normally this will entail the installation of wire-reinforced glass to a minimum thickness of 6 mm set in hardwood beading of not less than 13 mm in overall dimensional thickness.

CHAPTER 11

ROOF COVERINGS

11.1 PITCHED ROOFS

In the past, the selection of a suitable roofing covering seldom permitted choice and protection was mainly dictated by availability and the manner in which a local material could be applied to combat climatic exposure. This, in turn, had a fundamental influence on architectural style and resulted in the creation of many regional forms throughout the British Isles.

Roof profiles can sometimes be an indication of age, with older roofs normally being constructed to a steeper pitch (Figure 11.1). Many traditional materials relied on a steep pitch to shed snow and rain-water speedily in order to maintain adequate weathering and protection. This encouraged designers to develop roofing as a design feature, but during the late seventeenth century the fashion started to wane, mainly as a result of a fundamental change in the relationship between design and construction. By the late eighteenth century the widespread availability of Welsh slate enabled the classical architecture to flourish and roofs to be laid to a flatter pitch and to be hidden by features such as parapets.

The contrasts in roof forms are even more pronounced at vernacular level, where either natural slate or stone have been used for roofing purposes. The key zones of influence are to be found in the Lake District and areas of north Wales, Cornwall and some parts of Devon and Leicestershire. The weather and local circumstances have dictated variations in working methods, which have become prominent features in the local landscape.

11.1.1 Repair and renewal

With repair and renewal work, it is vital for the historical values and features of the past to be maintained and preserved. There may be circumstances, however, where the provision of a more recent roof covering is out of keeping with the period of the structure and will need to be replaced with a historically correct alternative. In all cases it is essential the following rules are observed:

- Check to ensure replacement materials are of the correct type and style for the architectural period and theme.

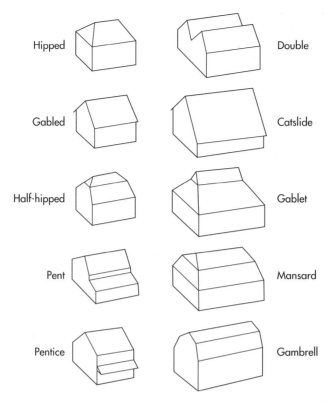

Fig. 11.1 Diagrammatic summary of historic roof forms

- All work must be capable of being reversed.
- Replacement materials must be functionally reliable and ideally from the original source of supply.
- Determine the extent and degree of any deterioration in the roof covering and establish the reasons for failure, i.e. poor workmanship, incorrect gauging, inferior materials etc.
- If renewal of the roof covering is necessary, seek approval before introducing changes in the replacement work.
- Calculate the pitch of the roof and measure the gauge and lap used for slating/tiling and check for functional suitability.
- Check the condition of the roof timbers and ensure the load-bearing capacity of the roof structure is adequate.
- Check the condition and method of construction of all ridges, valleys, hips and verges.

Much of the charm and character of an older building is in the easy and undulating lines of the structure, which contrast with the geometrical uniformity of more modern times. For this reason, movements in the ridge line and roof carcassing should be left untouched unless there is a need for structural interference. Before roof stripping, take photographs and drawings of the original so that the new covering can be laid as near as possible to the old profile.

Roof renewal can involve the need to comply with the ventilation requirements of Part F in the Building Regulations, but it is essential to select a solution that is unobtrusive, such as the Keymer in-line system (Figures 11.2 and 11.3)). Many traditional forms of roofing cannot meet the cross-ventilation requirements for roof timbers without modifying the original method of construction. It is a problem that sometimes has to be resolved through innovation and requires a close dialogue between the builder, the building control officer and the conservation officer if compliance is to be achieved in a concealed form.

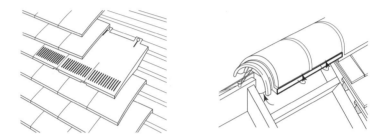

Fig. 11.2   Examples of the Keymer in-line system for roof ventilation

Fig. 11.3   An example of how the Keymer in-line ventilation system maintains the original roof line without impediment (photograph by kind permission of Keymer Tiles Ltd)

11.2   SLATES

Climatic conditions and local circumstances have dictated the manner and form in which local variations in working slate have developed. Some are especially individualistic, such as in the Lake District, where tradition has followed the use of round-headed slates using a single fixing hole and peg, with the slates being laid in a series of diminishing courses, ranging from 610 mm at the base to 150 mm at the ridge. In the same region wrestler slates are to be found, so called because they are dressed to interlock to prevent uplift and slippage from wind and other movements (Figure 11.4). By contrast, slating in Cornwall is regularly found to be bedded in mortar with a dressing of either a cement slurry, red lead or tar to counter the severe weather problems caused by the Atlantic gales.

In general terms, the mineral constituents found in most slates quarried in the British Isles are stable, but some are vulnerable to attack from acids found in polluted environments. Slates which are affected in this way usually contain quantities of calcite, pyrites and carbon, and deterioration appears in the form of delamination, general softening (porosity), crumbling and the development of pits, holes and cracking. Most failures, however, are caused by the corrosion of the nail fixings rather than the failure of the actual slates. The manner of fixing can also be a cause of slates breaking and slipping. Slates are secured either by head or centre nailing, with the latter being preferred due to the reduced risk of lifting from wind pressure. It is essential to ensure slates of the correct size are used. The size should increase dimensionally in proportion to the lowering of the roof pitch. While large slates can be used on steep pitches, it is bad practice to fix small slates on roofs that are to a low pitch. Fixing nails should be either copper or stainless steel and have large flat heads with annular rings in the shanks for improved grip to the wood battening. Nails that have been driven home too hard are likely to damage and enlarge the fixing holes, to cause excessive movement and eventual damage in high winds. Natural slates are normally classified as being either best, mediums, seconds or thirds. These terms relate to weight and thickness and not to quality.

Roofing slates are broadly classified as being either sized or random in shape. When selecting replacements the following considerations apply:

Fig. 11.4   Wrestler slates. When laid, the slates are interlocked, which gives greater resistance to uplift and slippage from wind and other movements

- A good slate when cut has no signs of being friable at the edges.
- Slates should not be too brittle and should be free from splinters.
- Welsh slates can easily be distinguished from Westmorland slates, being thinner, smaller and finer.
- Test for absorbency by placing a sample slate in water to half its height for twelve hours. The water line on the slate should not rise more than 4 mm above the level of the water in the vessel.
- Leave the rough side of a slate exposed to the weather, with the grain running in the direction of the length of the slate.

11.3   STONE SLATES (SOMETIMES KNOWN AS TILES)

11.3.1   Preparation

In locations where stone was used, the application of the material depended on how it could be split and trimmed and has resulted in an interesting variation in styles throughout the country. To be suitable, this purpose stone has to be naturally fissile. In the case of limestone, the lamination process was accelerated by a time-honoured practice of saturating with water and allowing the action of frost to either assist or complete separation. After winning, the stone was trimmed into selected shapes and sizes and then sorted into various categories, often being given quaint sounding names. In the Cotswolds for example, terms such as wivetts, muffities, tants and cussems all have a meaning. The limestone belt in particular has produced a wide variety of styles including well-known names such as Collywestons from Northamptonshire. Sandstone was also used, but the slates are usually much thicker and heavier and this tended to place limitations on roof configurations, which needed to be more simple in shape and to a lower pitch. Most early stone roofs are found torched in either clay or lime mortar with horse hair added to act as a binder. Some districts have localised preferences, such as stone slates being fixed at eaves level only with other materials, including thatch, being used further up the slope. Owing to their greater permeability, stone slates had to be much thicker than true slate.

Limestone

Limestone was usually laid to a steep pitch of 50° or more in diminishing courses, with either swept or laced valleys. The method of fixing was normally by means of a simple oak peg, but sometimes an alternative in the form of small animal bones can be found. The slates should always be hung over stout wood battens and never nailed directly to them. Eaves under slates (often known as cussomes) are bedded in mortar and are hooked under the first batten for good anchorage, but the length of this slate needs to be shorter to enable the end to terminate equally with the eaves course slate. The stone slates found in the Cotswolds, Dorset and Devon are much thicker and heavier than those used elsewhere and, in consequence, need more robust roof structures to carry the extra weight. Special stone ridge pieces were often made to a V shape and are now very difficult to replace. In some cases the problem has been overcome by using purpose-made ceramic ridge tiles. The historic method of fixing often entails the need to strip and re-lay stone slate roofs every 80 to 100 years or more, but the work must be planned so that the slates can be fitted back into position in a similar way to a jigsaw puzzle. This is because most limestone slates become extremely hard once the quarry sap has dried out and cannot be readily redressed, cut or trimmed. Limestones suitable for roofing are found in Dorset, Somerset, north west Wiltshire, the eastern half of Gloucestershire, parts of Oxfordshire and Worcestershire. Also in some districts in Northamptonshire, Rutland and the Kesteven area of Lincolnshire.

Sandstone

This is mostly found on old buildings where a good supply was available in the immediate locality. In consequence, sandstone roofing occurs along the sandstone belt running from the Pennines into Yorkshire and into Scotland. It can also be found in the region of north Wales that borders the Midlands.

Sandstone slates are often found laid in diminishing courses similar to limestone with the largest sizes commencing at the eaves and gradually reducing up to the ridge. Normally, riven oak laths were used with the slates being fixed with a single oak peg or a nail, but a variation does occur whereby the pegging is fixed between double battens.

Stone flags

Stone flags are thick and heavy slabs of large-sized stone and are mostly derived from sandstone. Sometimes the dimensions are enormous and can be as much as 1.2 m in width and at least 75 mm in thickness. Usually laid to a pitch of about 30°, they were often used at the eaves with other forms of roof cover especially thatch.

11.3.2   Inspection and assessment

- Check the condition of the slate cover and look for signs of delamination and similar defects.
- Examine the underside of the roof and pay particular attention to the pegging and nailing to the slates.
- Check the roof timbers and the method of construction. Look for deformations due to possible overloading, particularly if stone flags have been used.
- If different stone has been used for repair work, determine the nature of the replacement stone and check for compatibility with the original.
- Take particular care in examining the condition and overhang of the eaves under slate.
- Check the method of fixing between the eaves under slate and the oversailing course. A system of stone wedging was often used between the two courses.
- Examine wooden pegging for insect infestation.
- If torching or moss has been used in fixing, check for signs of dampness and decay in the surrounding timbers.

11.3.3 Renewal and repairs

- If a roof needs stripping, carefully calculate the number of replacement slates needed and take particular care when matching new to the old.
- Most replacement supplies are now only obtainable from sources of architectural salvage.
- After stripping, considerable care needs to be taken in sorting the slates correctly. This is best achieved by laying the slates out on the ground in an orderly form.
- Only allow cleaning or trimming of reclaimed slates to be done by skilled labour.
- Always make a generous allowance for breakages when ordering supplies.
- It is impracticable to introduce sarking in pegged replacement work unless counter-battening is provided. Alloy pegs are now available in lieu of wood.
- The final course at the ridge was traditionally bedded in lime mortar rather than being pegged or nailed.
- Ridge tiles are usually bedded in lime mortar supported by piles of small broken stones.
- Roof valleys are difficult to sweep unless the slates are very small. Normally valleys are formed with valley boards covered with valley slates.
- Replacing single slates entails lifting the surrounding slates by means of small wedges until sufficient space has been formed to insert new slates.
- Bed all verges in lime mortar.
- If the slates have a narrow width, the ratio between the pitch, depth and width is particularly important, otherwise water in the margin joints tends to creep up to the heads of the slates underneath.
- The mellow effect from weathering can be accelerated by coating with a slurry of cow dung, which encourages the growth of vegetation.

11.4 PLAIN CLAY TILES

11.4.1 The first tiles

During the thirteenth century, plain roof tiling started to become a feature in many parts of south east England, which in time extended into the Midlands as far as the Welsh border and into the southern parts of East Anglia. The original peg tiles were not uniform in shape or size. They were fixed with oak pegs on riven oak battens. Occasionally small animal bones were used instead of the oak pegs.

11.4.2 Sizes

In 1477 Edward IV decreed tile sizes should be standardised to $10\frac{1}{2}'' \times 6\frac{1}{4}'' \times \frac{5}{8}''$ (267 mm $\times$ 159 mm $\times$ 16 mm) but in practice this was never achieved due to inadequate supervision, the strength of local tradition and the difficulties encountered in firing clay to accurate dimensions. As a result, old tile dimensions in Leicestershire increased to $11'' \times 7''$ (280 mm $\times$ 180 mm) and the normal tile width in Sussex became $6\frac{3}{4}''$; in Kent $9'' \times 6''$ sizes (229 mm $\times$ 152 mm) were more usual. In many parts of the country, sizes reduced later to $9\frac{1}{2}'' \times 5\frac{3}{4}'' \times \frac{1}{2}''$ (242 mm × 146 mm × 13 mm) before being standardised to $10\frac{1}{2}'' \times 6\frac{1}{2}'' \times \frac{1}{2}''$ (267 mm × 153 mm × 13 mm). At the end of the eighteenth century knibs started to replace peg holes, thereby reviving a practice that had originally been introduced to these shores by the Romans. To reduce draughts and the penetration of snow, the underside of the tiling was often 'torched' with either a mortar of lime putty and hair or clay and hair. Moss was sometimes packed between the tiles to make the pegging more secure and less prone to the effects of wind.

11.4.3 Machine manufacture

It was not until the nineteenth century that machine-made mass-produced tiles appeared and at first they could not match the quality of their handmade counterparts. Problems arose initially from inferior mixes as a result of the early methods of mechanised blending and grinding and in the system of kilning, which often resulted in under-burning in the outer parts of the stacking. Under-burnt tiles are usually lighter coloured, snap more easily and when tapped lack the distinctive ring of a well-burnt tile. Many of the early machine-made tiles had no camber, which resulted in them being subjected to longer periods of saturation and in consequence they deteriorated more rapidly and unevenly.

11.4.4 Variations

The lack of uniformity in many of the early handmade peg tiles means great care is necessary when seeking replacements. Some only have a slight camber while others have a camber in the direction of both the length and width (double camber) (see Figure 11.5). Such shapings mean that modern tiles cannot be used with older tiles. Purpose-made facsimile products are often used. The double camber (sometimes described as a cross-camber) was devised to convey rain-water onto the middle surface of the tile immediately underneath. When machine manufacture began, the double

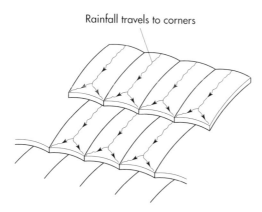

Rainfall travels to corners

Fig. 11.5

camber was discontinued in the belief that heavy winds could cause dislodgement more easily. The later introduction of a British Standard omitted any reference to the double camber. In the early roofs, weathering at intersections was achieved by using either swept or laced valleys with mortar fillets at the abutments. Small pieces of tile can be found embedded in the fillets and in some regions corbelled oversailing bricks were laid to protrude about 2″ (50 mm) above the abutments, with the tops being sloped with mortar for added protection and improved weathering.

Particular attention needs to be given to the following items before undertaking renewal or repair work.

11.4.5   Inspection and assessment

- Accurately record the condition and profile of the roof paying particular attention to the fixing methods used at the valleys, verges and eaves.
- Look for signs of delamination and surface failure of the tiles, also for excessive accumulations of moss and other forms of vegetation.
- Consider whether any nearby trees should be felled or lopped.
- Provide for the clearance and cleaning of all valleys, gutters and downpipes.
- Assess the effect of any nearby overgrowth such as Virginia creeper which clings by suction pads attached to the tendrils. In reality this is not particularly harmful, but it does tend to keep tiling in a prolonged state of saturation. On the other hand, ivy can cause considerable damage when its root formations penetrate under and between the tiles.
- Check the condition of the underside of the roof. Pay particular attention to the state of the battening and examine for nail sickness.
- Look for signs of crystalline salt deposits on the underside of the tiles. If present, this is a sign of undue water absorption and can result in rapid deterioration particularly around the tile head and at the nibs (if present).
- Check the tile courses for sagging. Sometimes the fixing nails to the battens corrode and the collective weight of the tiles causes the battening to droop and sag before total failure occurs.
- Check the pitch of the roof, which for plain tiling should not be less than 40°.
- Consider how any requirement for roof ventilation under the Building Regulations can be met (see Figure 11.2).

11.4.6   Renewal and repair

- If the roof pitch is less than 45°, have particular regard to the lap, which should be not less than 65 mm. If the existing gauge needs to be narrowed, make provision for more tiles.
- If the roof is to be stripped, ensure the tiles are stored in sequence and in size order. Many of the early peg tiles are not uniform in shape or size and need to be kept in piles which have similar dimensions and peg hole alignments.
- Tile and a half sizes for many of the early varieties of tile are very difficult to obtain and it may be necessary to cut half tiles in lieu.

- Use modern 'breathable' sarking felt.
- Always use either copper or aluminium alloy fixing nails. Stainless-steel nails are not ideal as they are difficult to draw if later repair work is necessary and this often results in breakages to the surrounding tiles.
- Do not alter the historic method of fixing and detailing unless bad practice is involved and needs to be changed.
- Pay particular attention to ensuring safe access to the roof, particularly with regard to ladder fixings. If tiles are unsafe or insecure, the weight of a ladder can cause large areas of tiling to slide.
- Bedding mortars should be mixed in the proportions of either 1:2 or 1:3 lime/sand. Cement/sand mortars must not be used as they are too hard and encourage cracking and the ingress of moisture. Also, tiles cannot be cleaned and reused if later repairs prove to be necessary.
- Ensure verge tiling is provided with a good tilt.
- If lead soakers are used at the abutments, either code 3 (green colour banded) or code 4 (blue colour banded) is the minimum standard that is acceptable.
- The lichens and other vegetation which appear on well-weathered tiles can be encouraged to colonise the surfaces of new replacement tiles by coating with a wash made from cow dung and water.
- Old roofs tend to settle and consolidate. When re-laying or replacing tiles, check whether as a result of any excessive movement the tiles can marry and interfix sufficiently to remain weathertight. Sometimes there is a need to level and block up parts of the roof carcassing before work can commence.
- The variations in shape and size found in old handmade tiles become more pronounced when they are hung on riven oak battens which are not completely straight lengthwise or uniform in size. As a result, the use of sawn battens in matching repair work is likely to produce slight but clearly discernible differences between those hung on riven laths and those on sawn laths.
- If they are to be laid alongside original tiles, avoid the use of new handmade clay tiles that have been darkened during manufacture to simulate the appearance of natural weathering. With time, the darkening intensifies to give a highly unsatisfactory and non-conforming appearance.

11.5 CLAY PANTILES

11.5.1 Continental influence

Single-lap tiling has a different origin and first appeared in the eastern counties of England towards the end of the seventeenth century as a result of trade links with Holland. This continental influence also had an impact in the Bridgwater area of the south west of England for the same reason. At first pantiles were imported, but eventually a thriving industry developed in East Anglia and they became a popular material due to their lightness, which made them an ideal replacement for thatch. Eventually the influence of pantiling extended into other parts of the country including

Yorkshire (excluding the Dales), but is rarely found elsewhere, especially the west, the Midlands and the south east. Whereas plain tiles are laid with butt side joints with three thicknesses at the lap and two thicknesses between laps, pantiles are laid with overlapping side joints with two thicknesses only at the head joints and a single thickness at the unlapped points. This created difficulties in adequately weathering the rough and crudely formed early tiles and additional protective measures were necessary. They mostly took the form of torching the underside of the roof or pointing the tail and side joints. Another technique involved lathing and bedding the side joints. Known as strip lathing, it entailed fixing plasters' laths at 'finger spacing' to the tiling battens running from the eaves to the ridge. Lime mortar was then spread over the laths while the tiles were being fixed and bedded. A variation of this method was the laying of reed bundles between the battens and fixing them into position with short laths. The tiles were then bedded in mortar at their side joints.

11.5.2   Sizes

Standard dimensions for pantiles were originally fixed by George I as being 13″ × 9″ (330 mm × 228 mm), but in practice variations are found with lengths extending from 14″ to 15″ (355 mm to 381 mm) and widths can range from 9″ to 11″ (228 mm to 279 mm).

11.5.3   Inspection and assessment

- Check the pitch of the roof, which should not be less than 30° (35° is more suitable). Conversely, the pitch should not be more than 47°. With steeper pitched roofs, check to ensure rain-water run-off is not overshooting the guttering at eaves level.
- Carefully examine all eaves, verges and abutments which are particularly vulnerable to water penetration.
- Examine for adequate overlapping. Pantiles are affected by movements in the roof structure which can result in gaps occurring between the tiles.
- Check the condition of the nailing and the battening. The early pantiles relied on nailing to remain in position.
- Measure the overhang at the verges, which should not be more than 75 mm (3″). Pantiles must not be permitted to tilt inwards, as for plain tiling.

11.5.4   Renewal and repair

- Considerable care is needed in the fixing and spacing of replacement battens, otherwise the tail of each tile will not seat properly over the head of the tile immediately underneath.
- In addition to variations in colour and texture, concrete pantiles are unsuitable for repair work on account of a difference in thickness.
- Whereas with plain tiling undulations in the roof structure can be retained, the reverse applies to pantiling. It is important for all alignments to be true and

accurate, otherwise the interlocking between the tiles will not be satisfactory. To achieve this it may be necessary to use firrings, false rafters and packing pieces before felting and battening.

- A slight upward tilt at the eaves can improve weathertightness. Normally this can be done by marginally increasing the height of the fascia board or by fixing a tilting fillet. Plain tiles should also be laid as an undercloak with the gap between the rolls being galleted with tile slips in a 1:1:6 cement/lime/sand mortar or similar containing horse hair.
- Fix ridge tiles in a 1:1:6 cement/lime/sand mortar on a shallow bed with tile slips set in the channels. Hip and valley tiles should also be set on shallow beds of mortar.
- The provision of lead flashings to the abutments in lieu of mortar fillets is sounder practice, but is not always approved for reasons of appearance and tradition. Code 5 lead (colour banded red) should be used.
- In locations which are exposed to heavy winds and driving rain, the use of sprockets is often advisable.
- All mortar mixes used in repair and renewal work need to be tested before use for correct colour.
- The tile lap may have to be adjusted according to the degree of exposure.
- Always use non-ferrous nails.

11.6 OAK SHINGLES

11.6.1 Roman origins

A shingle is, in essence, a wood tile which in size, shape and application is similar to a plain clay tile. Shingles may be either riven or sawn, with those that have been cleft being more durable due to an age-old method of splitting. The clefting should always be made along the grain of the wood, which allows rain to fall upon the surface and drain along the channels formed by the natural fibres in the wood. By contrast, sawn shingles enable rain-water to penetrate directly into the timber to cause warping, shrinkage and splitting. A legacy of the Roman invasion, oak shingles were a common feature in the Middle Ages but as the cost of oak increased, usage steadily dwindled and finally went out of fashion in the eighteenth century. Elm shingles were used as an alternative at one stage but clearly must have been unsuitable.

11.6.2 Sizes

Oak shingles vary in size from 304 mm (12″) to 685 mm (27″) long to 101 mm (4″) to 152 mm (6″) in width and 3 mm ($\frac{1}{8}$″) to 6 mm ($\frac{1}{4}$″) in thickness. The shingles are more usually fixed to close boarding, but it is essential to leave a small air space between the underside of the shingles and the boarding to enable adequate drying to occur after periods of heavy rain. In the past they were mostly fixed by means of wooden pegs. Copper nails have been substituted in more recent times.

11.6.3   Inspection and assessment

- Check the pitch of the roof, which should not be less than 45° under normal conditions. Lower pitches are acceptable subject to the gauge being decreased accordingly.
- Shingles can often be found fixed to undersized roof carcassing. In such cases some of the roof strength may depend on the battening, when sizes in the region of 100 mm × 17 mm may be necessary.
- Check the system of nailing. Shingles should be double nailed, but are sometimes single nailed, which causes the shingles to split down the length, mostly as a result of wind pressure.
- Examine the shingles for biodeterioration.
- Check all flashings and cover flashings for close fitting.

11.6.4   Renewal and repair

- New shingles need to be left to mature for at least twelve months before use.
- Laps are normally set at two and a half to three times.
- A double row of shingles is necessary at eaves level resting on a tilting fillet.
- Do not butt joint shingles, otherwise they are likely to buckle during periods of damp weather. A 3 mm ($\frac{1}{8}''$) gap is necessary between each shingle.
- Use annular ring-shaped stainless-steel or copper nails for fixing.
- Upon completion of work, arrange for the roof to be swept and check the valleys and gutters for loose nails.
- Treat the surface with an approved fire-retardant preparation.
- Use skilled and experienced labour at all times.
- Only breather quality sarking should be used with renewal and repair work.

11.7   THATCH

11.7.1   Tradition

In the past, limited availability in some regions meant a variety of materials were used for thatching including bent (marram grass), furze, meadow rushes, ling (heather), bracken roots and broom. Turf thatch was also used, with the grass side being laid uppermost, but wheat, rye, barley and oat straw were the more widely used materials. Today the choice is normally between long straw, combed wheat reed and water reed, with sedge sometimes being used for the dressings (Figure 11.6). Thatching was frequently used with pole rafter roofs.

Long straw thatch: This can be identified mainly from the clearly visible long straw lengths. It can also be recognised by the method used for the rodding at the eaves and gables, which is usually done with hazel, a method rarely used with other forms of thatching.

Combed wheat reed thatching (Devon reed): This has a closely packed finish in which the butt ends of the wheat reed form the face of the thatch. Another important detail is the flush cut at the eaves and gable ends.

Fig. 11.6   Thatched roofing held secure by a network of ropes fastened at the gable ends. An essential feature in windswept locations

Water reed (Norfolk reed): This is mostly seen in East Anglia and differs from combed wheat reed in that the eaves and gables are dressed in position with a tool known as a legget. The ridges are normally capped with sedge.

11.7.2   Inspection and assessment

- Check the condition of the roof structure.
- Check the pitch of the roof, which should be at least 45°. The condition and life expectancy of thatch depends not only on the roof pitch but also on the quality of the materials used and on the workmanship. Normally long straw has a lifespan of 25 years, combed wheat reed 30 to 40 years and Norfolk reed 60 years.
- Trees must not be permitted to brush or overhang thatch and need to be at a clear distance.
- When thatch is in good condition, rain penetration is superficial. Where there are signs of excessive penetration expert advice should be sought.
- Check the thickness of the thatch and look for evidence of erosion and wear. Erosion may well be present if the fixings are more visible than they ought to be.
- Assess the condition of leadwork or mortar fillets around the chimney, valleys, aprons and suchlike.
- Examine the fixing and condition of any netting.

- Pay particular attention to the condition of the ridges, which normally need to be replaced every twelve to fifteen years.
- Check the condition of the underside of the roof and the thatching.
- Pay particular attention to the colour of the thatching. New thatch is a warm yellow which weathers to a darkish brown. After two years this darkening starts to appear in the exposed locations, with the more protected areas tending to remain less affected for a longer period of time.
- Look for any signs of scorching to the timbers around the chimney stacks.

11.7.3   Engaging a thatcher

- As far as is practicable, stipulate the use of authentic local materials and features.
- Ensure any change from the original form of roof cover has listed building consent or planning permission before the commencement of works.
- Sometimes the original thatching will be found undisturbed since the property was built. Such historic thatching may be concealing important aspects of the past which should be investigated by an archaeologist. Likewise smoke blackening on the underside of the timbers and on thatching is protected in a listed building and must be left untouched.
- Extra care is necessary to reduce the risk of fire. Special attention must be given to electrical and television installations and fittings. The roof space may also need to be draught-proofed.
- The Rural Development Commission and the Master Thatchers' Associations can offer guidance on the engagement of a skilled thatcher.

11.8   PAPER ROOFS

Sheets of tarred paper nailed onto roof boards were used as a roofing material in England and Scotland from about 1770 to around 1850 and some examples have survived to the present day. It is, however, more likely to be masked under a later roofing material and when found, it is important that it is correctly identified and recorded. In addition to tarred paper, roofs were also covered with a paper sheathing over which was laid a composition coating made from bone-ash, sand, whiting and pounded charcoal. This was added to a mixture of boiling tar and black rosin and then spread evenly over the paper sheathing. Any discoveries of this nature have an important historical significance and are currently the subject of research by Dr M. Airs of Oxford University. They are mostly found on properties which have an uncharacteristic low pitch to the roof carcassing. If construction of this type is discovered, it is essential to notify the conservation officer to the local authority.

Lead and copper roofing: see Chapter 9.

FURTHER READING
See section on Roofing in the References.

CHAPTER 12

RENDERS, CLADDINGS, PAINTS AND FINISHES

12.1 EXTERNAL RENDERS

The use of rendering as an external coating has a long history and a number of different forms and techniques have developed. These variations revolve mostly around the constituent materials and the mixing ratios which determine strength, density, porosity and durability. While primarily intended to protect from rain penetration and draughts, it also provided scope for artistic licence which many of the early builders exploited to the full. Today this legacy can be seen in features such as pargetting and the precision-worked plaster details in many classical buildings. Sometimes renders have been added to satisfy a later fashion or fad and may not be an appropriate or correct embellishment for the property in question. If renewal is necessary, it is advisable to take expert advice before making a final commitment to the operation.

Before the advent of Portland cement in 1824, most renders were lime/sand based, but the outcome and durabilty of the work depended on the nature of the aggregate and the quality of the lime. Where there is a need to match an existing render, laboratory analysis of the original is essential. Trial mixes should be made on test panels until a comparable composition has been found (see also Section 2.2). Many of the early renders contain additives such as casein, linseed oil, tallow and animal blood, which materially alter the colour and texture of the render and are unlikely to be correctly identified without laboratory assistance.

12.1.1 Materials

Lime: Most of the early lime mortars were non-hydraulic, being derived from lump lime which was slaked on site. Setting was slow and relied solely on carbonation and for this reason it was usual in later work to add a small proportion of Portland cement to the mix. Some hydraulic limes were however available which set chemically in combination with water (see also Section 2.3). When working with lime renders, care must be taken to prevent rapid drying, otherwise a momentum can be established which results in the translocation of the lime, which passes through the aggregate to the outer surfaces. This weakens the mix in the inner parts and creates a differential in the mix proportions between the inner and outer parts of the same mortar. The likely effect is a splitting away of the outer surface. A similar problem can occur due to over-trowelling.

Keene's cement or Parian cement: The term cement is a misnomer, as this product is a hard-burnt anhydrous gypsum plaster suitably accelerated. Produced by a more intense heat process, the amount of water removed prevents setting unless an accelerating agent such as alum is added. It is used for a hard, smooth finish and has the advantage of setting in a uniform and continuous manner up to the point of the complete set, but it also has a tendency towards poor adhesion. A modified form of Keene's cement is now obtainable as a class D plaster. Under no circumstances should Portland cement be added; otherwise ettringite will be formed and a destructive expansion of the material will result.

Roman cements: These were made by kilning nodules of septaria and became popular on account of their quick-setting properties and high durability. They also proved ideal for working fine detail and for making intricate mouldings and other features. Supplies have now been exhausted. Existing examples can be identified from a distinctive brown colour. Many eighteenth-century and early nineteenth-century houses were rendered in Roman cement.

Masonry cements: These are a possible option where sandstone is vulnerable to deterioration from lime. Such mortars have good water retention and excellent plasticity, being formulated from a mixture of ordinary Portland cement, plasticisers and inert fillers.

White Portland cements: These have less strength than ordinary Portland cement but are ideal where matching mortars and renders need to be light in colour. The main constituents are chalk and china clay.

Devonite rendering: Suitable for both external and internal use, this can be an effective barrier against damp. A particular advantage is the resistance it provides to salt migration, providing the render is applied in one coat to a thickness of not less than 13 mm. Often thicknesses of up to 50 mm are more suitable and slow natural drying is essential to avoid cracking. A proprietary product, it is made from a mixture of lime/sand/cement/clay and fibre fillers.

Pozzolanic cements: Most pozzolanic cements are a mixture of ordinary Portland cement and PFA (pulverised fuel ash) which produces a low-heat cement with good resistance to sulphates.

Gypsum content in renders: This was first imported from France but later won from deposits in various parts of the British Isles. The regular use of this material began in the middle of the thirteenth century and was selected for work involving fine detail. Gypsum was also used in external renders as a gauging. Although it is soluble in water, it has sometimes survived in the sheltered parts of a structure.

12.1.2   Method and techniques

Pargetting: The homeland of this unique form of external decoration is Essex and Suffolk, but it can also be found in parts of Hertfordshire, Cambridgeshire, Norfolk, the north of Kent and along the eastern regions of England as far north as York and in isolated locations elsewhere. It is usually associated with timber-framed construction, but also has strong connections with clay lump. The technique passed through a number of decorative phases and basically features a series of repetitive designs that have either been incised, hand-moulded or worked in relief. The highly intricate pargetting now found in East Anglia first appeared during the sixteenth century, reached its artistic zenith at around the middle of the seventeenth century, and later declined in quality. At the turn of the eighteenth century the fashion went into complete decline, though it did enjoy a brief revival around 1900. Working and repairing pargetting is an individual skill and should only be undertaken by an experienced craftsman with a proven record. It is unwise to engage labour without first obtaining exemplars and checking previous work (Figure 12.1).

Stucco: Whereas there is good reason to believe pargetting was used for improved protection and weathering, it is known that stucco evolved for purely economic reasons. Widely used in the second half of the eighteenth century, it became a low-cost substitute for stone. The effect of simulating the appearance of stone was achieved by scoring, working and cutting the wet render to the fashion of stonework. Prior to

Fig. 12.1 Intricate pargetting to a jettied house in Clare, Suffolk

the eighteenth century, English renders had been coarse-textured, but with the advent of stucco there was a demand for smoother and harder renders. This resulted in the appearance of a host of patent products formulated for this purpose. They were especially suited for the moulding of fine detail and other intricate work, but the most successful product was Parker's Roman cement (see also Section 12.1.1 on Roman cement). The dexterity and skill used in the application of stucco made an important contribution to the resurgence of classical architecture during this period. From the mid-nineteenth century, other materials were gradually superseded by Portland cement (Figure 12.2).

Roughcasting: Roughcasting is generally perceived to be a feature of speculative developments built between the two World Wars, but it has a long tradition. The original renders are derived from a mixture of stone chippings, sand and slaked lime. Later work also contains Portland cement. In some parts of the British Isles, the technique is known as **Harling**.

Pebble dash: Is similar to roughcasting. The difference being that the small stones are left out of the render but are thrown onto the surface later while it is still wet.

Depeter work: Small stones, pebbles and flints are pressed into the rendering while it is still wet, causing the stones to be held more firmly than with pebble dashing. The technique often features elaborate designs and patterns.

Oil mastic: Is an oil-based render developed for the dual function of working in fine detail and as a protection against water penetration. The first recorded patent appeared in 1773 as Liadet's cement, only to be generally known later as Adam's cement. Subsequently other patents appeared, such as Dahl's cement (1815) and Hamelim's cement (1817). The basic component was linseed oil, to which was added an inert filler such as well-ground porcelain clay or clean, fine sand. Some formulations also included additives such as litharge, lime and turpentine. Application was by way

Fig. 12.2 Elevations worked in stucco

of an initial coating of linseed oil painted onto the background surface, followed by the oil mastic, which was worked on in one coat. Use of the material was largely superseded by the development of natural cements such as Parker's Roman cement. Modern cement/sand renders will not bond with oil mastics.

English cottage-style renders: A popular feature at one stage, it is worked from a thin coat of finishing render. While it is still wet, dabs of the same material are applied with a firm arm action which produces an undisciplined and overlapping daub effect.

12.1.3 Inspection and assessment

- Examine for signs of cracking and assess the extent of any moisture penetration.
- Determine whether the cracks are the result of structural movement, thermal movement, the action of frost or sulphate attack. If there is a Portland cement content in the render, the presence of sulphates is likely to produce horizontal or 'map cracking'. If this is the suspected to be the cause, a chemical analysis will be necessary.
- Check for any peeling or detachment due to inadequate bonding.
- Pay particular attention to rendered cornices, mouldings and other projections.
- Parapets and chimneys are particularly vulnerable to sulphate problems. With chimneys, this fault is likely to be far more acute due to the accumulation of sulphates from salts in the flue.
- Examine for indications of surface crumbling and powdering, which is usually the result of salt contamination in either the aggregate or the backing coat. Rising damp can be an alternative cause of salt impregnation.
- Pay special attention to historic renders that have been patched. When Portland cement is used in repair work, this often results in problems accumulating in original renders containing other materials such as Roman cement.
- Excessive thickness in render coats can result in separation between the coats. A lack of suction control at the time of application leaves the render vulnerable to the same fault.

12.1.4 Repairs and maintenance

- Avoid using mixes with a high Portland cement content and aim for a relatively porous render. With older structures lime/sand compositions are more suitable, but they may need regular coatings with a limewash to ensure full protection.
- If an ordinary Portland cement render over brickwork has been specified, test for the presence of soluble sulphate salts. If present, the use of sulphate-resisting cement will be necessary. (In the presence of moisture, the tricalcium aluminate content in ordinary Portland cement is attacked by the soluble sulphates to cause an expansion in volume.)
- Traditional lime/sand mixes are likely to have better weathering qualities if they are coarse textured. Smooth finishes cause a rapid run-off of rain-water, which tends to accumulate in particular areas to cause streaking.

- The re-facing of features such as cornicing and other projections should be worked to a fall to ensure adequate rain-water run-off.
- Avoid rendering window cills, which should ideally be of a hard impervious natural material.
- As far a practicable always provide a 'bell mouth' over plinths, skirtings and similar parts (Figure 12.3).
- Always use a clean aggregate. Dust and foreign matter can cause shrinkage cracks in the render and mixes which are too dense produce a similar effect.
- If the surface to be rendered is made up of differing materials, the whole needs to covered with either a non-ferrous mesh or a bituminous finished expanded metal in order to avoid differential expansion. Soft under-burnt bricks are unsuitable as a key.
- Ensure that the surface to be worked is clean and dust-free and where the adequacy of the key is suspect, apply a rough spadderdash coat beforehand.
- If dubbing out is necessary, this needs to be built-up with a series of thin coats.
- With traditional coatings, areas which are exposed to severe climatic conditions require three applications of render. In moderately exposed and sheltered parts, two-coat work is normally sufficient.

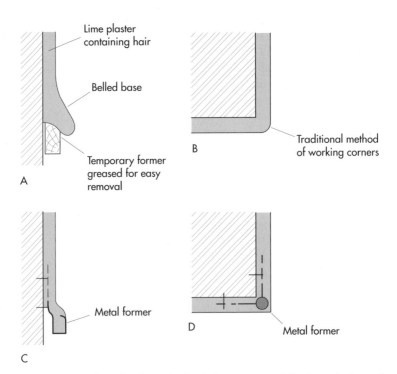

Fig. 12.3 External renders. At vernacular level, the corners and details at the base of external renders appear softer and less defined (see A and B). Sharper and more distinctive finishes are necessary for some other periods such as Victorian Gothic and the classical styles (see C and D)

- In situations where the existing riven lath background has decayed, expanded metal lathing is not a suitable substitute for wood.

12.1.5 Repair mix proportions

- Many stucco mixes are composed of hydraulic lime and sand, with the addition of cow hair in the undercoating. Hydraulic lime should be used within four hours of mixing and must not be 'knocked up'. Ensure any finishing or tooling is completed within four hours of application. Do not allow mixes to become too wet and use them in the proportions of 1:3 (hydraulic lime/sand) in normal situations.
- When Portland cement started to be added to non-hydraulic lime renders, old specifications indicate the undermentioned mix proportions were the most used:

    Undercoat (cement/lime/sand): one part Portland cement, three parts lime putty, and ten parts clean sand.

    Finishing coat (cement/lime/sand): one part Portland cement, three parts lime putty, and twelve parts clean sand.

However, a good hydraulic lime or a pozzolan with a non-hydraulic lime are also suitable for repair and replacement work (see Section 2.2).

The lime can be knocked up into lime/sand coarse stuff beforehand, but if cement is to be introduced this needs to be added just before use, with the completed mix being applied within two hours of mixing. Renders that are to be patched and left unpainted must be sampled for analysis and a matching aggregate prepared to order, otherwise the result is likely to be unsightly.

There has been a growing tendency to use 'hybrid' mortar mixes in repair work by combining hyralic and non-hydraulic limes in the same mix. A number of failures have occurred and are under investigation. Before working with a specification of this type, advice should be sought from English Heritage.

Rough cast: The mix should be as for cement/lime/sand renders, but the dash work needs to follow within half an hour of the application of the render. It is important for pebbles or gravel to be thrown on violently as the force of the impact improves adhesion by dispelling air pockets within the mix. The work should be phased so that each wall is completely covered before being left overnight, otherwise demarcation points can occur.

Oil mastic: If a traditional repair is required, a suitable mix is one part litharge, five parts clean fine sand and five parts whiting (finely ground chalk) mixed with linseed oil. The backing must be well primed with linseed oil and be allowed to dry before the mastic is applied in one operation. If replacement is extensive, a sample of the existing render needs to be analysed before compounding a matching mix. An alternative replacement render is one using a $1:1\frac{1}{2}:6$ cement/lime/sand mix, the quality of the lime being critical for good adhesion. The surface needs to be well cleaned beforehand. This is also an acceptable repair mix for Roman cement renders adjusted to 1:1:6 cement/lime/sand.

Lime renders gauged with gypsum: Lime renders which have been gauged with gypsum can be repaired with materials that are compatible with the gypsum, but on no account should Portland cement be used. If original materials have been stipulated, a suitable mix is one containing three to four parts of lime putty with one part plaster of Paris and six parts of clean sharp sand.

Pargetting: Decorative repair and replacement work requires a particular skill and should only be undertaken by suitably experienced craftsmen. The undercoat needs to be well textured to provide a good key for the finishing coat. It is important for the water content of the mix to be kept to the minimum. Normal mix proportions are $\frac{1}{2}$:3:4 cement/lime/sand with well teased out hair being added to the undercoat.

FURTHER READING
See section on Renders in the References.

12.2 EXTERNAL WALL COATINGS

12.2.1 Limewash

Buildings from the past were constructed of materials that are more absorbent than most of those used today. A critical difference between the past and the present is the composition of mortars, plasters and renders. The early lime-based materials allowed water that was absorbed into the fabric to evaporate out at the surface. This fundamental difference needs to be understood and perpetuated so that the structure can continue to 'breathe'. The use of hard impervious coatings which prevent this is not compatible with the lime-based materials of earlier times.

Traditionally, limewash has been used on lime renders, clay lump, cob, clunch, and wattle and daub panels. Adequate preparation before application is necessary and all surfaces to be treated must be clean and free from loose particles. It is essential to prevent excessive suction by first damping down and then applying the limewash while the surface is still moist. The first coat is likely to give an opaque appearance, with density being achieved with the subsequent coats. Normally three coats are necessary, with each coat being allowed to dry before the next one is applied. The wash should be applied with a soft hand brush and well worked in (thick limewashes soon craze). Pigments used for colouring can come from a variety of sources including sheep dyes, artists' colours and natural earths. Beeswax, tallow and linseed oil seem to have been the more popular choices for use as water repellents. Tallow was often selected for outside work and was mostly tempered with alum to help bind the mix. Linseed oil was usually preferred for inside work as it has a less objectionable smell. Many later washes contained either milk or casein, which formed an almost insoluble protective layer possessing longer lasting properties. Some very reliable proprietary limewashes are now on the market, with good weathering and water resisting qualities.

12.2.2 Painting external walls

In the case of listed buildings, formal consent is necessary for any form of limewashing, painting or decoration. The colours chosen should accurately reflect the character and period of the structure. The paint can be chosen from a wide range of options, namely oil bound, cement based, emulsion formulated and those compounded from silicates. Selection normally needs to be made according to the composition and condition of the substrate and particular care is necessary where new rendering has been introduced. All new surfaces must be allowed to dry thoroughly before any attempt is made at painting. There may also be a need to consider the presence of soluble salts in the fabric, which could later crystallise out and cause efflorescence on the newly decorated surface. The most practical way to rectify an existing problem is to wipe the surface with a damp (not soaking) cloth, repeating the process regularly until the salts have disappeared. The dampening of the surface will, however, necessitate further drying out. If decoration to new work is required immediately, then alkali-resistant paints must be used. The painting of surfaces which have developed piecemeal may result in differences in the quality of the finish, due to the varying porosities in the render. Adequate preparation and careful priming are necessary to stabilise such surfaces. If permission has been granted to use a traditional lead-based paint, ensure there is no residual free lime left in the render, otherwise there will be a tendency for the linseed oil in the paint to saponify.

12.3 FACADES AND CLADDINGS

The modern tendency towards the use of alternative products adapted to replicate another material is not new. Many of the earliest records describe how lime/sand renders were successfully scored and worked to give the appearance of stone.

As architectural tastes altered, it became fashionable at various stages in the past to give buildings from an earlier period a facelift by means of a facade. The technique was widely used in the eighteenth century, when many Medieval and Elizabethan mansions underwent dramatic changes in the Palladian style. Stone was the more prestigious material, but most of this work was undertaken in stucco. Brick was used in a similar way, either as a facing or as a means of introducing additional structural support. Facades seldom envelope an entire building and typical 'give away' signs are the use of boarding at the ends with timber plinths and quoins being worked to simulate stone. In the course of time, the fashion descended down the social scale to buildings of lesser importance and quality and works often included new windows, a central door and staircase, and a parapet wall. Many of these facades were tagged onto the timber frame, with each effectively being independent structures expanding and contracting at different rates. Where sash windows were built into the brick facade, the box frame was generally fixed to the original timber frame, causing them to be set back by half a brick.

Although facades are associated with fashion, claddings have traditionally been used for weather protection. They can also be a possible indicator that at least part of an original structure has a timber frame, even if the outward appearance suggests otherwise. Occasionally they were also used to create a harmonising effect where later additions had been built in materials different to the original. If cladding is removed during building operations, it is vital for any out-of-the-ordinary or unexpected discoveries to be accurately recorded. This information needs to be put in a place of safe keeping and if a property is listed, a copy should also be lodged with the local planning authority.

12.3.1　Weatherboarding (also known as clapboarding)

Weatherboarding dates from the late sixteenth century and for a long time its use seems to have been confined to farm buildings and other non-domestic properties. All available evidence indicates it did not appear on dwellings until the late eighteenth century and at that stage was restricted to housing lower down the social scale. It is mostly found fixed to timber frames, but plenty of exceptions can be found.

Weatherboarding originated as rough dressed and unpainted lengths of oak or elm fixed horizontally by means of wood pegs, the exception being buildings located near the sea or in exposed positions, when it was the custom to coat the external surface of the boards with tar. In the fullness of time, pine and other soft woods replaced oak and elm and fixing altered to nailing. A number of different ways of working and dressing the boards evolved and boarding is now found either feather-edged, tongued and grooved, lapped or rebated. Occasionally vertical fixing with cover strips was preferred, especially for tall thin structures such as towers. If total replacement is essential, it is important to ensure the new boarding complies with the original form and style. With old buildings it is likely that re-cladding has occurred more than once and the existing boarding may be inappropriate. Time spent investigating the correct style and finish for replacement boarding can reap a rewarding dividend. Discernible saw marks on old weatherboarding can, for example, assist an expert in identifying the date when the existing planks were worked and dressed. Head and tail nailing should not be used, as this will cause the timber to split as a result of restrained movement (Figures 12.4–12.6).

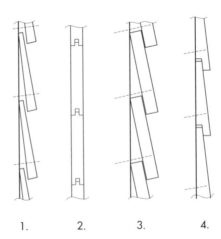

1.　　2.　　3.　　4.

Fig. 12.4　Methods of shaping and fixing weatherboarding. (1) Feather-edged; (2) Tongued and grooved; (3) Lapped; (4) Rebated

Fig. 12.5 Weatherboarding © David Parmiter photography

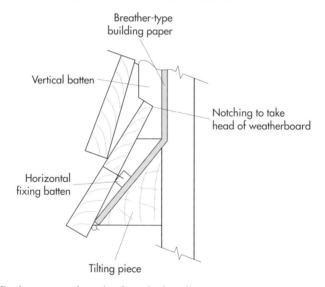

Fig. 12.6 Replacement and repair of weatherboarding

12.3.2 Tile hanging

Tile hanging first appeared towards the end of the seventeenth century and is mostly found in the south east of England. It became a popular method of weatherproofing, as it provided better protection than either brick nogging or wattle and daub panels. It also offered a convenient method of dressing the upper elevations of a building where jettied overhangs were bricked up to extend the ground-floor area (Figure 12.7).

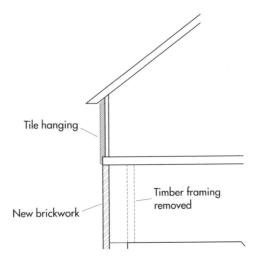

Tile hanging

Timber framing removed

New brickwork

Fig. 12.7

Later, tile hanging became a design feature and was sometimes fixed to brickwork in rat-trap bond, which commenced at first-floor level and went up to the eaves and verges. Normally wood plugs were set into the mortar joints, with the lathing being spiked to the plugs. Sometimes, however, the tiles are found nailed directly into the mortar joints, which makes the nails more vulnerable to the destructive effects of corrosion and rust, causing them to fail or work loose. Buildings that are fully tile hung are likely to have been designed in this style and derive from a later period.

The early tiles had no nibs and were hung on riven oak laths with pegs usually of oak, hazel or willow, the tile heads being regularly embedded in a lime/sand/mortar containing animal hair. Many of the early fixings have a distinctive wood tilting fillet and an under tile to the bottom course with a protective weather drip which helps to shield the underlying parts from surface water run-off. In later brick buildings, this feature can take the form of corbelled-out tile creasing. The problem of dressing corners was at first solved with timber cover beading, but eventually external angle corner tiles, which give a better functional and visual result, became available.

In the eighteenth century a number of decorative tiles appeared on the market including club, fish-tail, vee, hammer-head and arrowhead. Many are still in use. Over the years these variations have been applied to good effect to produce some pleasing and interesting designs. Salvaged replacement tiles from another source that are the same colour, texture and design are unlikely to have weathered in the same way as the existing tiles and can produce an unacceptable contrast. The only satisfactory way of overcoming this problem is to allow for a general rearrangement of the whole in a manner that enables them to blend together. This is always an acute problem with freshly manufactured tiles and when glaring contrasts between the old and the new cannot be avoided, total replacement is normally the better option.

12.3.3 Mathematical tiles

Mathematical tiling is an ingenious form of vertical tiling devised to simulate the appearance of brickwork. The idea probably originated towards the end of the seventeenth or beginning of the eighteenth century, with the tiles normally hung on boarding, or oak or hazel laths nailed to a timber frame. The joints were pointed in mortar in the same manner as brickwork, although the tiles can also be found bedded and back bedded in mortar (Figure 12.8). As a cladding it could serve as a means of weatherproofing or as a way of up-dating the appearance of a building to a fashion for brick. Mathematical tiles could also be conveniently used where brick extensions were added to timber-frame construction and enabled the new and the old to blend well together.

Mathematical tiling can be extemely difficult to detect on observation alone. But it is usually confined to the front elevation, with the remaining areas being covered by an alternative material. There are also a number of give-away indicators, such as the shallow depth of the cladding which is usually more apparent around windows. Another clue is the presence of a lead flashing along the bottom course. Timber cover strips around door and window openings, which are moulded to imitate dressed stone, are also a likely sign.

Failure is mainly caused either by rotted battens or corroded nailing, which leads to bulging and slipped tiles. The interlocking nature of the tiles means repairs can be difficult to undertake without stripping and re-fixing large areas. Sometimes individual tiles can be re-secured or replaced by sliding out from the end tiles in the overhead course, but special care is necessary to prevent damage. New nailing needs to be of non-ferrous metal and the mortar should, permit the evaporation of moisture through the joints. If the mix is too strong, any penetrating water will migrate out through the tiles to cause excessive saturation and eventual deterioration. Replacement tiles are difficult to obtain, but some manufacturers such as Keymer in Burgess Hill will make new components to special order.

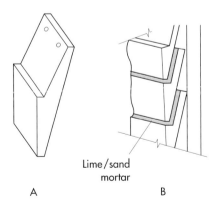

Lime/sand
mortar

A   B

Fig. 12.8 Mathematical title (A) and method used to fix it (B)

12.3.4   Slate hanging

The use of slate hanging can be traced back to the early part of the seventeenth century, when it became a popular method of weathering in the natural slate-bearing regions of the British Isles. As a result, it is seen mostly in the coastal regions of Devon and Cornwall, some parts of Wales and in the Lake District. The heyday of the fashion was in Georgian and Regency times, when it was often used to good architectural effect at and above first-floor level.

When fixed to stone walling, it was normal practice to batten and counter-batten owing to the rough and uneven nature of the wall surface. At one stage, most of this work was carried out using head-nailed 'Countess' slating [500 mm × 250 mm (20″ × 10″)]. Centre nailing with the heads bedded in mortar is better practice, as this minimises the risk of damage or movement from wind pressure. Double coursing is necessary at the bottom edges, with the slates being mitred at the corners and fixed over lead soakers. With brick surfaces, the slates are more likely to be found nailed directly into the mortar joints, which can result in premature failure (Figure 12.9).

Slate hanging sometimes developed into an art form, with slates being worked to different shapes which gave highly pleasing effects. Occasionally slaters went further

Fig. 12.9   Vertical slate hanging

and created attractive variations using different coloured slates. Slate hanging should not be confused with set slating. In some districts, notably the west of England, walls are often found rendered with the slates having been pressed into the mix while it was still wet.

FURTHER READING
See section on Facades in the References.

12.4 INTERNAL WALL FINISHES

12.4.1 History

During the Middle Ages, plaster mixes were mostly of lime and sand with hair being used as a binder in the undercoats. Good results were achieved, but the time lag between the application of successive coats caused unwelcome delays and frustrated the follow-on trades. In the fullness of time, gypsum became more readily available which resulted in lime/sand mixes often being gauged with gypsum, which speeded the setting process. Many alternative options are available today but more traditional choices are still based on lime, Portland cement, or gypsum and anhydrous plasters.

The influence of the Renaissance inspired the fashion for ornate plasterwork throughout the sixteenth and seventeenth centuries. During the eighteenth century, the artistry in plaster working became more elaborate and intricate, due in part to the availability of a number of different materials and cements specially compounded to give improved workability for the crafting of fine detail. To a lesser extent, decorative plasterwork continued into the early Victorian period, but changes in building practices at around 1840 created a different emphasis. A fundamental shift occurred at the end of World War I, when a scarcity of skilled plasterers resulted in the introduction of plasterboard. Produced by sandwiching gypsum plaster between sheets of strong paper this answered a need, only to dwindle in popularity until after World War II, when modern production methods and marketing techniques established plasterboard as a primary building material.

12.4.2 Lime plaster

Preparation

Meticulous care is necessary when slaking lime so that all lumps are either broken down or removed; otherwise caustic lime will enter the plaster mix and cause 'blowing', blisters and cracks to the finished work. It is equally important to ensure the lime used does not have a low carbonate of lime content, as this causes a lack of strength. Some limes contain inert matter such as clay, which diminishes the quality of the work. The best limes are normally those derived from the upper chalk strata, which possess a high carbonate of lime content and are known as high calcium or fat limes.

After the slaking process has been completed, the putty needs to be passed through a fine screen (about 5 mm) to ensure any remaining lumps or particles are removed. The final product known as 'plasterers' putty' must be lightly covered with slaking water and left to mature for a minimum of two weeks before use. Lime which has already been hydrated is now available commercially and is supplied in either a dry powder state or in drums as lime putty.

Hydraulic limes are mostly produced from limestones containing carbonate of lime, clay and a proportion of silicate of alumina. The lias or blue lias limes come within this grouping and set through a combined process of carbonation and chemical action. It is possible, however, to achieve a chemical set with a non-hydraulic lime through the use of a pozzolanic additive such as PFA (pulverised fly ash), HTI (high temperature insulation) and brick or tile dust.

Repair and replacement

Traditional lime plaster applied to internal walling is mostly of three coats applied as a render, float and set. The first rendering and the second, or floating, coat consists of coarse stuff, usually to the ratio of one part lime to three parts of clean sharp sand, plus the addition of cow hair in the proportions of 1.5 kg to every cubic metre of mortar. The render or first coat should be at least 12 mm thick, the floating coat about 17 mm thick and the finishing or setting coat at least 6 mm thick. Old wall surfaces are often uneven and out of plumb and may require screeding to produce a true surface finish. The screeds are formed from narrow strips of plaster which are plumbed, lined up and allowed to harden. They guide the plasterer applying the floating coat and as this is worked, the surface is levelled off using a floating rule over the screeds. The fine stuff used for the setting coat should be thoroughly slaked lime putty in the proportions of one to one and a half parts of lime putty to one part clean sand. The plaster needs to retain sufficient moisture to enable the setting process to be fully completed, as rapid evaporation will result in a loss of strength and eventual failure. The process must be complete before adding a successive coat, especially before applying the final coat, as this minimises the effects of drying shrinkage.

If a harder and smoother surface finish is required, it can be achieved by using three to four parts of fine stuff to one part of plaster of Paris. As gypsum tends to expand on setting, this helps to restrain drying shrinkage. The inclusion of Portland cement in a lime/sand mix produces a faster set and a harder plaster, the degree of hardness depending on the amount of Portland cement used. Suitable mixes for cement/lime/sand plaster are 1:1:6 cement/lime/sand or 1:2:9 cement/lime/sand. If lime putty is used as a finishing coat, caution needs to be exercised before facing with a wallpaper. Fresh lime may sometimes affect the colour of the paper, but the problem can be overcome by neutralising the alkalinity of the lime plaster with a wash of ordinary household vinegar.

Dinging: This is a form of rough one-coat coarse work normally found in the service and storage areas of a building and in cellars. Applied as a thinnish layer, it was either brushed or rubbed on with sacking and limewashed.

12.4.3 Gypsum plasters

In Britain the first recorded use of plaster of Paris dates from around 1255, but as a building material it was not much used until the time of Henry VIII, being reserved for fine finishes in prestigious buildings. This situation continued until substantial deposits of gypsum were discovered throughout the British Isles, which resulted in gypsum plasters becoming readily available from the nineteenth century onwards. Until then the best quality material came from the Montmartre area of Paris, hence the name plaster of Paris. This form of plaster is produced by heating natural deposits of calcium sulphate to a temperature sufficient to form calcium sulphate hemihydrate. In this condition the plaster will set when mixed with water to reform as calcium sulphate.

Class A plaster is used for fibrous plaster work and for patching and repairs. It is hemihydrate, that is, it has one molecule of water of crystallisation for every two molecules of compound. Class B plaster is a retarded hemihydrate plaster and is produced from a much coarser form of gypsum to which retarding agent is added during manufacture. It is available in two categories, one being suitable as an undercoat for browning and metal lathing, the other for final-coat work. It can be used neat or as a gauged plaster. It is, however, important to keep the lime content down to a level of not more than 25 per cent by volume in two- or three-coat work. Class C plaster is an anhydrous gypsum plaster which sets slowly and must not be permitted to dry too rapidly, owing to the fact it has two sets, the first being hemihydrate and the other anhydrous (anhydrous means without water). Class D Keene's cement, which is harder than retarded plaster of Paris, is also anhydrous and has a slow set of about eight hours, which is accelerated by the addition of salts such as alum or potassium sulphate. It is best used for working surfaces to a fine hardwall finish and for filling cracks in mouldings and cornices.

12.4.4 Fibrous plaster

Fibrous plaster is a method of pre-forming plasterwork features by casting wet plaster into moulds containing reinforcement, which when set is fixed into position. This form of pre-fabricated enrichment can be produced from a number of variations in the basic technique and is normally secured with countersuck screws. It first appeared in 1856 as a result of an innovation by Frenchman Leonard Desachy, who quickly established a new approach to the casting and fixing of continuous plaster embellishment. Prior to this, the traditional method had been to run cornices and similar features on site using a 'horse and runner'. Fibrous plaster is made from gypsum which is reinforced with hessian mesh and wood laths, the cast plaster sections being joined by a combination of jute hessian and plaster.

12.4.5 Other methods

Enrichment in high and low relief was originally achieved by moulding and working suitable material into desired shapes and forms. Lime-based plaster was not always used for this purpose and special formulations were also employed. If these alternative techniques are discovered, any necessary work must be left to expert craftsmen. It is important to understand the significance of such a legacy, which may not only be a rare representation of a particular artist, but also a feature of some relevance to the historical development of a structure. It is essential the following methods are correctly identified and protected:

Carton Pierre: This is a mixture of pulped paper, whiting and size stirred to a dough-like consistency and then either pressed into a mould for shaping or worked to a particular profile.

Papier-mache: Used for making ornamental features which are set into the plaster. This form of embellishment was very much a feature in the enriched plasterwork of the eighteenth century and continued into nineteenth century.

Scagliola: Is a plaster finish that is worked in a way that conveys the impression of veined marble. The effect is achieved by mixing Keene's cement with dyes and by dragging strings soaked in dye across the face to simulate natural veining. Repair work should only be undertaken by approved craftsmen. High-class scagliola can be most difficult to differentiate from genuine marble, but it is not so cold to the touch, and when viewed from a slanted position in an angle of light is likely to reveal slight undulations or surface ripples that are not seen with polished marble. Minute fissures on the surface are also a telling sign, caused by the highly brittle nature of the material which is unable to resist even the slightest of movements in the building structure.

Stucco-duro: Is suited for certain forms of moulded work. It is made from equal parts of fat slaked lime and finely powdered white marble gauged with lime water.

Gesso: Is a form of fine moulded relief worked in freehand. Most mixes are compounded from a mixture of one part powdered resin, four parts linseed oil and six parts melted animal glue. The whole is taken to the boil with whiting that has been soaked in pure water, being added while the mix is still hot but off the boil. When dry it can be polished with either a wood spatula or pumice powder.

Sgraffito: Is an unusual art form and rare in the British Isles. Pointed tools are used to incise designs into wet plaster to a depth which reveals the underlying surface. Normally the final coat is applied over a different coloured undercoat which highlights the worked designs by way of contrast. The technique enjoyed a brief and limited revival during the middle of the nineteenth century. The presence of sgraffito can be easily missed where over-painting has occurred and a finding should be left untouched until inspected by an expert. It was also used as a feature on external renders.

Lathing: The different forms of lathing used in earlier times, including wattle or reeds, can be a useful indicator in dating plasterwork. Oak, chestnut and hazel have a long tradition and were originally riven, but by the middle of the nineteenth century sawn laths in softwood had come into general use. Wire lathing also appeared at around the same time.

Inspection and assessment

- Look for signs of damp such as discoloration in the plaster and rust stains around nailing and determine the cause. No work should be put in hand until any defects of this nature have been remedied.

- Try to identify the materials used in the plaster mix. The presence of gypsum can normally be detected by a rough site test. Place a small plaster sample into dilute hydrochloric acid and allow it to stand. Gypsum produces a fine, white powder sediment. When in doubt, seek expert advice.
- Also take a sample for laboratory analysis to ensure replacement materials are compatible with the old and are capable of producing the correct texture to the finished work. If results indicate the presence of a Selenitic cement, any further use of this material should be avoided. Patented in 1870, it is formulated from a mixture of hydraulic lime and plaster of Paris which encourages the transfer of calcium sulphate into masonry to cause decay.
- Establish the number of coats applied to the existing work. Until about 1930, most plastering involved the application of three coats.
- Diagnose the pattern and form of any cracking and establish whether there is evidence of structural movement, defective backing or similar causes.
- Test for blistering and shelling by lightly tapping with the knuckles.
- Accurate recording of the condition of the plasterwork at the time of the inspection is essential. It should include photographs and drawings.
- Make provision for casts to be taken of any work to be replaced or repaired.
- Check the condition of any lathing, joists or background timbers which support the plasterwork.
- Where plaster has been applied to lathing, check the state of the extrusions which form the keying. Sometimes old lathing is found too closely spaced and an inadequate key results. The distance between laths should be at least 7 mm.
- Look for signs of bowing and deflection in ceiling timbers.
- Fine crystals on the face of gypsum plaster are a likely sign of intermittent dampness.
- A useful test is to gently press the plaster face with the finger tips. If there is any perceptible give to pressure, suspect a fault in the backing or key.
- Test for the presence of hygroscopic salts.
- Check the condition and nature of any decorative coatings. The stripping of some inappropriate modern paints can be a difficult and time consuming activity.
- Do not assume original plaster that has become either very loose or completely detached is dispensable. In skilled hands it can often be re-attached.
- Consider the effect any building work will have on the original plaster if heavy impacts or vibration are likely to occur.
- As far as possible, provide for minimum interference with the existing plasterwork unless safety and stability are a problem.

Maintenance and repairs

- Always observe the primary rule: top coats should be weaker than undercoats.
- While the risk is considered to be extremely low, isolated cases of anthrax spores present in the animal hair of old plasterwork have been reported. With this in mind, protective measures may be necessary after consultation with the Health and Safety Executive.

- With lime plasters, the scouring of the undercoat is crucial. It is important for the scouring to have wide channels with sharp angles as this has an important effect on the strength of the key.
- Allow wet plaster to dry slowly.
- Aggregates must be properly graded.
- Gauge boxes should always be used in preparing a mix.
- It is well to be cautious before replacing lime/sand plasters with more brittle gypsum. Natural movements in older structures differ from those in modern buildings and a neat gypsum plaster applied to historic construction could be prone to cracking. A much safer solution is the use of lime/sand plaster gauged with gypsum.
- Do not add Portland cement to hydraulic lime mixes.
- The use of PFA provides a low sulphate pug for use with lime and for grouting.
- When laths have become detached, they can be screwed back to the ground using brass screws and washers. In cases where laths have separated from joists, an alternative option is to refix them with wire straps.
- If ceiling plaster is bowing due to a faulty key or lathing, temporary support should be provided using plywood panels held into position by a system of braced framing. Any overlying floor boards should be removed. After clearing away loose debris, copper gauze can be laid over the top plaster surface and dressed up and fixed to the joists (Figure 12.10). The whole must then be run with an overlying

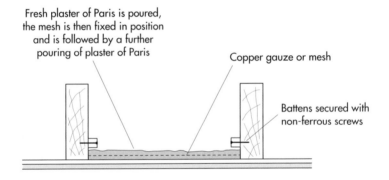

One of the more difficult challenges in conservation is the saving of badly deteriorated historic plasterwork. The problem mainly occurs from the loss of key due to either the extrusions between the lathing fracturing or the rusting of the lathing nails, plus a gradual accumulation of debris between the plaster and the underside of the lathing, which encourages detachment. Sometimes failure is exacerbated as a result of sand pugging which imposes an unacceptable load on the supporting plaster.

Detached wall plaster can normally be re-secured using screws and wide washers with mesh discs and/or injecting a prepolymerised polyurethane foam between the back of the plaster and the wall

Existing mouldings and cornices should be carefully preserved in situ. Many of the modern fibrous plaster castings are not to the correct detail and are unsuitable for conservation work

Fig. 12.10   Repairing old ceiling plaster

plaster bed. An alternative to plaster is the use of glass-fibre cloth set into position with resin.

■ Voids which have developed behind wall plaster as a result of detachment can be usefully filled with polymerised polyurethane foam. Defer any patching until this has matured.

■ Ensure plaster mixes for patch work are comparable to the original.

■ Retarded hemihydrate plaster should be used for repairs to gypsum-based plaster.

Specialist advice is essential for work to carton pierre, papier-mache, scagliola, stucco-duro, gesso and sgraffito.

FURTHER READING
See section on Plasters and plastering in the References.

12.5 HISTORIC PAINTS AND COLOURS

Many historic paints and coatings have an aesthetic and functional significance that is not always understood or recognised. In reality, the restoration of an original decorative scheme should be an important feature of any conservation programme. This is likely to require some research to accurately determine issues such as colour and the correct use of materials. In this, expert opinion is essential and may also necessitate laboratory facilities for the analysis of samples and fragments. A paint layer stratigraph should be compiled from these findings work before commences.

The constructional differences between old and more modern buildings are also of relevance in the selection of suitable paints and other decorative materials. The thickly dimensioned walls found in many ancient structures rely on porosity to permit the evaporation of absorbed moisture. Consequently, painted surfaces must provide for the fabric to 'breathe', which makes a large number of the paints currently on the market unsuitable for this type of work. Coatings most capable of perpetuating the natural balance are whiting, limewash, distemper and whitening. Some emulsions can also be used, but technical advice should be sought from the manufacturers beforehand.

Whitewash (or whiting): This is prepared from finely ground chalk mixed with water and relies on the evaporation of the water to form a surface coating. The particles of hydrated lime are not bound together and can be easily rubbed away by friction.

Whitening (or ceiling white): This is made from finely ground chalk which is poured into water tanks and then allowed to settle. The water is drawn off and the fine sediment is scooped out and dried. When in powder form the chalk is passed through a series of sieves before being mixed with size (animal glue) which acts as the binder.

Distemper: This is made from the same mixture as whitening, the only difference being the introduction of colouring pigments.

Washable distemper: Contains a binder made from drying oils which have been emulsified with either size or casein. The proportion of oil is low enough for the mixture to be classified as water paint and enables water to be used for thinning.

External paints: In the Middle Ages it was the practice to coat external timbers with either limewash or raddle, which is a mixture of ox blood and soot. For a considerable period, lead-based oil paints remained the only reliable protection but modern technology and the health hazards associated with lead substances have established a new era in paint production. If lead-based paint is specified, it can only be used under existing legislation in Grade I to Grade II* buildings, subject to formal permission being obtained from English Heritage.

Lime-tallow washes: With external wall protection, hot tallow was regularly added to the limewash, which caused the fat to be saponified by the lime to form water-insoluble calcium soap compounds. The chemical conversion also acted as a binding agent and inhibited wear on the coating.

12.5.1   Decorative themes and features

The selection of paints containing the correct pigments and density of colour is essential if an accurate representation is to be made of historic decor. A significant change in taste began in the early eighteenth century, which resulted in a steady drift away from wood panelled interiors in favour of decorated wall and ceiling treatments in lighter colours. During this phase, paints changed to a matt finish, replacing the sheen-like surfaces which had hitherto been popular. Inspired by the colours used in Etruscan pottery, Robert Adam introduced an innovative theme which he used to good effect and created a much admired new fashion of the time. The preference for matt finish paint persisted, however, until well into the nineteenth century. Graining and marbling came into fashion in the early part of the nineteenth century. In the Georgian period, there was a craze for ironwork in greened bronze, which involved bronze powder being worked into the surface while the paint was still wet. The examples mentioned are only some of the complex considerations which relate to the preservation or re-creation of decorative schemes from the past. It is important for a contractor to be alert to these fashions and to ensure work is undertaken in accordance with the period concerned.

Old paint formulations can still be obtained by special order through many paint manufacturers.

12.5.2   Inspection and action

- Check whether the building is listed under the Town and Country Planning Acts. Listed Building Consent is necessary for any form of external or internal decorative work to a listed building.
- Determine the nature of the decorative surface and the substrate.
- Test for dampness and the presence of hygroscopic salts and undertake any necessary remedial action.
- An indication of the number of surviving paint layers can be gained by slicing the paint film at an angle using a scalpel. This will expose the paint sequences.
- Take samples for analysis, retaining some for record purposes. These should be placed in a suitable container and lodged in a place of safe keeping.

12.5.3 Paint preparation

- Blow lamps or blow torches must never be used.
- Lime-coated surfaces need to be thoroughly brushed and all loose and friable particles removed before re-coating.
- Soft distemper coating can be removed by repeated washing and rubbing with warm water.
- Emulsion paints applied to plaster and masonry need to be steam-stripped.
- Oil bound distempers and paints are best removed by light rubbing with a mild abrasive or by using scrapers with a superheated jet of steam. A specialist service is now available which involves very little excess moisture being produced. The system is particularly suitable for the removal of lead based paints as it reduces lead vaporisation.
- Caustic paint strippers are not normally suitable, as they leave harmful salt deposits which can damage sensitive areas. If paint strippers are necessary, it is safer to use those made from solvent-based formulations containing methylene chloride.

FURTHER READING
See section on Colour and paints in the References.

REFERENCES

Accessing

Construction (Design and Management) Regulations 1994. HMSO.

Foster, L. 1997 *Access to the historic environment – meeting the needs of disabled people.* Donhead.

Health and Safety at Work Act 1974. HMSO.

Health and Safety Executive. There are a number of useful publications issued by the Health and Safety Executive.

Management of Health and Safety at Work Regulations 1992. HMSO.

Manual Handling Operations Regulations 1992. HMSO.

National Federation of Master Steeplejacks and Lightning Conductor Engineers' Code of Practice (not dated).

Workplace (Health, Safety and Welfare) Regulations 1996. HMSO.

Aggregates and sands

English Heritage 1997 *English Heritage directory of building sands and aggregates.* Donhead.

Architecture and architectural history

Airs, M. 1995 *The Tudor and Jacobean country house: a building history.* Allan Sutton.

Brown, R.J. 1979 *The English country cottage.* Robert Hale.

Brunskill, R.W. 1997 *Illustrated handbook of vernacular architecture.* Faber.

Cave, L.F. 1981 *The smaller English house.* Robert Hale.

Curl, J.S. 1990 *Victorian architecture.* David and Charles.

Georgian Group, 1996 *Georgian vernacular.* Georgian Group.

Gray, E. 1994 *The British house.* Barrie and Jenkins.

Lloyd, N. 1975 *History of the English house.* Architectural Press.

Powell, C. 1984 *Discovering cottage architecture.* Shire Publications.

Wade Martins, S. 1991 *Historic farm buildings.* Batsford.

Yarwood, D. 1980 *The architecture of Britain.* Batsford.

Bricks

Baer, N.; Fitz, S.; Livingstone, S. 1988 *Conservation of historic brick structures.* Donhead.

Bidwell, T.G. 1977 *The conservation of brick buildings: the repair, alteration and restoration of old brickwork.* Brick Development Association.

Brunskill, R.W. 1990 *Brick building in Britain*. Victor Gollancz – Peter Crawley.
Lynch, G. 1990 *Gauged brickwork – a technical handbook*. Gower Technical Press.
Lynch, G. 1993 *Brickwork – history, technology and practice*. Donhead.
Sowden, A.M. 1990 *The maintenance of brick and stone structures*. E. and F.N. Spon.
Wight, J. 1972 *Brick building in England from the Middle Ages to 1550*. John Barker.

Chalk

Pearson, G. 1992 *Conservation of clay and chalk buildings*. Donhead.

Chimneys

SPAB 1976 Chimneys in old buildings. *SPAB Technical Pamphlet 3*.

Clay and cob – see Unbaked earth

Cleaning

Ashurst, N. 1993 *Cleaning historic buildings*. Vols 1 and 2, Donhead.
BRE 1972 Control of lichens, mould and similar growths. *BRE Digest 139*.
Cooper, M. 1998 *Laser cleaning in conservation – an introduction*. Butterworth – Heinemann.
Historic Scotland 1994 *Stonecleaning: a guide for practitioners*. Historic Scotland.
Historic Scotland 1997 *Stone cleaning of granite buildings*. Historic Scotland.
Webster, R.G.M. (Ed.) 1992 *Stone cleaning and the nature, soiling and decay mechanisms of stone*. Donhead.

Colour and paints

Bristow, I.C. 1996 *Architectural colour in British interiors 1615–1840*. Yale University Press.
Bristow, I.C. 1996 *Interior house painting colours and technology 1615–1840*. Yale University Press.
SPAB 1989 Removing paint from old buildings. *SPAB Technical Pamphlet No. 5*.

Damp in old buildings

BRE 1981 Rising damp in walls – diagnosis and treatment. *BRE 245*.
SPAB (not dated) Treatment of dampness in old buildings. *SPAB Technical Pamphlet 8*.
SPAB 1989 An introduction to the treatment of rising damp in buildings. *SPAB Information Sheet 6*.
SPAB 1990 The need for old buildings to 'breathe'. *SPAB Information Sheet 4*.

Ecclesiastical exemption

Department of Culture, Media & Sport 1994 Code of Practice 'The Ecclesiastical Exemption: what it is and how it works'. HMSO.
The Ecclesiastical Exemption (Listed Buildings and Conservation Areas) Order 1994. HMSO.

Facades

Highfield, D. 1991 *The construction of new buildings behind historic facades.* E. and F.N. Spon.
Richards, J. 1994 *Facadism.* Routledge.

Finance and economics

Architectural Heritage Fund 1998 *Funds for historic buildings in England and Wales – a directory of sources.* Architectural Heritage Fund.
Burman, P.; Pickard, R.; Taylor, S. (Eds) 1995 *Economics of architectural conservation.* Institute for Advanced Architectural Studies, York.
Cunnington, P. 1988 *Change of use; the conversion of old buildings.* Alphabooks.
Wilkinson, P. 1989 *Alternative uses for redundant farm buildings.* College of Estate Management, Whiteknights, Reading.

Fire protection

Historic Scotland 1997 *Fire protection measures in Scottish historic buildings.* Historic Scotland.

Fixtures and fittings

Hill, L.; Alcock, N.W. 1994 *Fixtures and fittings in dated houses 1567–1763.* Council for British Archaeology.
Miller, J.; Miller, M. 1993 *Period details: a source book for house restoration.* Mitchell Beazley.
Victorian Society 1997 *Victorian fireplaces.* Victorian Society.
Williams, K. 1992 *The David and Charles manual of stoves, hearths and chimneys.* David and Charles.

Floors and flooring

Barnard, J. 1979 *Victorian ceramic tiles.* Cassell.
Eames, E. 1985 *English Medieval floor tiles.* British Museum.

General topics

Innocent, C.F. 1971 *The development of English building construction.* David and Charles.
Salzman, L.F. 1952 *Building in England down to 1540.* Oxford University Press.

Glass

Ashurst, J.; Ashurst, N. 1988 *Practical Building Conservation.* Vol. 5 (English Heritage Technical Handbook), Gower Technical Press.
Council for the Care of Churches, 1995 *The repair and maintenance of glass in churches.* Council For the Care of Churches.
Dodsworth, R. 1982 *Glass and glassmaking.* Shire Publications.
Newton, R. 1987 *Caring for stained glass.* Ecclesiastical Architects and Surveyors Association.

Interiors

Yarwood, D. 1983 *English Interiors.* Lutterworth Press.

Legislation

Mynors, C. 1985 *Listed buildings and conservation areas.* Sweet and Maxwell.

Parnell, A. 1987 *Building legislation and historic buildings.* Architectural Press/Butterworth Architecture.

Lightning conductors

Allen, N.L. 1988 *The protection of churches against lightning.* Council for the Care of Churches.

BSI 1992 BS 6651: 1992 – Protection of structures against lightning. British Standards Institution.

Golde, R.H. 1973 *Lightning protection.* Edward Arnold.

Metals

Ashurst, J.; Ashurst, N. 1988 *Practical building conservation.* Vol. 4. (English Heritage Technical Handbook), Gower Technical Press.

Copper Development Association Various publications on copper available from the Copper Development Association.

Evans, V.R. 1972 *The rusting of iron: causes and control.* Edward Arnold.

Eveleigh, D.J. 1990 *Firegrates and kitchen ranges (metal).* Shire Publications.

Fearn, J. 1990 *Cast iron.* Shire Publications.

Gale, W.K.V. 1985 *Ironworking.* Shire Publications.

Lead Sheet Association/English Heritage 1998 Leadwork – Lead roofs in historic buildings (See also various publications issued by the Lead Sheet Association.).

Lister, R. 1960 *Decorative cast ironwork in Great Britain.* G. Bell & Sons.

Mortars

Ashurst, J. 1983 *Mortars, plasters and renders in conservation.* Ecclesiastical Architects and Surveyors Association.

Ashurst, J.; Ashurst, N. 1988 *Practical building conservation.* Vol. 3 (English Heritage Technical Handbook), Gower Technical Press.

Cowper, A.D. 1998 *Lime and lime mortars.* Donhead.

Schofield, J. 1998 *Lime in building – a practical guide.* Black Dog Press.

SPAB 1988 An introduction to building limes. *SPAB Information Sheet 9.*

Philosophy

BSI 1998 BS 7913: 1998 Guide to the principles of the conservation of historic buildings. British Standards Institution.

Earl, J. 1996 *Building conservation philosophy.* College of Estate Management, Whiteknights, Reading.

Historic Scotland 1997 The Historic Scotland guide to international charters. *Technical Advice Note No. 8.*

IHBC 1997 Reconstruction and regeneration: the philosophy of conservation. *Proceedings of the IHBC Canterbury School (1997).* Institute of Historic Building Conservation.

Plasters and plastering

Historic Scotland 1994 *Conservation of plasterwork*. Historic Scotland.

Miller, W. 1998 *Plastering plain and decorative*. Donhead.

Stagg, W.D.; Masters, R. 1983 *Decorative plasterwork – its repair and restoration*. Orion Books.

Pointing

SPAB 1979 Pointing stone and brick walling. *SPAB Technical Pamphlet No. 5.*

SPAB (not dated) Tuck pointing in practice. *SPAB Information Sheet No. 8.*

Renders

Ashurst, J.; Ashurst, N. 1988 *Practical building conservation*. Vol. 3 (English Heritage Technical Handbook), Gower Technical Press.

SPAB 1988 The need for old buildings to breathe. *SPAB Information Sheet No. 4.*

SPAB 1989 Roughcast for historic buildings. *SPAB Information Sheet No. 11.*

Repairs and maintenance

Brereton, C. 1991 *The repair of historic buildings*. English Heritage.

Burman, P. 1994 *Treasures on earth – a good housekeeping guide to churches and their contents*. Donhead.

Edinburgh New Town Conservation Committee 1981 *The care and conservation of Georgian houses*. Edinburgh New Town Conservation Committee.

Johnson, A. 1984 *How to restore and improve your Victorian house*. David and Charles.

Powys, A.R. 1981 *Repair of ancient buildings*. Society for the Protection of Ancient Buildings.

SPAB 1989 An introduction to the treatment of rising damp in old buildings. *SPAB Information Sheet No. 6.*

Wright, A. 1991 *Craft techniques for traditional buildings*. Batsford.

Resins

Oates, D.W.; Rickards, M. 1984 *Epoxy resins in the repair of timber structures*. Chartered Institute of Building.

Roofing

Billett, M. 1979 *Thatching and thatched buildings*. Robert Hale.

DCC 1996 *Derbyshire stone slate roofs*. Derbyshire County Council.

Fearn, J. 1976 *Thatch and thatching*. Shire Publications.

Historic Scotland 1998 The archaeology of Scottish thatch. *Technical Advice Note No. 13.*

Keymer Tile Company *Keymer handmade clay tiles user's manual*. Keymer Tile Company.

Nash, J. 1991 *Thatch and thatching*. Batsford.

Rural Development Commission 1981 *The thatcher's craft*. Rural Development Commission.

SPAB 1986 The care and repair of thatched roofs. *SPAB Technical Pamphlet No. 10.*

Wright, A. 1991 *Craft techniques for traditional buildings (roofing section)*. Batsford.
Yeomans, D. 1992 *The trussed roof – its history and development*. Scolar Press.

Services

Newmark Kay G. 1992 *Mechanical and electrical systems for historic buildings*. McGraw Hill.
Phillips, D. 1997 *Lighting historic buildings*. Butterworth-Heinemann.
SPAB 1996 Electrical wiring in old buildings. *SPAB Technical Pamphlet No. 9*.

Stone

Ashurst, J.; Ashurst, N. 1988 *Practical building conservation*. Vol. 1 (English Heritage Technical Handbook), Gower Technical Press.
Ashurst, J.; Dimes, F.G. 1998 *Conservation of building and decorative stone*. Vols 1 and 2, Butterworth – Heinemann.
Caroe, A.D.R.; Caroe, M.B. 1984 *Stonework: maintenance and surface repair*. CIO Publishing.
Clifton-Taylor, A. 1972 *The pattern of English building*. Faber and Faber.
Clifton-Taylor, A.; Ireson, A.S. 1972 *English stone building*. Victor Gollancz–Peter Crawley.
Garner, L. 1992 *Dry stone walls*. Shire Publications.
Herald House 1999 *Natural stone directory*. Herald House.
Hill, P.R.; David, J.C.E. 1995 *Practical stone masonry*. Donhead.
Historic Scotland 1997 *Biological growths on sandstone buildings: control and treatment*. Historic Scotland.
Historic Scotland 1997 *Quarries of Scotland*. Historic Scotland.
Martin, D.G. 1970 *Maintenance and repair of stone buildings*. The Church Information Office.
Sowden, A.M. 1990 *The maintenance of brick and stone structures*. E. and F.N. Spon.

Structural aspects

Beckmann, P. 1995 *Structural aspects of building conservation*. McGraw-Hill.
Heyman, J. 1996 *Arches, vaults and buttresses*. Variorum.
SPAB 1971 Outward learning walls. *SPAB Technical Pamphlet No. 1*.
SPAB 1976 Chimneys in old buildings. *SPAB Technical Pamphlet No. 3*.

Surveying

Council for British Archaeology 1996 *Recording timber-framed buildings – an illustrated glossary*. Council for British Archaeology.
Smith, L. 1986 *Investigating old buildings*. Batsford.
Swallow, P.; Watt, D.; Ashton, R. 1993 *Measurement and recording of historic buildings*. Donhead.
Watt, D.; Swallow, P. 1995 *Surveying historic buildings*. Donhead.

Timber

Alcock, N.W. (Ed.) 1981 *Cruck construction – an introduction and catalogue*. Council for British Archaeology.
Ashurst, J.; Ashurst, N. 1988 *Practical building conservation*. Vol. 5 (English Heritage Technical Handbook), Gower Technical Press.

Brunskill, R.W. 1985 *Timber building in Britain.* Victor Gollancz – Peter Crawley.
Charles, F.W.B.; Charles, M. 1995 *Conservation of timber buildings.* Donhead.
Harris, R. 1978 *Discovering timber framed buildings.* Shire Publications.
Hewitt, C.A. 1980 *English historic carpentry.* Phillimore & Co.
Munn, H. 1983 *Joinery for repair and restoration contracts.* Orion Books.
SPAB 1986 Timber treatment – a warning about de-frassing. *SPAB Information Sheet No. 2.*
SPAB 1990 Patching old floorboards. *SPAB Information Sheet No. 10.*
SPAB 1990 Surface treatment of timber-framed buildings. *SPAB Information Sheet No. 3.*
SPAB 1989 Panel infilling to timber-framed buildings. *SPAB Technical Pamphlet No. 11.*
SPAB 1991 Repair of timber frames and roofs. *SPAB Technical Pamphlet No. 12.*
SPAB 1991 Strengthening timber floors. *SPAB Technical Pamphlet No. 2.*
SPAB (not dated) Repair of wood windows. *SPAB Technical Pamphlet No. 13.*
Swindells, D. 1989 *Restoring period timber frame houses.* E. and F.N. Spon.
West, T. 1971 *Timber framed houses in England.* David and Charles.

Unbaked earth construction

Ashurst, J.; Ashurst, N. 1988 *Practical building conservation.* Vol. 2 (English Heritage Technical Handbook), Gower Technical Press.
Cambridgeshire County Council (not dated) Cambridgeshire conservation notes. *Pamphlet No. 7.*
Devon Earth Building Association. Various publications.
Egeland, P. 1988 *Cob and thatch.* Devon Books.
Historic Scotland 1996 Earth structures and construction in Scotland: *Historic Scotland Technical Advice Note No. 6.*
McCann, J. 1983 *Clay and cob buildings.* Shire Publications.
Pearson, G. 1992 *Conservation of clay and chalk buildings.* Donhead.
Warren, J. 1999 *Construction of earth structures.* Architectural Press.

Wall coverings

Hoskins, L. (Ed.) 1994 *The papered wall – the history, patterns and techniques of wallpaper.* Thames and Hudson.
Rouse, E.C. 1991 *Medieval wall paintings.* Shire Publications.
Taylor, C. 1991 *Wallpaper.* Shire Publications.
Tristam, E.W. 1944 *English Medieval wall paintings.* Oxford University Press.
Tristam, E.W. 1955 *English wall paintings of the 14th century.* Routledge and Kegan Paul.

Windows

Historic Scotland 1996 *Performance standards for timber sash and case windows.* Historic Scotland.
SPAB 1992 Repair of wood windows. *SPAB Technical Pamphlet No. 10.*

APPENDIX A

Ancient Monuments Board for Wales,
Welsh Office,
Crown Building, Cathays Park,
Cardiff CF1 3NQ.
Tel: 01222 500200.

Ancient Monuments Society (AMS)
St. Ann's Vestry,
2 Church Entry,
London EC4V 5HB.
Tel: 0171 236 3934.

Architectural Heritage Fund,
Clareville House,
26–7 Oxendon Street,
London SW1Y 4EL.
Tel: 0171 925 0199.

Architectural Salvage Index,
c/o Hutton and Rostron,
Netley House, Gomshall,
Surrey GU5 9QA.
Tel: 01483 203221.
Fax: 01483 202911.

Association for Industrial Archaeology,
Ironbridge Gorge Museum,
Telford TF8 7AW.
Tel: 01952 432141.

Association of Specialist Underpinning
Contractors,
Association House,
235 Ash Road,
Aldershot, Hampshire GU12 4DD.
Tel: 01252 336318.

Avoncroft Museum of Historic
Buildings,
Stoke Heath,
Bromsgrove, Worcestershire
B60 4JR.
Tel: 01527 831363.

Brick Development Association
(BDA),
Woodside House,
Winkfield,
Windsor, Berkshire
SL4 2DX.
Tel: 01344 885651.

British Foundry Association,
6th Floor,
The McLaren Building,
35 Dale End,
Birmingham B4 7LN.
Tel: 0121 200 2100.

British Lime Association,
156 Buckingham Palace Road,
London SW1W 9TR.
Tel: 0171 730 8194.

British Society of Master Glass
Painters – Conservation
Committee,
5 Tivoli Place,
Ilkley, West Yorkshire LS29 8SU.
Tel: 01943 602521.

Brooking Collection,
University of Greenwich,
Oakfield Lane,
Dartford,
Kent DA1 2SZ.
Tel: 0181 331 9897.
(Window Museum).

Building Centre,
26 Store Street,
London WC1E 7BT.
Tel: 0171 637 1022.

Building Crafts and Conservation
Trust,
Kings Gate,
Dover Castle,
Kent CT16 1HU.
Tel: 0134 225066.

Building Research Establishment
(BRE),
Bucknalls Lane,
Garston,
Watford WD2 7JR.
Tel: 01923 664664.

Cadw (Welsh Historic Monuments),
Crown Building,
Cathays Park,
Cardiff CF1 3NQ.
Tel: 01222 500200.

Chartered Institute of Building (CIOB),
Heritage and Building Conservation
Group,
Englemere,
Kings Ride,
Ascot, Berkshire SL5 7TB.
Tel: 01344 630700.

Chiltern Open Air Museum,
Newland Park,
Gorelands Lane,
Chalfont St. Giles, Buckinghamshire
HP8 4AD.
Tel: 01494 871117.

Civic Trust,
17 Carlton House Terrace,
London SW1Y 5AW.
Tel: 0171 930 0914.

Civic Trust for Wales,
4th Floor,
Empire House,
Mount Stewart Square,
The Docks,
Cardiff CF1 6DN.
Tel: 01222 484606.

College of Masons,
42 Magdalen Road,
London SW18 3NP.
Tel: 0181 874 8363.

Conservation Unit,
The Museums and Galleries Commission,
16 Queen Anne's Gate,
London SW1H 9AA.
Tel: 0171 233 4200.

Construction History Society (CHS),
c/o Chartered Institute of Building,
Englemere,
Kings Ride,
Ascot, Berkshire
SL5 8TB.
Tel: 01344 630734.

Copper Development Association,
Verulam Industrial Estate,
224 London Road,
St. Albans, Hertfordshire AL1 1AG.
Tel: 01727 731200.

Cregneash Open Air Museum,
Manx National Heritage,
Manx Museum and National Trust,
Douglas,
Isle of Man.
Tel: 016214 648000.

Council for British Archaeology,
Bowes Morrell House,
111 Walmgate,
York YO1 2UA.
Tel: 01904 671417.

Council for Scottish Archaeology,
National Museum of Scotland,
Queen Street,
Edinburgh EH2 1JD.
Tel: 0131 225 7534.

Devon Earth Building Association,
c/o P. Child,
Environment Department,
Devon County Council,
County Hall,
Exeter, Devon EX2 4QW.
Tel: 01392 382261.

Dry Stone Walling Association
of Great Britain,
c/o YFC Centre,
National Agricultural Centre,
Stoneleigh Park,
Warwickshire CV8 2LG.
Tel: 0121 378 0493.

EARTHA – East Midlands Earth Structures
Society,
20 West Parade,
Lincoln LN1 1JT.

Earth Structures Section – International
Council on Monuments and other Sites.
Chairman: John Hurd,
20/22 West Parade,
Lincoln LN1 1JT.

East Anglian Earth Buildings Group,
Paperhouse,
West Harling,
Norfolk NR16 2SF.
Tel: 01953 717814.

Ecclesiastical Architects and Surveyors
Association (EASA),
Scan House,
29 Radnor Cliff,
Folkestone,
Kent CT20 2JJ.
Tel: 01303 254008.

English Heritage,
429 Oxford Street,
London W1R 2HD.
Tel: 0171 973 3000.

Fire Protection Association (FPA),
Melrose Avenue,
Borehamwood, Hertfordshire
WD6 2BJ.
Tel: 0181 207 2345.

Georgian Group,
6 Fitzroy Square,
London W1P 6DX.
Tel: 0171 387 1720.

Glass and Glazing Federation,
44–8 Borough High Street,
London SE1 1XB.
Tel: 0171 403 7177.

Guild of Architectural Ironmongers,
8 Stepney Green,
London E1 3JU.
Tel: 0171 790 3431.

Heritage Building Contractors Group (UK),
c/o Linford Group,
Quonians,
Lichfield, Staffordshire
WS13 7LB.
Tel: 01543 414 234.

Heritage Lottery Fund,
National Heritage Memorial Fund,
7 Holbein Place,
London SW1W 8NR.
Tel: 0171 591 6000.

Historic Churches Preservation Trust,
Fulham Palace, Bishops Avenue,
London SW6 6EA.
Tel: 0171 736 3054.

Historic Farm Buildings Group,
c/o Museum of English Rural Life,
University of Reading,
Whiteknights,
Reading, Berkshire RG6 6AG.
Tel: 0118 931 8663.

Historic Gardens Foundation,
34 River Court,
Upper Ground,
London SE1 9PE.
Tel: 0171 633 9165.

Historic Houses Association,
2 Chester Street,
London SW1X 7BB.
Tel: 0171 259 5688.

Historic Scotland,
Longmore House,
Salisbury Place,
Edinburgh EH9 1SH.
Tel: 0131 668 8600.

Institute of Archaeology,
University College London,
31–4 Gordon Square,
London WC1H 0PY.
Tel: 0171 387 7050.

Institute of Historic Building Conservation,
PO Box 301,
Brighton,
East Sussex BN2 1BQ.

Institute of Historic Buildings
Conservation – Scotland,
The Glasite Meeting House,
33 Barony Street,
Edinburgh EH3 6NX.
Tel: 0131 529 3913.

Institution of Civil Engineers –
Historic Engineering Works Panel,
1 Great George Street,
London SW1P 3AA.
Tel: 0171 665 2250.

Institution of Structural Engineers –
History Group,
11 Upper Belgrave Square,
London SW1X 8BH.
Tel: 0171 235 4535.

International Centre for the Study of the
Preservation and Restoration of Cultural
Property (ICCROM),
13 Via de San Michele,
I-00153 Rome,
Italy.
Tel: 00 39 6 58553 1.

International Council on Monuments
and Sites (UK),
10 Barley Mow Passage,
London W4 4PH.
Tel: 0181 994 6477.

Ironbridge Gorge Museums,
Ironbridge,
Telford TF8 7AW.
Tel: 01952 433522.

Lead Sheet Association,
Hawkeswell Business Park,
Maidstone Road,
Pembury,
Tunbridge Wells,
Kent TN2 4AH.
Tel: 01892 822773.

London Stained Glass Repository,
Glaziers Hall,
9 Montague Close,
London SE1 9DD.
Tel: 0171 403 3300.

Master Carvers Association,
Unit 20,
21 Wren Street,
London WC1X 0HF.
Tel: 0171 278 8759.

National Federation of Master Steeplejacks
and Lightning Conductor Engineers,
4d St. Mary Place,
The Lace Market,
Nottingham NG1 1PH.
Tel: 0115 955 8818.

National Federation of Roofing
Contractors,
24 Weymouth Street,
London W1N 4LX.
Tel: 0171 436 0387.

National Monuments Record for Wales,
Crown Buildings,
Plas Crug,
Aberystwyth,
Dyfed SY23 1NJ.
Tel: 01970 621233.

National Monuments Record of
Scotland,
John Sinclair House,
16 Bernard Terrace,
Edinburgh EH8 9NX.
Tel: 0131 662 1456.

National Monuments Records Centre,
Kemble Drive,
Swindon, Wiltshire
SN2 2GZ.
Tel: 01793 414600.

National Society of Master Thatchers,
20 The Laurels,
Tetsworth,
Thame, Oxfordshire
OX9 7BH.
Tel: 01844 281568.

National Trust,
36 Queen Anne's Gate,
London SW1H 9AS.
Tel: 0171 222 9251.

National Trust for Scotland,
5 Charlotte Square,
Edinburgh EH2 4DU.
Tel: 0131 226 5922.

National Trust (North Wales),
Trinity Square,
Llandudno,
Gwynedd LL30 2DE.
Tel: 01492 860123.

National Trust (South Wales),
The King's Head,
Bridge Street,
Llandeilo,
Dyfed SA19 6BB.
Tel: 01558 822800.

Natural Slate Quarries Association,
26 Store Street,
London WC1E 7BT.
Tel: 0171 323 3770.

North of England Open Air Museum,
Beamish,
Co. Durham DH9 0RG.
Tel: 01207 231811.

Orton Trust,
PO Box 34,
Rothwell,
Kettering, Northamptonshire NN14 6XP.
Tel: 01536 761303.
(training courses on stonework available).

Royal Commission on the Historical
Monuments of England,
National Monuments Record Centre,
55 Blandford Street,
London W1H 3AF.
Tel: 0171 208 8200.

Royal Commission on the Ancient and
Historical Monuments of Scotland,
John Sinclair House, 16 Bernard Terrace,
Edinburgh EH8 9NX.
Tel: 0131 662 1456.

Royal Commission on the Ancient and
Historical Monuments of Wales,
Crown Buildings,
Plas Grug,
Aberystwyth SY23 1NJ.
Tel: 01970 621233.

Scottish Civic Trust,
The Tobacco Merchant's House,
42 Miller Street,
Glasgow G1 DT.
Tel: 0141 221 1466.

Scottish Conservation Bureau,
Longmore House,
Salisbury Place,
Edinburgh EH9 1SH.
Tel: 0131 668 8668.

Sir John Soane's Museum,
13 Lincoln's Inn Fields,
London WC2A 3BP.
Tel: 0171 405 2107.

Society for the Protection of Ancient
Buildings (SPAB),
37 Spital Square,
London E1 6DY.
Tel: 0171 377 1644.
(courses and lectures on various topics).

Society of Architectural Historians
of Great Britain,
16 Hart Street,
Edinburgh EH1 3RN.

Stained Glass Museum,
The Chapter House,
Ely Cathedral,
Ely CB7 4DN.
Tel: 01353 667 735.

Stone Federation of Great Britain,
18 Mansfield Street,
London W1M 9FG.
Tel: 0171 580 5404.

Stone Roofing Association,
Ceunant,
Caernarfon,
Gwynedd LL55 4SA.
Tel: 01286 650402.

Thatching Information Service,
Thatcher's Rest,
Levens Green,
Great Mundon,
Nr Ware, Hertfordshire
SG11 1HD.
Tel: 01920 438710.

Tiles and Architectural Ceramics Society,
School of Cultural Studies,
Leeds Metropolitan University,
Calverly Street,
Leeds LS1 3HE.
Tel: 0113 283 2600 extn 3355.

Traditional Paint Forum,
c/o Simpson and Brown,
179 Canongate,
Edinburgh EH8 8BN.
Tel: 0131 557 3880.

Twentieth Century Society,
70 Cowcross Street,
London EC1M 6BP.
Tel: 0171 250 3857.

Ulster Architectural Heritage Society,
66 Donegall Pass,
Belfast BT7 1BU.
Tel: 01232 550213.

Ulster Folk and Transport Museum,
Cultra Manor,
Holywood,
Northern Ireland.

United Kingdom Institute for
the Conservation of Historic
and Artistic Works,
109 The Chandlery,
50 Westminster Bridge Road,
London SE1 7QY.
Tel: 0171 721 8721.

Vernacular Architecture Group
(VAG),
Ashley,
Willows Green,
Great Leighs, Chelmsford,
Essex CM3 1QD.
Tel: 01245 361408.

Victorian Society,
1 Priory Gardens,
Bedford Park,
London W4 1TT.
Tel: 0181 994 1019.

Wallpaper History Society,
c/o Cole and Son,
144–6 Offord Street,
London N1 1NS.
Tel: 0171 700 9122
(Ref: L. Hoskins).

Weald and Downland Open Air
Museum,
Singleton,
Nr Chichester,
West Sussex PO18 0EU.
Tel: 01243 811363.
(courses and lectures available on
various topics).

Welsh Folk Museum,
St. Fagans,
Cardiff CF5 6XB.

Woodchester Mansion Trust,
1 The Old Town Hall,
High Street,
Stroud,
Gloucestershire GL5 1AP.
Tel: 01453 750455.
(courses available on various topics).

Worshipful Company of Glaziers and
Painters of Glass,
Glaziers Hall,
9 Montague Close,
London SE1 9DD.
Tel: 0171 403 3300.

APPENDIX B

A SELECTION OF SPECIALIST SERVICES AND SUPPLIERS

Accessing

Church Conservation Ltd,
Unit 4, Manvers Business Park,
High Hazles Road,
Cotgrave
Nottingham NG12 3GZ
Tel: 0115 9894864

Architectural and sheet lead casting

Northwest Lead,
3 Sunnyfield Road,
Heaton Mersey, Stockport,
Cheshire SK4 3HS.
Tel: 0161 4432700.

St. Blaise Ltd,
Westhill Barn, Evershot,
Dorchester Dorset DT2 0LD.
Tel: 01935 83662.

Architectural salvage

The London Architectural Salvage and
Supply Company,
Saint Michael's,
Mark Street,
London EC2A 4ER.
Tel: 0171 739 0448.

Preservation in Action,
Tower Farm,
Norwich Road,
Mendlesham,
Suffolk IP14 5NE.
Tel: 01449 766095.

Solopark PLC,
Station Road,
Nr Pampisford,
Cambridgeshire CB2 4HB.
Tel: 01223 834663.

*Note: It is advisable to purchase salvaged
artefacts and materials from dealers who conform
to the SALVO CODE: For further details
Tel: 01890 820333 or Fax: 01890 820499.*

Brick suppliers for conservation work

Bulmer Brick and Tile Company,
Bulmer,
Nr Sudbury,
Suffolk CO10 7EF.
Tel: 01787 269 232.

Ibstock Building Products Ltd,
Ibstock,
Leicestershire LE67 6HS.
Tel: 01530 261999.

Phoenix Brick Co. Ltd,
The Brickworks,
Campbell Drive,
Barrow Hill,
Chesterfield S43 2PR.
Tel: 01246 473171.

Brickwork contractors: specialist

Gerard Lynch LCG,
23 Maple Grove,
Woburn Sands,
Milton Keynes,
Buckinghamshire MK17 8QN.
Tel: 01908 584163.

Tony Oliver Meaney,
26 Llanover Road,
Wembley,
Middlesex HA9 7LJ.
Tel: 0181 903 4539.

Building services engineers undertaking conservation projects

Oscar Faber and Partners,
Marlborough House,
Upper Marlborough Road,
St. Albans,
Hertfordshire AL1 3UT.
Tel: 0181 784 5784.

Peter Lawson-Smith Associates,
6 Longdale Court,
Market Square,
Witney,
Oxfordshire OX8 6FG.
Tel: 01993 776668.

Clay roofing tiles to historic sizes and profiles

Bulmer Brick and Tile Company,
Bulmer, Nr Sudbury,
Suffolk CO10 7EF.
Tel: 01787 269232.

Keymer Tiles Ltd,
Nye Road,
Burgess Hill,
West Sussex RH15 0LZ.
Tel: 01444 232931.

Damp-proofing old buildings

Quadric Ltd,
(A Chartered Building Company),
Quadric House,
66 Hammonds Drive,
Eastbourne, East Sussex BN23 6PW.
Tel: 01323 430503.
(also timber treatments).

Glass and glazing

Design and installation: Glasswood,
29 Beechwood Drive,
Crewkerne,
Somerset TA18 7BY.
Tel: 01460 72832.

Period glass: The London Crown
Glass Company,
21 Harpsden Road,
Henley-on-Thames,
Oxfordshire RG9 1EE.
Tel: 01491 413227.

Repair and restoration:
Bernard Becker Studios,
11 Canonbury Yard, 190A,
New North Road,
London N1 7BJ.
Tel: 0171 226 5226.

Handmade iron door furniture

Malvern Hills Furniture,
Unit 8,
Sixways Trading Estate,
Barnards Green,
Malvern,
Worcestershire WR14 3LY.
Tel: 01684 891644.

Historic timber frame: contractors

J. Bispham,
103 Ferry Road, Hullbridge,
Essex SS5 6EL.
Tel: 01702 230950.

McCurdy & Co.,
Manor Farm,
Stanford Dingley,
Nr Reading,
Berkshire RG7 6LS.
Tel: 0118 9744866.

St. Blaise Ltd, Westhill Barn,
Evershot, Dorchester,
Dorest DT2 0LD.
Tel: 01935 83662.

Lime

The Lime Centre,
Long Barn,
Morestead, Winchester,
Hampshire SO21 1LZ.
Tel: 01962 713636.

The Scottish Lime Centre,
The Schoolhouse,
4 Rock Road,
Charlestown,
Dunfermline,
Fife KY11 3EN.
Tel: 01383 872722.

Metalwork

Dorothea Restoration Ltd,
New Road,
Whaley Bridge,
Stockport,
Cheshire SK23 7JG.
Tel: 01663 733544.

Mortar analysis

The Lime Centre, Long Barn,
Morestead, Winchester,
Hampshire SO21 1LZ.
Tel: 01962 713636.

Non-destructive investigations

Demaus Building Diagnostics Ltd,
Stagbatch Farm, Leominster,
Herefordshire HR6 9DA.
Tel: 01568 615662.

Hutton and Rostron Environmental
Investigations,
Netley House,
Gomshall,
Surrey GU5 9QA.
Tel: 01483 203221.

Paint analysis

Rose of Jericho,
Westhill Barn,
Evershot, Dorchester,
Dorset DT2 0LD.
Tel: 01935 83676.

Paint removal

St. Blaise Ltd,
Westhill Barn,
Evershot, Dorchester,
Dorset DT2 0LD.
Tel: 01935 83662.

The Specialist Paint Removal Service,
50 Amersham Road,
London SE14 6QE.
Tel: 0181 692 2016.

Period roof lights and lanterns

The Metal Window Company,
Unit 8,
Wychwood Business Centre,
Milton Road,
Shipton-under-Wychwood,
Oxfordshire OX7 6XO.
Tel: 01993 830613.

Clements Window Group,
Clement House,
Haslemere,
Surrey GU27 1HR.
Tel: 01428 643393.

Plasterwork: plain and decorative

Acanthus, 5 Hansford Square,
Combe Down,
Bath BA2 5LQ.
Tel: 01225 837223.

S. & J. Whitehead, Derker Street,
Lower Moor, Oldham OL1 4EE.
Tel: 0161 624 4395.

Remedial treatments: historic structures

Consultants: Hutton and Rostron
Environmental Investigations,
Netley House,
Gomshall,
Surrey GU5 9QA.
Tel: 01483 203221.

Consultants: Ridout Associates,
147a Worcester Road,
Hagley,
Stourbridge,
West Midlands DY9 0NW.
Tel: 01562 885135.

Contractors: Building Solutions Ltd,
Abbey House,
Ashville Road,
Gloucester,
Gloucestershire GL2 5EU.
Tel: 01452 304490.

Roofing contractors: specialist

E.G. Swingler and Son,
27–9 Windsor Road,
Northampton NN5 5BE.
Tel: 01604 755055.

John Williams and Co. Ltd.,
Stone Street,
Lympne,
Hythe,
Kent CT21 4LD.
Tel: 01303 265198.

Sash windows: traditional

Dask Timber Products Ltd,
Dublin Road,
Banbridge,
Northern Ireland BT32 3PB.
Tel: 01762 318696.

Ventrolla,
11 Hornbeam Square,
South Harrogate,
North Yorkshire HG2 8NB.
Tel: 01423 870011.

Steeplejacking and difficult accessing

Church Conservation Ltd,
Unit 4,
High Hazels Road,
Manvers Business Park,
Cotgrove,
Nottingham NG12 3GZ.
Tel: 0115 989 4864.

Stone conservators

Nimbus Conservation Ltd,
Wadbury Barn,
Mells, Frome,
Somerset BA11 3PA.
Tel: 01373 812545.

St. Blaise Ltd,
Westhill Barn,
Evershot,
Dorchester,
Dorset DT2 0LD.
Tel: 01935 83662.

Stone masons

Formasons Ltd,
398 Freelands Road,
Bromley,
Kent BR1 3HZ.
Tel: 0181 460 8216.

Wells Cathedral Stonemasons,
Brunel Stoneworks,
Station Road,
Cheddar,
Somerset BS27 3AH.
Tel: 01934 743544.

A.F. Jones, 33 Bedford Road,
Reading,
Berkshire RG1 7EX.
Tel: 0118 957 3537.

Structural engineers: historic works

The Morton Partnership,
61 Islington Park Street,
London N1 1QB.
Tel: 0171 359 0202.

Terracotta

Shaws of Darwen Ltd,
Waterside,
Darwen,
Lancashire BB3 3NX.
Tel: 01254 775111.

Timber for historic works: suppliers

English Woodlands Timber,
Cocking Sawmills,
Cocking,
Nr Midhurst,
West Sussex GU24 0HS.
Tel: 01730 816941.

Jameson Joinery,
Hook Farm,
West Chiltington Lane,
Billingshurst,
West Sussex RH14 9DP.
Tel: 01403 782868.

John Boddy Timber Ltd,
Riverside Sawmills,
Boroughbridge,
North Yorkshire YO5 9LJ.
Tel: 01423 322270.

Whippletree Hardwoods,
Milestone Farm,
Barley Road,
Flint Cross,
Heydon, Royston,
Hertfordshire SG8 7QD.
Tel: 01763 208966.

Traditional lime washes and distempers

Rose of Jericho,
Westhill Barn,
Evershot,
Dorchester,
Dorset DT2 0LD.
Tel: 01935 83676.

Traditional paint suppliers

Farrow and Ball,
Uddens Estate,
Wimborne,
Dorset BH21 7NL.
Tel: 01202 876141.

Unbaked earth construction

Carruthers Building Conservation,
Meadowside,
Main Street,
Kirkmichael,
Blairgowrie,
PH10 7NT.
Tel: 01250 881216.

John Hurd Conservation,
20/22 West Parade,
Lincoln LN1 1JT.
Tel: 01522 526139.

Wood carving

Carvers and Gilders,
Eltringham Street,
London SW18 1TD.
Tel: 0181 870 7047.

APPENDIX C

EXTRACTS FROM THE BURRA CHARTER

Preamble

Having regard to the International Charter for the Conservation and Restoration of Monuments and Sites (ICOMOS 1966), and the resolutions of the Fifth General Assembly of ICOMOS (Moscow 1978), the following charter has been adopted by Australia ICOMOS.

Definitions

Article 1: For the purpose of this charter:

Place means site, area, building or other work, group of buildings or other works together with pertinent contents and surroundings.

Cultural significance means aesthetic, historic, scientific or social value for past, present or future generations.

Fabric means all physical material of the *place*.

Conservation means all the processes of looking after a *place* so far as to retain its *cultural significance*. It includes *maintenance* and may according to circumstances include *preservation*, *restoration*, and *adaptation* and will be commonly a combination of more than one of these.

Maintenance means the continuous protective care of the *fabric*, contents and setting of a *place*, and is to be distinguished from repair.

Repair involves *restoration* or *reconstruction* and should be treated accordingly.

Preservation means, maintaining the *fabric* of a *place* in its existing state and retarding deterioration.

Restoration means returning the EXISTING *fabric* of a *place* to a known earlier state by removing accretions or by reassembling existing components without the introduction of new material.

Reconstruction means returning a *place* as nearly as possible to a known earlier state and is distinguished by the introduction of materials (new or old) into the fabric. This is not to be confused with either re-creation or conjectural reconstruction which are outside the scope of this charter.

Adaptation means modifying a *place* to suit proposed compatible uses.

Compatible use means a use which involves no change to the culturally significant fabric, changes which are substantially reversible, or changes which require a minimal impact.

206

Conservation principles

Article 2: The aim of conservation is to retain or recover the cultural significance of a place and must include provision for its security, its maintenance and its future.

Article 3: Conservation is based on a respect for the existing fabric and should involve the least possible physical intervention. It should not distort the evidence provided by the fabric.

Article 4: Conservation should make use of all the disciplines which can contribute to the study and safeguarding of a place. Techniques employed should be traditional but in some circumstances they may be modern ones for which a firm scientific basis exists and which have been supported by a body of experience.

Article 5: Conservation of a place should take into consideration all aspects of its cultural significance without unwarranted emphasis on any at the expense of others.

Article 6: The conservation policy appropriate to a place must first be determined by an understanding of its cultural significance and its physical condition.

Article 7: The conservation policy will determine which uses are compatible.

Article 8: Conservation requires the maintenance of an appropriate visual setting, e.g. form, scale, colour, texture and materials. No new construction, demolition or modification which would adversely affect the settings should be allowed. Environmental intrusions which adversely affect appreciation or enjoyment of the place should be excluded.

Article 9: A building or work should remain in its historical location. The moving of all or part of a building or work is unacceptable unless this is the sole means of ensuring its survival.

Article 10: The removal of contents which form part of the cultural significance of the place is unacceptable unless it is the sole means of ensuring their security and preservation. Such contents must be returned should changed circumstances make this practicable.

Conservation processes

Preservation

Article 11: Preservation is appropriate where the existing state of the fabric itself constitutes evidence of specific cultural significance, or where insufficient evidence is available to allow other conservation processes to be carried out.

Article 12: Preservation is limited to the protection, maintenance and where necessary, the stabilisation of the existing fabric but without the distortion of its cultural significance.

Restoration

Article 13: Restoration is appropriate only if there is sufficient evidence of an earlier state of the fabric and only if returning the fabric to that state recovers the cultural significance of the place.

Article 14: Restoration should reveal anew culturally significant aspects of the place. It is based on respect for all the physical, documentary and other evidence and stops at the point where conjecture begins.

Article 15: Restoration is limited to the reassembling of displaced components or removal of accretions in accordance with Article 16.

Article 16: The contribution of all periods to the place must be respected. If a place includes the fabric of different periods, revealing the fabric of one period at the expense of another can only be justified when what is removed is of slight cultural significance and the fabric which is to be revealed is of much greater cultural significance.

Reconstruction

Article 17: Reconstruction is appropriate where a place is incomplete through damage or alteration and where it is necessary for its survival, or where it recovers the cultural significance of the place as a whole.

Article 18: Reconstruction is limited to the completion of a depleted entity and should not constitute the majority of the fabric of a place.

Article 19: Reconstruction is limited to the reproduction of fabric the form of which is known from physical and/or documentary evidence. It should be identifiable on close inspection as being new work.

Adaptation

Article 20: Adaptation is acceptable where the conservation of the place cannot otherwise be achieved, and where the adaptation does not substantially detract from its cultural significance.

Article 22: Fabric of cultural significance unavoidably removed in the process of adaptation must be kept safely to enable its future reinstatement.

Conservation practice

Article 23: Work on a place must be preceded by professionally prepared studies of the physical, documentary and other evidence, and the existing fabric recorded before any disturbance of the place.

Article 24: Study of a place by any disturbance of the fabric or by archaeological excavation should be undertaken where necessary to provide data essential for decisions on the conservation of the place and/or to secure evidence about to be lost or made inaccessible through necessary conservation or other unavoidable action. Investigation of a place for any other reason which requires physical disturbance and which adds substantially to a scientific body of knowledge may be permitted, provided that it is consistent with the conservation policy for the place.

Article 25: A written statement of conservation policy must be professionally prepared setting out the cultural significance, physical condition and proposed conservation process together with justification and supporting evidence, including photographs, drawings and all appropriate samples.

Article 26: The organisation and individuals responsible for policy decisions must be named and specific responsibility taken for each such decision.

Article 27: Appropriate professional direction and supervision must be maintained at all stages of the work and a log kept of new evidence and additional decisions recorded as in Article 25 above.

Article 28: The records required by Articles 23, 25, 26 and 27 should be placed in a permanent archive and made publicly available.

APPENDIX D

EXTRACTS FROM THE VENICE CHARTER

Imbued with a message from the past, the historic monuments of generations of people remain to the present day as living witness of their age-old traditions. People are becoming more and more conscious of the unity of human values and regard ancient monuments as a common heritage. The common responsibility to safeguard them for future generations is recognised. It is our duty to hand them on in the full richness of their authenticity.

It is essential that the principles guiding the preservation and restoration of ancient buildings should be agreed and be laid down on an international basis, with each country being responsible for applying the plan within the framework of its own culture and traditions.

By defining these basic principles for the first time, the Athens Charter of 1931 contributed towards the development of an extensive international movement which has assumed concrete form in national documents, in the work of ICOM and UNESCO and in the establishment by the latter of the International Centre for the Study of the Preservation and Restoration of Cultural Property. Increasing awareness and critical study have been brought to bear on problems which have continually become more complex and varied; now the time has come to examine the charter afresh in order to make a thorough study of the principles involved and to enlarge its scope in a new document. Accordingly the Lind International Congress of Architects and Technicians of Historic Monuments, which met in Venice from 25th May to 31st May 1964 approved the following text.

Definitions

Article 1: The concept of an historic monument embraces not only the single architectural work but also the urban or rural setting in which is found the evidence of a particular civilisation, a significant development or an historic event. This applies not only to great works of art but also to more modest works of the past which have acquired cultural significance with the passing of time.

Article 2: The conservation and restoration of monuments must have recourse to all the sciences and techniques which can contribute to the study and safeguarding of the architectural heritage.

Aim

Article 3: The intention in conserving and restoring monuments is to safeguard them no less as works of art than as historical evidence.

Conservation

Article 4: It is essential to the conservation of monuments that they be maintained on a permanent basis.

Article 5: The conservation of monuments is always facilitated by making use of them for some socially useful purpose. Such use is therefore desirable but it must not change the lay-out or decoration of the building. It is within these limits only that modifications demanded by a change of function should be envisaged and may be permitted.

Article 6: The conservation of a monument implies preserving a setting which is not out of scale. Wherever the traditional setting exists, it must be kept. No new construction, demolition or modification which would alter the relations of mass and colour must be allowed.

Article 7: A monument is inseparable from the history to which it bears witness and from the setting in which it occurs. The moving of all or part of a monument cannot be allowed except where the safeguarding of that monument demands it or where it is justified by national or international interests of paramount importance.

Article 8: Items of sculpture, painting or decoration which form an integral part of a monument may only be removed from it if this is the sole means of ensuring their preservation.

Restoration

Article 9: The process is a highly specialised operation. Its aim is to preserve and reveal the aesthetic and historic value of the monument and is based on respect for original material and authentic documents. It must stop at the point where conjecture begins, and in this case moreover any extra work which is indispensable must be distinct from the architectural composition and must bear a contemporary stamp. The restoration in any case must be preceded and followed by an archaeological and historical study of the monument.

Article 10: Where traditional techniques prove inadequate, the consolidation of a monument can be achieved by the use of any modern technique for conservation and construction, the efficacy of which has been shown by scientific data and proved by experience.

Article 11: The valid contribution of all periods to the building of a monument must be respected, since unity of style is not the aim of a restoration. When a building includes the superimposed work of different periods, the revealing of the underlying state can only be justified in exceptional circumstances and when what is removed is of little interest and the material which is brought to light is of great historical, archaeological or aesthetic value, and its state of good preservation enough to justify action. Evaluation of the importance of the elements involved and the decision as to what may be destroyed cannot rest solely on the individual in charge of the work.

Article 12: Replacements of missing parts must integrate harmoniously with the whole, but at the same time must be distinguished from the original so that restoration does not falsify the artistic or historic evidence.

Article 13: Additions cannot be allowed except in so far as they do not detract from the interesting parts of the building, its traditional setting, the balance of its composition and its relation with its surroundings.

Historic sites

Article 14: The sites of monuments must be the object of special care in order to safeguard their integrity and ensure that they are cleared and presented in a seemly manner. The work of conservation and restoration carried out in such places should be inspired by the principles set forth in the foregoing articles.

Excavations

Article 15: Excavations should be carried out in accordance with scientific standards and the recommendation defining international principles to be applied in the case of archaeological excavation adopted by UNESCO in 1956. Ruins must be maintained and measures necessary for the permanent conservation and protection of architectural features and of objects discovered must be taken. Furthermore, every means must be taken to facilitate the understanding of the monument and to reveal it without ever distorting its meaning. All reconstruction work should however be ruled out *a priori*. Only anastylosis, that is to say, the reassembling of the existing but dismembered parts can be permitted. The material used for integration should always be recognisable and its use should be at least that which will ensure the conservation of a monument and the reinstatement of its form.

Publication

Article 16: In all works of preservation, restoration or excavation, there should always be precise documentation in the form of analytical and critical reports, illustrated with drawings and photographs. Every stage of the work of clearing, consolidation, rearrangements and integration, as well as technical and formal features identified during the course of the work, should be included. This record should be placed in the archives of a public institution and made available to research workers. It is recommended that the reports should be published.

INDEX